AF477767

Precarious Spaces

Precarious Spaces
The Arts, Social and Organizational Change

Edited by Katarzyna Kosmala and Miguel Imas

intellect Bristol, UK / Chicago, USA

First published in the UK in 2016 by
Intellect, The Mill, Parnall Road, Fishponds, Bristol, BS16 3JG, UK

First published in the USA in 2016 by
Intellect, The University of Chicago Press, 1427 E. 60th Street,
Chicago, IL 60637, USA

A catalogue record for this book is available from the
British Library.

Copy-editor: MPS Technologies
Cover designer: Jane Seymour
Cover image: Katarzyna Kosmala, Santa Marta, Rio de Janeiro, 2010
Production manager: Amy Rollason
Typesetting: Contentra Technologies

Print ISBN: 978-1-78320-593-6
ePDF ISBN: 978-1-78320-594-3
ePUB ISBN: 978-1-78320-595-0

Printed and bound by TJ International

Contents

Acknowledgements

This book has had a lengthy gestation process, and several people have contributed to its fruition in the Global South and the Global North. Most of all, we would like to acknowledge the contribution of now deceased Professor Marcelo Milano Falcão Vieira for his involvement in the early stages of this project and in ideas development, as well as his enthusiasm for a positive change; aimed at transforming the current conditions while working towards more 'liveable' lives in peripheral spaces. We are grateful to all authors who feature in this edited collection. Most authors have contributed new texts, written especially for this book, and we particularly appreciate their time and commitment to the project. A few chapters have also been developed from contributors' ongoing research and activism in the area, with authors sharing their ongoing journeys of discovery in seeking innovative means for change. Equally, we would like to thank all artists and researchers whose images feature in this volume for their generosity as well as for permissions to reproduce their images, which made the visual element of this project possible. Last, but not least, we would like to thank John Mullen for his work on image reproduction and editorial work.

Preface

Precarious Spaces: The Arts, Social and Organizational Change is a timely contribution that fills a gap in both the arts and social sciences literature concerning arts-informed interventions in peripheral spaces and creative practices of the poor and marginal.

The concept of precarious spaces and the use of arts-based inquiry as a research method in this context provides a valuable contribution to several academic fields, including social sciences, urban studies, geography, organisation studies, visual studies, as well as arts and philosophy. The remarkable aspect of this volume is a unique blend of different theoretical and conceptual approaches that brings together research on space, precarity, and art-centred interventional practices. Indeed, the first section of the volume provides an enriching and *avant-garde* set of ideas on how to conceptualise issues associated with social and organizational change in relation to marginal spaces. The breadth and critical appreciation of interdisciplinary engagement with the conceptualisation of creativity and precariat opens an important window for reflection upon the human condition in precarious realms, as well as how space can be constructed, negotiated and re-constructed at the periphery of society. Following from this refreshing conceptual framing, the chapters in Parts II and III bring cases and experiences from different locations of the Global South, including original insights into the world of favelas, and how we can learn and reflect back on our own communities while appreciating their richness 'differently'. We get a glimpse of the complexities of settlement strategies – how communities have to improvise with scarcity of resources, embrace temporary conditions and deal with day-to-day challenges necessary to preserve and reproduce life locally. We also learn how community practices transform, as for instance in the case of the *Mbyá-Guarani,* to assert their dwelling culture in unimagined urban spaces.

Another significant contribution of this volume is an engagement with local histories through interdisciplinary dialogue, articulating theoretical reflections without privileging philosophical framings originating from the Global North. This is extremely relevant, as the inclination in producing knowledge of this nature tends to privilege the voice of the Global North and English-language framings, giving less importance to the knowledge produced in 'other' localities. This volume embeds theory as a reflection of the experiences of living communities.

This book, a testimony to the work and dedication of all the contributors bringing insight into the world of marginal dwellers, reflects the intellectual contribution of

Professor Marcelo Milano Falcão Vieira, who sadly died in December 2011. He significantly contributed to the formation of ideas in the early stages of this project, especially with his work on Brazilian culture and the impact of neo-liberal managerialism on local community practices. Among his outstanding work, relevant for this volume, was the importance he placed on studying favelas and peripheral neighbourhoods while probing the limits of culture in societal transformation. Henceforth, it is with this mix of sadness – as Marcelo Milano Falcão Vieira is not here to see this volume published – and joy – that I thank the authors and editors for bringing this valuable project to completion. Thus, I could not recommend this book more to anyone who wants to challenge their own understandings and perceptions of precarious spaces or simply explore how the intersection of precarity, community and intervention-centred art practices are negotiated in localities of the Global South.

Maria Ceci Misoczky

Part I

Introducing the Volume

Chapter 1

Why precarious spaces?

Katarzyna Kosmala and Miguel Imas

Precarious?

This volume addresses current concerns in art discourse around the instrumentality and agency of art in the context of the precarity of daily living, urban informality and the proliferation of alternative forms of organizing. Authors from South America as well as Europe, the United States and Canada engage with spatial strategies behind the utilization of precariousness, and examine ways of challenging forms of precarity, and indeed, the instigation of precarity.

The volume draws upon interdisciplinary research including cultural and visual studies, art theory, organization studies, architecture, urban planning, geography and contemporary philosophy, and supplements local histories and experiences in the Global South, as well as their theoretical frameworks, with theories of art and socio-political practice as they have been debated and developed in European and North American contexts. The book offers a survey of socially and community-engaged art practices in South America and from there expands to address similar issues in the Global North. The individual chapters examine examples of projects based on performances of space that can be seen as exceeding the norm, as well as case studies concerning art-informed inquiry aimed at social and transformative consequences, set against the backdrop of neo-liberal economies that have contributed to the emergence of precarity in both life and work. Such an inquiry implies not only a particular philosophical and theoretical position, but equally demonstrates how, in practice, groups, individuals, and communities can challenge constructed, established orders to create spaces of emancipation. Thus, the book offers a unique interdisciplinary perspective for engaging with some of the themes of precarious spaces by mobilizing the use of arts-based inquiry both as a research method and as an intervention that aims at social and organizational change; drawing on resources that originate from South America, including examples from Brazil, Mexico, Peru, Argentina and Chile, supplemented with insights and resources emerging from the North, including the United Kingdom, the United States and Canada.

The key phrases surrounding precarity, such as unstable condition of today's living; flexible, context-dependent and time-contingent employment; self-organization, disposability and contingency, have opened up new thresholds in theory development as well as in art-centred activism and the arts more generally. Foster (2009) identifies contemporary art practice with the precarious condition many artists share and respond to by creating meanings from uncertain circumstances, especially through a comment or an evocation of discourse, in response to a political confusion, and in association with socio-economic unrest. Such processes associated with reimaging the precarious condition into spaces of opportunity also require a theoretical reflection upon the processes of intervention and self-organization. At the same time, the scope of the critique of contemporary Capitalism and neo-liberal sentiments threatens to generalize precarity as a somewhat undifferentiated and ubiquitous condition.

We could argue, following on from Judith Butler's investigation into human vulnerability in *Precarious Lives: The Power of Mourning and Violence* (2004), that, while what can be termed as precariousness is common to all life and contemporary living, a state of precarity associated with the contemporary moment of neo-liberalism is largely politically induced and, we would add, requires to be problematized. Precarity commonly refers to a living condition based on temporality, fragmentation and job insecurity in increasingly flexible labour markets. Precarious spaces are often seen as not being stable, settled or well staked out; these spaces are perceived as unstable, unsettled and relatively unmapped or less visible. Precarious places reflect exposure to spaces that are marginal in our societies (Wacquant, 2008) and yet, often, informality of marginalized groups becomes a groundwork for 'inverse colonialism' (Yiftachel, 2009).

Butler (2004) returns to Emmanuel Levinas and his analysis of the meaning of being human, and, from such a basis, argues for a kind of political and ethical work needed to achieve peace globally, and indeed, for creating a condition for better, 'liveable' lives. Zygmunt Bauman refers to contemporary times as an era of uncertainty, a state of 'liquid modernity' and 'liquid times,' where instability and unpredictability are reshaping the society as a network rather than conforming to a solid structure. Bauman (2007) also notes that the responsibility to shape a liveable life has fallen on the individual, as a life, demarcated by a series of short-term projects, requires most of all flexibility and adaptability to the rigours of the social factory and demands for increased productivity. In this frame, he argues for solutions emerging from the 'local' organization or a community rather than institutional structures or a state authority.

There is also the precariat. What has been commonly referred to as the precariat – a term describing a recent, tangible phenomenon – is a social class in the making, and approaches the consciousness of common vulnerability that Butler, Bauman and others have been hinting at (Harvey, 2010: 243). The precariat consists of those who feel their living and identities are made up of fragmented and fractured elements, in which it seems impossible to construct a desirable narrative by weaving work and quality time for a life outside work (Harvey, 2010, 2014; Standing, 2011). Under neo-liberal Capitalism, the balance of power has switched from labour to capital, resulting in occupational insecurity, precariousness and individualization of life (McGuigan, 2010).

We would argue that a notion of precariat can be viewed as an umbrella term, encompassing experiences of all those who need to train themselves – regardless of their origin – in order to compete on labour markets and to find a source of income, often on a temporary basis, and without social security in the case of illness or when needing assistance (e.g. Neilson and Rossiter, 2006; Kalleberg, 2009). Thus, precariat refers to experiences of people that have been made redundant, those on zero-hours contracts, migrants, asylum seekers as well as the so-called creative class, and, in particular, those who are most likely to be in debt at the time of entering the labour market.[1] Referring to the latter, Gregory Sholette in his book *Dark Matter: Art and Politics in the Age of Enterprise Culture* has pointed out, drawing on an astrophysics-derived metaphor of 'dark matter,' that 'without this obscure mass of "failed" artists the small cadre of successful artists would find it difficult, if not impossible, to sustain the global art world as it appears today' (2011: 3). Sholette describes a complex division of labour in the art world whereby many excluded creative practices as well as marginalized and 'unsuccessful' artists sustain the functioning of the system through volunteering practice; serving as interns at art galleries, taking underpaid art teaching positions or other jobs and consuming art experience more generally. The author argues that it is the system that keeps the creative class in a state of subservience, and, in a sense, a state of co-dependence.

Bauman, Butler, Wacquant, and to some degree Harvey as well as others, all imply an individual pressure in the struggle to make a living in relation to precarity. And such a positioning of individual agency, indeed, implies vulnerability. Analysing Butler's ethical position, Lloyd points out that for Butler, the body is central to a conceptualization of vulnerability since it is precisely the body that exposes us and opens us to the other, their gaze, touch and various forms of violence (2008: 94).

The main focus of the collection is a critical reflection upon the concepts of space, precariousness and broadly defined, art-based activities as well as their dynamic relationship, in seeking a change and transformation of living conditions, associated with what Butler (2004) described as 'liveable' lives. Similarly, Anna Dezeuze debating precariousness in art practices in the context of socio-economic development refers to Hannah Arendt's conceptualisation of human condition as 'human existence as it has been given' (Ardent, 1958: 2 in Dezeuze, forthcoming) and argues that 'it is a matter of addressing the situation of the individual, here and now, in the concrete world, on a human scale' (Dezeuze, forthcoming: 27).

The chapters in this volume examine various urban spaces and locations associated with the imaginary of precariousness, seek practices within such contexts that are neither formally managed nor organized, as well as explore examples of interventions in the geographical imaginary of the precarious that emerge out of architecture, design, visual arts, music and performative practice. The chapters articulate different discourses of social change, instigated by arts-based intervention that can imply a cross-cultural engagement, neighbourhood-driven action, politically infused activism in a particular area and community building. The volume also explores uses of media discourse as platform for a social change and a forum for asking questions on established perceptions of existence in the imaginary of precarious realms, including examples of urban voids, derelict buildings, self-built communities, such as a favelas or shantytowns, as well as dwellings based on occupation of urban infrastructure, such as an underpass or roadside.

Precarious Spaces is devoted to explorations of the South, pointing out that some locations and geographical imaginings appear more vulnerable to enactments and investigations of precarity than others. The Latin American Modernist movement, with its often unacknowledged debt to the vernacular architecture of the 1920s and 1930s, has drawn inspiration from local communities' experiences of communal living and reflected upon the ways of coping with exclusion in different socio-economic environments. By looking at the South American experience, and Brazil's 'informal' situation in particular, for transferable methodological processes and from such a position, expanding to the North, the volume contributes to a debate on the possibilities of change through social, environmental and ecological solutions offered to the spatial problems and socio-economic challenges associated with 'liveable' life.

Artistic engagement with the imaginary of the precariousness

Precarity signifies many things and is commonly associated with socio-economic challenges of contemporary living, uses of public space, political issues of the creative classes, agency in arts, interventions and social movements. More broadly, it reflects contemporary interests in political philosophy and cultural theory, including the writings of Michael Hardt, Antonio Negri, Achille Mbembe, Paolo Virno, Zygmunt Bauman, Judith Butler, Claire Bishop and others.

This edited collection is concerned with a set of broadly defined arts-based relational practices and their potentiality to creatively facilitate knowledge exchange and to instigate social change. A closer examination of the agency, emerging out of relational or participatory art practices in precarious contexts, or addressing imaginary of precariousness, puts the role of self-organizing systems and its micro-politics at the centre of discussion.

In aesthetic terms, associated with broadly defined participatory or relational practice, that is, in dialogical aesthetics, the art object appears less important than the participatory process, or transgresses the purely artistic enactment of and engagement in a particular context; as argued by Claire Bishop, Grant Kester and others. The book seeks alternative answers as to how the artistic engagement within the participatory and relational paradigm can provide a tangible platform for an exploration of political alternatives for social change. The book also examines organizational practices that emerge from the grassroots, including circumstances of impoverished and dis-possessed communities and their bottom-up organizational forms. The question is: What kind of aesthetic lens is required for such an engagement?

Theoretical framings of dialogical aesthetics appear complex, oscillating between structuralist and post-structuralist positions and critical hermeneutics. Referring to Jürgen Habermas' concept of discursive interaction and the importance of openness, Jean-Francois Lyotard and his aesthetics of the *differand* and Ken Hirschkop's take on Mikhail Bakhtin's redemptive inter-subjectivity, Kester in *Conversation Pieces* provided a useful definition by describing dialogical aesthetics as being 'based on the generation of a local consensual knowledge that is only provisionally binding and that is grounded at the level of collective interaction' (2004: 112). Within a set of art practices that broadly aspire to dialogic aesthetics, a reflective positioning can act as a catalyst for change, potentially revealing more of the experiential specificity of the world as the context-focus unfolds. In a dialogic aesthetic frame, artistic practice embraces the importance of a dialogue, as an integral component to an engaged practice (Kosmala, 2010).

Nicolas Bourriaud, putting aside criticism associated with his writing, pointed out that the way of working for some contemporary artists today is governed by a concern to 'give everyone their chance,' through forms that do not establish any precedence, a priori, of the producer or the artist over the beholder, but rather negotiate open relationships (Bourriaud, 2002: 58). Representational conventions of the arts and aesthetics, therefore, may be challenged by the creative facilitation of knowledge exchange. It is also a site-specificity that can become a space for encounter. The space and its specificity can facilitate the possibility of change, with a shift away from art as object-making to art conceptualized as an open form of exchange or co-production, whether in reference to the gallery context, as Bourriaud discussed in *Relational Aesthetics* (1998/2002), or outside the gallery realms, as Kester delineated in *Conversation Pieces* (2004), and further developed in *The One and the Many: Contemporary Collaborative Art in a Global Context* (2011) in relation to politically engaged practice, blurring the line between community activism and art production. Yet, participative, interventional action does not necessarily embrace a 'positive' paradigm, as some artists and activists may be drawn to the 'good vibe' and 'social activism' promoted by Bourriaud (2002) or 'community art' (Kester, 2011: 2004), while others may incorporate 'aestheticisation' of poverty (Dezeuze, 2006) or an act of antagonism (Bishop, 2004) in artistic renegotiation and political reframing. There is also a wider problem associated with the way of art functioning in the processes of neo-liberal appropriation and the proximity of art and politics (Kosmala, 2015). Sholette (2011) has warned that political agency in art and collective action, although initially aimed at challenging the hegemony of the art world, risks being eventually co-opted or absorbed by the dominant system, appropriated by its institutions, or simply forgotten and marginalized.

Structure of the volume

This edited collection focuses on precarious spaces associated with or located in public realms, predominantly drawing on the South American experience, where alternative forms of urban informality may be emerging as a 'new paradigm for understanding urban culture' (Roy and AlSayyad, 2004). Some chapters also address the concepts of 'site-specificity' (Kwon, 2002) and location, pointing out the privilege of the artist's agency and origin in relation to cultural and social regeneration of precarious spaces and working with peripherally located communities around the globe. Artists can be seen as agents that can simulate change but also may act as those who contaminate space by their enacted roles in specific time-defined moments, challenging the boundaries of art production between politics and aesthetics. The authors in their chapters discuss various encounters and alternative strategies that can express experiential effects of intervention for being and becoming a more 'liveable' place. By doing so, the book's individual contributions help to invent archives and utilize modes of engagement for unleashing the hidden potential, aimed to transform the current condition (less 'liveable' place) and to discover innovative means for change.

The book consists of three Parts: **I: Introducing the Volume** explores the key terms advanced throughout, including a notion of precariousness, autonomy, community at periphery in global realms and social and organizational change, as well as introduces the context of the book; **II: Emancipating: The Arts and the Possibility of Change** discusses examples of artistic engagement in and with the precarious, and examining interventions addressing the questions of socio-economic change; **III: Resisting: Opening Organizations, Altering Organizing** explores the potentiality of cultural and other forms of organizations in engaging with the precarious, as well as discusses how forms of (self-)organizing can alter the political dynamics of neighbourhood and community building.

This opening chapter contextualizes the volume by introducing key terms associated with the notion of precarity and precariousness, as well as briefly discussing types of arts-based interventions that feature in the volume; reflecting upon a trend that revisits modernist artistic and social utopias, particularly in seeking positive cultural openings in specific sites and communities perceived as being vulnerable to precarious living. The Introduction supplements Chapter 2, which theorizes and discusses two particularly rich categories – planetarity and autonomy – that together can help reframe contemporary precarity debates by providing directions for renewed creativity in interactively responding to, and directing, social change. Brydon argues that although change is challenging, contemporary living provides opportunities for the kind of decolonizing project, linking global cognitive and social justice, as envisioned by Boaventura de Sousa Santos, Walter Mignolo, Gayatri Spivak and others.

Part II of the volume, **Emancipating: The Arts and the Possibility of Change** opens with Chapter 3, a case study of the *Complexo da Maré*, in Rio de Janeiro, Brazil, an area formed by abandoned industrial infrastructures and expanding slums. Vaz and Seldin discuss the processes of historical formation and transformation of architectural spaces within the *Maré* hybrid realms, and examine the relationship between the emerging culture in *Maré* and the existing, expanding city. The analysis draws on interdisciplinary inquiry, including writings of Brazilian geographers Milton Santos and Rogério Haesbaert, French cultural geographer Joël Bonnemaison, Brazilian cultural theorist Teixeira Coelho, Argentinian anthropologist Néstor García Canclini, among others. Kosmala in Chapter 4, drawing on the examples of site-specific works realized under the umbrella of 'Favela Painting', the arts-based interventions that are site-specific and targeted at the socio-disadvantaged areas, debates the potentiality of their critical dimension, bringing the voices of art theorists and critics in relational practice, including Grant Kester and Nicolas Bourriaud, as well as Brazilian geographer Milton Santos. Parry in Chapter 5 examines spontaneous vernacular architecture, its origins in indigenous building forms and construction methods, through the art practice of the artist Abraham Cruzvillegas who grew up in a squatter settlement on the then vacant periphery of Mexico City, in the so-called 'unofficial zone' of Ajusco. Cruzvillegas' artistic project *Autoconstrucción* relates the story of his childhood through the self-build construction of a family home on the volcanic lands. The chapter includes the associated discourse of artists such as Francis Alÿs, Santiago Sierra, Marijetica Potrc, as well as writings by art theorists and critics such as Claire Bishop, Grant Kester, Anna Dezeuze, among others. Olmos and Biffi in Chapter 6 present FOLi Lab, a museographic urban experiment from the First Biennial of Photography in Lima, Peru, aimed to provide an alternative space for reflection and appreciation of photographic culture locally. FOLi Lab made humble efforts towards public engagement across the wider social spectrum of Lima's population, fostering not only social integration, but increasing shared collaboration and local communities' participation during the Biennial. Imas and Weston in Chapter 7, building on Mouffe's agonistic pluralism and Boje's notion of ante/organized, introduce 'organsparkZ' defined as: 'forms of co-participative art-activist practices of spontaneous and an unrestrained nature, which are enacted in primarily (but not exclusively) precarious spaces.' In such a frame, the authors discuss the examples of creative responses to the crisis situation, emerging from local organizations: (1) Buenos Aires, Argentina, in occupied printing factory, Chilavert; (2) Cape Town, South Africa in non-profit organization Salesian Life Choices; and (3) Valparaíso, Chile, in the Valopo Hills' communities.

Part III: Resisting: Opening Organizations, Altering Organizing commences with Chapter 8 in which Carvalho and Marquesan discuss the historical formation of *Mbyá-Guarani* indigenous camps in Rio Grande do Sul state, Brazil, and their land occupation strategies. The authors analyse local histories of the camps, drawing on writings of Santana, Oliveria, Lima and others. The chapter explains the idea behind the *Mbyá-Guarani's* resistance strategy, based on exposing their own misery as an instrument of struggle for constitutional rights. In Chapter 9, Lima, Pires and Martins discuss examples of *Fábricas Recuperadas* and co-operatives from across Brazil's industrial sectors, varying from metallurgy to canvas textile production, focusing on the dilemmas of their origins and development. The authors make comparisons with the Argentinean case of *Fábricas Recuperadas*,[2] and argue that Brazilian recovery experiences did not manifest as a popular movement and never had back-up support from the trade unions. In Chapter 10, Darbilly presents examples of social practices associated with media activism in Brazil, such as Movement of Progressive Bloggers BlogProg and Mídia Ninja, and explores possibilities of resistance to the organizing practices of traditional dominant media corporations. In Chapter 11, Peci, Lacerda and Brulon probe how cultural organizing practices can produce space, transforming it in terms of its symbolic, political and technical dimensions, drawing on writings of Marcello Vieira, Milton Santos and Henri Lefebvre, among others. The authors examine how organizing practices encompassing a variety of cultural initiatives in an exemplary Brazilian favela, which they termed as favela *Fluminense*, can mediate the effects of precarity through the transformation of space within the confines of a so-called 'slum' territory. The volume closes with Chapter 12, written in a form of a performative letter exchange. Molina and Rockwell address each other with questions, hinting at the nature of human interdependency and the need to theorize what a political practice that takes human interdependency and vulnerability to others might consist of in searching for more 'liveable' lives.

References

Banks, M. and Hesmondhaugh, D. 2009. 'Looking for work in creative industries policy', *International Journal of Cultural Policy*, 15 (4), 415–430.

Bauman, Z. 2007. *Liquid Times: Living in an Age of Uncertainty*, Cambridge: Polity Press.

Bishop, C. 2004. 'Antagonism and relational aesthetics', *October Magazine*, 110 (Fall), 51–79.

Bourriaud, N. 1998/2002. *Relational Aesthetics*, Dijon: Les Presses du Reel.

Butler, J. 2004. *Precarious Lives: The Power of Mourning and Violence*, London: Verso.

Dezeuze, A. 2006. Thriving on adversity: The art of precariousness', *Mute* 2 (3) http://www. metamute.org/editorial/articles/thriving-adversity-art-precariousness   Accessed 12 June 2015.

Dezeuze, A. forthcoming. *Almost Nothing: Observations on Precarious Art Practices*, Manchester: Manchester University Press.

Foster, H. 2009. 'Precarious', *Art Forum*, December.

Harvey, D. 2010. *The Enigma of Capital and the Crisis of Capitalism*, Oxford: Oxford University Press.

Harvey, D. 2014. *Seventeen Contradictions and the End of Capitalism*, London: Profile Books.

Kalleberg, A. L. 2009. 'Precarious work, insecure workers: Employment relations in transition', *American Sociological Review*, 74 (February), 1–22.

Kester, G. 2004. *Conversation Pieces: Community and Communication in Modern Art*, Berkley, LA and London: University of California Press.

Kester, G. 2011. *The One and the Many: Contemporary Collaborative Art in a Global Context. Context*, Durham, NC: Duke University Press.

Kosmala, K. 2010. 'Expanded cities in expanded Europe: Resisting identities, feminist politics and their utopias', *Third Text*, 24 (5), 541–555.

Kosmala, K. 2015. 'Artistic tactics of the everyday: Ideology reframings in Gržinić and Šmid's practice'. In Thorsen, E., Savigny, H., Jackson, D. and Alexander, J. (Eds), *Media, Margins and Popular Culture*, London: Palgrave Macmillan.

Kosmala, K. and Imas, M. 2012. 'Narrating a story of Buenos Aires' Fabricas Recuperadas', *The International Journal of Management and Business*, 3 (1), 103–121.

Kwon, M. 2002. *One Place after Another: Site Specific Art and Locational Identity*, Cambridge, MA: The MIT Press.

Lloyd, M. 2008. 'Towards a cultural politics of vulnerability: Precarious lives and ungrievable deaths'. In Carver, T. and Chambers, S. A. (Eds), *Judith Butler's Precarious Politics: Critical Encounters*, London and New York, NY: Routledge.

McGuigan, J. 2010. 'Creative labour, cultural work and individualization', *International Journal of Cultural Policy*, 16 (3), 323–335.

Neilson, B. and Rossiter, N. 2006. 'From precarity to precariousness and back again: Labour, life and unstable networks', *Variant*, 25 (Spring), 10–13.

Roy, A. and AlSayyad, N. (Eds) 2004. *Urban Informality: Transnational Perspectives from the Middle East, Latin America, and South Asia*, Lanham, MD: Lexington Books.

Sholette, G. 2011. *Dark Matter: Art and Politics in the Age of Enterprise Culture*, London and New York, NY: Pluto Press.

Standing, G. 2011. *The Precariat: The New Dangerous Class*, London and New York, NY: Bloomsbury Academic.

Wacquant, L. 2008. *Urban Outcasts: A Comparative Sociology of Advanced Marginality*, Cambridge, MA: Polity Press.

Yiftachel, O. 2009. 'Theoretical notes on "gray cities": The coming of urban apartheid', *Planning Theory*, 8 (1), 87–99.

Notes

1   Linking to conflation of precarity debates, ways of living and creative labour, Banks and Hesmondhaugh have usefully summarized problems commonly related to experiences of creative class, as they argued that creative labour is:

> project-based and irregular, contracts tend to be short-term and there is little job protection; that is there is a predominance of self-employed or freelance workers; that career prospects are uncertain and often foreshortened; that earnings are usually slim and unequally distributed and that insurance, health protection and pension benefits are limited; that creatives are younger than other workers and tend to hold second or multiple jobs; and that women, ethnic and other minorities are under-represented and disadvantaged in creative employment.

> (2009: 420)

2   *Fábricas Recuperadas* is an umbrella term that refers to abandoned bankrupt businesses that were recovered at the time of the crisis initially in Argentina by workers themselves, promoting alternative organizing practices such as an elimination of operational management and flattening of the hierarchy in the organizational structure (Kosmala and Imas, 2012).

Chapter 2

How emergent cultural imaginaries of autonomy and planetarity can reframe contemporary precarity debates

Diana Brydon

Introduction

This chapter argues, first, that how communities imagine the spaces open to their agency is crucial in shaping the futures their members can devise; and secondly, that the concepts of autonomy and planetarity, when thought of together, can provide helpful directions for a renewed creativity in interactively responding to and directing social change. Although change can be frightening, our changing times provide new opportunities for the kind of decolonizing projects linking global cognitive and global social justice, as envisioned by Boaventura de Sousa Santos and his colleagues (2007a, 2007b). Santos attends to the epistemic violence that accompanied modernity and finds alternative modes of knowing in previously subjugated cultures of the world. His project of validating what he calls an 'ecology of knowledges' (2007a: ix–xvix), will eventually require rethinking many of the categories through which both scholarly knowledge systems and everyday common sense make meanings. This chapter attends to two particularly rich and problematic categories – planetarity and autonomy – which together can help reframe contemporary precarity debates addressed in this volume. To substantiate this argument, this chapter offers a literature review of some of the key ways in which planetarity is being used to elaborate on an emergent imaginary and redefine autonomy. These two cultural concepts carry important political implications for the organization of social relations at all scales of communal involvement.

Globalization, precarity and neo-liberal imaginaries

Contemporary cosmopolitan, feminist, decolonial, postcolonial and globalization studies have converged in recent years around discussions of precarious spaces. The production of 'precarity,' a complex and contested term as pointed out in Chapter 1, a neologism coined to describe new forms of labour organization (Neilson and Rossiter, 2005), is linked to trends in globalizing processes, especially to pressures that are often summarized as inspired by neo-liberal ideologies. Arguing that 'neo-liberalism has become the stamp of our age,' Marnie Holborow explains that it is 'at root an economic theory' that argues for the untrammelled efficiency of the market in shaping economic, political and social relations (2012: 14–15). This theory also functions as 'a dominant ideology emanating from a dominant class' (2012: 29) and as such works in contradictory ways. This perception of neo-liberalism emerged strongly in the aftermath of the financial crisis of 2008. Whereas previously many thinkers had been celebrating the autonomy afforded to individuals by freeing market flows from state regulation before the crisis, after 2008 the balance of attention began to shift towards redefining such flexible freedoms in terms of precarity. The emergent discourses of precarity now seem to have replaced earlier concerns about globalization that centred on the autonomy of the nation-state. A consensus now seems to have emerged that these earlier fears that globalization was weakening nation-state autonomy had diverted attention from growing inequalities within nation-states, as well as within areas beyond their control. An increased awareness of precarity now accompanies concerns about governance and legitimacy, while also motivating new social movements and re-energizing critique.

Pavan Kumar Malreddy defines precarity as 'an experiential and affective subject position that is produced by a lack of access to institutional structures that ensure safety, stability, income opportunities and protection' (2015: 14). Although he defines the term in relation to 'the normative categories of subalterns or proletarians (e.g. detainees of internment camps, sweatshop labourers and domestic workers),' the deprofessionalizing middle class is increasingly identifying with this subject position, as exemplified by the Occupy Movement. One might argue that precarity has been part of globalization discourse at least since Anthony Giddens (1999) wrote about 'our runaway world' and Ulrich Beck (1992) theorized the rise of 'the risk society.' Its more current manifestations, while continuing to stress a growing awareness of humanity's environmental dependencies, and the fragility of many multi-nation-states, centre more strongly than ever on growing economic disparities and the changing nature of employment. Insofar as awareness of human vulnerability can turn understanding of agency towards communal action, it can prove a potentially useful counter to neo-liberal indifference to human suffering. But it can also lead towards a sense of hopelessness that can be expressed through apathy, protest without offering alternatives, or even an increased selfish drive to succeed at any cost. This is why attention to autonomy, understood as self-determination, still matters, and why this chapter links that attention to emergent understandings of planetarity, providing a context for a renewed understanding of autonomy as fundamentally relational. 'Relational autonomy,' as theorized by feminist thinkers in particular, provides an important corrective to neo-liberal theorizations of autonomy as aggressively individualist (Code, 2000).

Globalization and autonomy

The theorization in this chapter builds on my experience in the 'Globalization and Autonomy' collaborative research group, funded by the Social Sciences and Humanities Research Council of Canada. In 2000, I joined this interdisciplinary research team, which framed its understanding of the challenges posed by globalization in terms of investigating *the relationship between globalization and the processes of securing and building autonomy* (Pauly and Coleman, 2008: viii; original emphasis). Implicit in our choice of theme was the emerging common sense of the time that globalization was creating a 'risk society,' in which precarious spaces were multiplying, and precarity was becoming the social norm – with each of these developments potentially impairing the capacity of nation-states and individuals within them to exercise their autonomy. Over subsequent years, my understanding of social change within shifting contexts of community formation has been shaped by this work and the demands it has made to question the ways in which people make meanings within different cultural contexts under changing historical and economic pressures. My theoretical approach derives from my background in feminist postcolonial studies and the teamwork that led to my co-edited volume in our Globalization and Autonomy series: *Renegotiating Community: Interdisciplinary Perspectives, Global Contexts* (Brydon and Coleman, 2008). In asking what happens to the autonomy of individuals and communities due to globalization, we addressed both the coercive and comforting dimensions of community while seeking to redraw the conceptual maps through which community, globalization and autonomy are understood. Those maps were largely created through the partnerships formed between Capitalism, colonialism and imperialism, through which a localized view of the world, grounded in imperialist knowledge formations, claimed universality for its values.

Decolonizing the mind

Postcolonial theory and cultural production set out to decolonize this dominant imaginary, but the decolonizing project has yet to be realized in either the academy or in the world beyond academia. While philosophically, there is a sense that justice will always be 'to come,' that recognition, while inspiring humility, should not deter efforts to move towards ending injustice now. In this chapter, my first concern is with epistemic injustice, whose ties to other forms of injustice are too often neglected. Decolonization of the imagination is an ongoing project, and takes different forms in different times and places. Internal disputes within the postcolonial field often miss the potential of postcolonial thinking to recast a shared project within a different mould. Ongoing disputes pitting theory against practice, university work against political work and resistance against complicity, are signs of a discourse that misrepresents the challenge of the postcolonial field to re-conceptualize human relations to each other, and to the world, beyond these disabling divisions. These opposed arenas, once understood as separate, are now being understood as connected within a larger epistemic frame associated with the ebbing dominance of European modernity.

The work of Walter Mignolo, in bringing Latin American decolonial analysis of 'the darker side' of modernity to a global audience, has been central in drawing attention to the 'cracks' in Eurocentric knowledge construction, and thus has actively advanced the project of 'provincializing Europe,' as advocated by Chakrabarty (2000). Even more importantly, however, this work retrieves alternative modes for making meaning and organizing human relations among themselves and the world. The success of the decolonial approach may be seen in the emerging consensus in certain circles that European thought is being displaced from its centrality, in Europe and the Americas, by other de-Westernizing configurations, as depicted in the 2015 study: *The Anomie of the Earth: Philosophy, Politics, and Autonomy* (Luisetti et al., 2015). This displacement is largely being facilitated by the increased visibility of the world's indigenous peoples on the global stage and by their success in getting the UN Declaration of the Rights of Indigenous Peoples ratified. But the potentially transformative impact of such decolonizing thinking has yet to be felt within either the academy or the wider societies of the West more generally. Malreddy (2011: 669) concludes that 'a neo-assimilatory process is already underway as most mainstream disciplines (sociology, psychology) list postcolonialism as just *another* methodology in their respective disciplinary traditions' (original emphasis), instead of considering the more fundamental challenges it poses. Most assessments concur – postcolonial critique has had an additive impact, enlarging the scope of disciplinary investigations, but without achieving a fully transformative impact. Gayatri Spivak argues the same process has blocked feminist analysis.

In both fields, the research imagination has yet to be 'de-parochialized' (Appadurai, 2000, 2006). Yet, at the same time, under other names, similar projects are underway. The editors of *Decolonizing European Sociology* conclude their introduction with the claim that 'our aim is to open up a space for a multiplicity of critical projects that may not use the same term for labelling themselves, but which pursue common goals' (Boatca, Costa and Rodriguez 2010: 2). This openness to multiple inflections of naming represents a promising redirection, especially for scholars and activists engaging in border-crossing team-based research. For example, Gluck and Tsing's collection, *Words in Motion: Toward a Global Lexicon* (2009), and Cassin, Apter, Lezra and Wood's *Dictionary of Untranslatables: A Philosophical Lexicon (Translation/Transnation)* mark a growing willingness to understand the network of travelling influences that shape concepts growing out of multiple contexts so that certain keywords of the Western civilizational imagination are now seen to be unable to indicate understandings of the world generated out of other, previously marginalized and now resurgent imaginative experiences. Other keywords, such as autonomy, need to be reclaimed from their neo-liberal appropriations.

The work of Nishnaabeg author Leanne Simpson, in *Dancing on Our Turtle's Back: Stories of Nishnaabeg Re-creation, Resurgence, and a new Emergence* (2011) and *Islands of Decolonial Love* (2013), returns to her language as the source of modes of thinking for reclaiming community and alternative understandings of culture and governance. As she explains: 'Our languages house our teachings and bring the practice of those teachings to life in our daily existence. The process of speaking Nishnaabewowin, then, inherently communicates certain values and philosophies that are important to Nishnaabeg being' (2011: 49). She further explains: 'Our social movements, organizing, and mobilizations are stuck in the cognitive box of imperialism and we need to step out of the box, remove our colonial blinders and at least see the potential for radically transformed ways of existence' (2011: 148). That potential will be found in the language. 'Bringing the old into the new is our way forward' (2011: 148–149), she concludes. Her texts put English into dialogue with her language of origin, to pull readers into an embodied understanding of her truth. She explains, 'our word for truth, (o)debwewin, literally means "the sound of the heart"' (2011: 94). That grounding in what she terms 'a Michi Saagig Nishnaabeg-constructed world' (2011: 95) exemplifies an understanding of the world literally danced into a renewed existence, which corresponds to what I see gestured towards in Gayatri Spivak's theorization of planetarity.

Planetarity and autonomy

In this context, Spivak's notion of 'planetarity' (2003) offers a complementary emergent cultural imaginary for revived research and social engagement. 'Planetarity,' as Spivak conceives it, offers an alternative to globalization and a way of defining the self that does not depend on opposition to an Other, or separation from a sense of communal responsibility. The problem with planetarity is its abstract quality, something it shares with globalization. In that sense it contrasts with Simpson's stress on land. Yet Simpson's land, 'our turtle's back,' in her people's cosmology, is part of what planetarity is attempting to signal; that is, a world outside Capitalist systems of relation, a world not constituted by a nature/culture binary.

'Transnational literacy' (Spivak, 2003: 81), a companion concept, refers to the modes of meaning-making that will arise as people educate themselves in the differences of planet-thought, and the linguistic diversity that 'was closed by colonialism' (Spivak, 2010: 34). What might such a project look like? Simpson's books, setting up a dialogue between Nishnaabeg and English concepts, grounded in the humanly experienced every day and rotating outwards, provide one example. Her thinking is in dialogue with Cree writer Neal McLeod, who explains: 'ê-ânisko-âcimoki, literally translated, means: "they connect through telling stories." The central strand in which Cree poetic discourse flourished and continues is through the connection of contemporary storytellers and poets to the ancient poetic pathways of our ancestors' (2014: 91). Such a process is open-ended and critical. It challenges Western notions of theory and tradition, grounding theory in 'concrete situations,' as well as noting that Cree traditions are built upon open-endedness and radical questioning (2014: 97). For such indigenous thinkers, local and global are not in contradiction but in complex and fluid relation.

From within what Simpson terms 'the cognitive box of imperialism,' planetarity and the transnational invoke large-scale border-crossing possibilities not usually associated with autonomy, which, at first glance, does not seem to belong in this grouping. I will make the case, however, that autonomy is precisely what is at stake in successfully negotiating change, within local and global contexts. Self-governance is not a concept the West can claim as solely its own, nor can it claim the sole right to define it.

Autonomy is generally viewed as a liberal concept, tied to Western traditions, and is often criticized as far too readily adaptable to neo-liberal demands. It is either ignored or attacked by mainstream postcolonial theory, yet, I would suggest, it requires renewed attention. Timothy J. Reiss (2002) addresses key problems with how the liberal concept of autonomy has been deployed in the cultural field. I take his arguments seriously, yet still believe that autonomy designates a value that is worth retaining, in a modified form. Redefining autonomy is what is at stake in Spivak's groundbreaking essay, 'Can the subaltern speak?' (1988; revisited in 1999).

In *Nationalism and the Imagination*, Spivak defines the subaltern as 'people who accept wretchedness as normality' (2010: 16). In *An Aesthetic Education in the Era of Globalization*, she names her preferred definition, as referring to 'those removed from all lines of social mobility' (2012: 430). These are the conditions of precarity. If autonomy refers to that system of relations that gives some people access to audibility, visibility and agency, while blocking others from access to such lines of social mobility, then it needs to be asked: How do the liberal definitions of autonomy, as a right and a value, need to be revised? This question formed part of the early postcolonial feminist insistence that Western women could not assume their definitional priority over the views of women in what was then called the Third World (Mohanty, 1984). If Western definitions of the human, agency and responsibility need to be rethought to address the situatedness of women in different parts of the world, as well as to more carefully understand what makes the subaltern, then interrogating autonomy must be part of that process of rethinking. Contemporary feminist philosophy continues to wrestle with these questions, asking, in response to some Muslim women's acceptance of Sharia law, for example, whether a decision to limit one's autonomy in certain ways can ever be made autonomously.

Although autonomy in many Western contexts is broadly understood to mark an individual's separation from community, I have come to see autonomy as always, in the end, relational autonomy. When understood as the capacity to give laws to oneself, autonomy functions as a social rather than an individual enterprise. At the same time, full recognition of a woman's right to autonomy also requires revision of what constitutes sociality; what Nancy calls 'being-in-common' (1991: xxxvii) and 'being together' (xxxvix) or, throughout his book of that title, 'being singular plural' (2000). In other words, autonomy needs to be freed from its role in legitimizing the possessive individualism, analysed by Macpherson (1962). The liberal notion of autonomy that produced a self-consolidating otherness for agents of imperialism, as described by Spivak, should not be allowed to strangle the more democratic potential of the concept. Rethinking autonomy involves respect for the other as fully representative of the human rather than as confined to particularity in opposition to the Western-determined universal. That respect for the other is now being taken even further, beyond assuming the centrality of humanity, into recognizing the agency of animals and objects. That expanded definition of relationality is linked by some to a type of planetary thinking in terms of geological eras, linked to the concept of the Anthropocene, but those extensions are not my focus here.

Yash Ghai claims that 'autonomy is increasingly becoming the metaphor of our times' (2000: 2). Yet, mainstream postcolonial and cultural theories have engaged this metaphor much less often, at least directly, than have democratic, feminist, philosophical and political theories. Closer attention to current debates over autonomy will be necessary for postcolonial cultural theory to move beyond its current position. Too often, postcolonial theorists simply dismiss the idea of autonomy as a Eurocentric imposition, without interrogating its complex and sometimes contradictory usages and its undeniable importance within current discourses of democracy, human rights, medical care and social justice. Neo-liberalism, based on an ideology of the possessive individual cast in opposition to the state and society, has led to a version of autonomy that feminist philosopher Lorraine Code labels 'a perversion of autonomy' (2000). That is not the kind of autonomy I am advocating here.

I am influenced by the work of feminists such as Code (2000) on 'relational autonomy' and by Cornelius Castoriadis' work (1991, 1998) in changing how the social imaginary is understood. For him, autonomy is the meaning-making creative power that constitutes society and enables people to imagine what is real. As Dilip Parameshwar Gaonkar explains, 'Castoriadis' account of the social imaginary as the matrix of innovation and change is linked to his central political project of promoting autonomy. According to Castoriadis, one cannot strive for autonomy without striving simultaneously for the autonomy of others' (2002: 8). This was the conclusion our Globalization and Autonomy research team arrived at in composing the volume, *Renegotiating Community: Interdisciplinary Perspectives, Global Contexts* (Brydon and Coleman, 2008). To engage in that project of collectively striving for autonomy, from a postcolonial perspective, requires moving away from what Gaonkar calls Castoriadis' 'staggering Eurocentrism' (2002: 9) and his masculinist bias. Postcolonial and indigenous theories encourage us to question the distinction Castoriadis makes between heteronomous traditional societies and autonomous modern societies, a distinction accepted by Charles Taylor in his *Modern Social Imaginaries*. I see Spivak's embrace of planetarity as an attempt to get beyond theories that distinguish between static traditional societies, where norms are assumed to be incapable of change, on the one hand, and self-identified modern societies, where self-questioning enables change, on the other.

Indigenous, decolonial and postcolonial work often refuses the tradition/modernity distinction and the assumptions on which it is based, which include assumptions about autonomy. From the modern point of view, individuals from so-called traditional cultures are seen as victims of their culture, unable to revise their inherited social norms, whereas modern individuals are autonomous, capable of critique and effecting change. Spivak describes one dimension of this thinking, when she dismisses the colonial trope of 'white men saving brown women from brown men,' and she moves away from this 'tradition versus modernity' optic in suggesting that her idea of planetarity is perhaps 'best imagined from the precapitalist cultures of the planet' (Spivak, 2003: 101). She sees in these precapitalist imaginaries an alternative to the need for self-consolidating others that characterizes European modernity. The challenge posed by these alternative imaginaries constitutes part of her project of training 'the imagination to be tough enough to test its limits' (Spivak, 2010: 47), 'unlearning our privilege as our loss' (Spivak, 1990: 9), and 'learning to learn from below' (Spivak, 2008: 43). Writing out of the eclipsed imaginaries of her people, Simpson seeks to escape the 'cognitive box of imperialism' through her own process of understanding loss and learning from the ancestors to revalue dreams and visions as routes into forms of imagining that align her community 'with the emergent and creative forces of the implicate order' (2011: 146). Revaluing orality is part of Simpson's method for simultaneously learning and teaching, an expanded form of transnational literacy.

Transnational literacy

Spivak introduces transnational literacy as a singular concept, designed to revise what literacy means beyond conventional notions of reading and writing, by insisting that it includes an awareness of the power relations built into knowledge production in local and cross-cultural contexts. As such, this kind of critical literacy is a task for everyone. How it is to be achieved will depend on the local circumstances in which learners function and what it involves will vary with those circumstances. At a general level, it requires in learners an aptitude for self-critique, vigilance and openness to challenge. In Spivak's formulation, transnational literacy also requires multilingualism, what she calls 'deep language learning,' and a special attentiveness to what she terms the precapitalist cultures of the world. For an academic audience based in the United States, she suggests transnational literacy can be developed through a process of mutual interruption between the multidisciplines of comparative literature and Area Studies, as practised within their nation (Spivak, 2003). Her prescriptions for other constituencies are different.

This chapter suggests there is much to learn from indigenous resurgence in the Americas. Simpson and McLeod write out of eastern and western North American indigenous understandings, respectively, interrupting, redirecting and expanding what the English language can articulate. In a related enterprise, Candice Amich analyses indigenous Chilean performance as documented in Cecilia Vicuña's formally innovative film to show how it 'refigures precarity, as the fragility of life and culture under conditions of neo-liberal globalization, into planetarity, an alternative that looks to precapitalist cultures to imagine a postcapitalist future' (2014: 135). What resonates for Amich in Spivak's theorization of planetarity is the ethical framework it provides 'for rethinking collectivity' in terms of 'receptivity and reciprocity' (2014: 148), a framework she finds exemplified in Vicuña's film. For Amich, a 'poetics of planetarity' must first 'register the sensory violence of globalization' and secondly, 'retreat from the desire to dominate time and space and embrace instead the alterity of the planet' (2014: 149). Although I appreciate her insights, I would argue that a focus on autonomy can enable a 'poetics of planetarity' to start from a different place, a recognition of the meaning-making systems that were occluded by colonialism but that survived in ceremony and memory.

Literature and culture: Versions of autonomy

Literature and culture are often assumed to exist within an autonomous sphere, freed from the market and the state. Some postcolonial theorists still defend this autonomy of the aesthetic, holding it to be an important value (Bongie, 2008). Culture holds a more complex position due to the interests of several disciplines in claiming culture as their terrain. Lawrence Grossberg notes that 'culture has increasingly moved from a transcendental autonomy to a form of quotidienization' but without necessarily shedding belief in its autonomy (2010). Grossberg defines this kind of autonomy as a particular form of 'embedded disembeddedness' (2010: 147). This allows the cultural sphere to claim a separate and privileged status within an often invisible system of unquestioned assumptions about how things are, even as this order is changing. Teasing out how this definition of autonomy as 'embedded disembeddedness' connects to autonomy, understood as self-determination, is a task that postcolonial cultural community and border studies are well suited to consider.

In *Cultural Studies in the Future Tense* (2010), Grossberg first notes, but then sidelines this kind of attention to the conditions available for knowledge production today. He provides a list of important issues he is unable to address: 'the environment (and the materiality of the world); religion; globalizations; various structures of belongings; militarism and violence; and the changing practices of knowledge production (under specific conditions of new technological, institutional, and postcolonial developments)' (2010: 5). A long list, these are questions that postcolonial and globalization studies prioritize and they are not so easily dismissed. In this chapter, however, I take issue only with his suggestion that all these problems are somehow equivalent, and their omission can be discounted given that 'cultural studies need not seek completeness' (2010: 5). In my view, the changing practices of knowledge production are not just one domain like the others; they constitute the changing context out of which we work and the emergent challenges we face within an academic system that is increasingly becoming internationalized in some respects while remaining dangerously parochial in others. Furthermore, currently dominant paradigms of internationalization stress competition between nation-states over transnational cooperation. Yet, cooperation is needed if solutions are to be found. In other words, how we make sense of the other issues he lists depends on the changing practices of knowledge production.

Grossberg does not quite see the connection when he admits another weakness of his book is that of the particular location out of which he writes:

> I know that the fact that I am trying to tell a story from inside the United States limits me in profound and sometimes disabling ways, for I can only follow the lines of transformation and struggle so far. And I know that the conversations I am calling for are already taking place in various regions of the world. I have tried to acknowledge and even enter into conversation with some of them, but I realize it remains too gestural.
>
> (2010: 5)

This is an honest and important admission, but a more serious problem than he implies. I work with a similar sense of my own limitations and a recognition that my Canadian location, and within Canada, my prairie location, while in some ways ex-centric to the academy he addresses – which in his words is 'largely the highly professionalized, capitalized, and formalized U.S. and European university systems' (Grossberg, 2010: 5) – is still insufficiently differentiated from them so as to afford much of an alternative view. In this sense, even those supposedly at the heart of the new empire inhabit precarious spaces. What is needed now is more than what any single individual or location can provide. Scholars need the kind of interregional, interdisciplinary, intergenerational and collaborative dialogue that carefully designed team-based research can provide. If scholars truly believed the UNESCO statement that 'the cultural wealth of the world is its diversity in dialogue,' then how might the spaces for dialogue be opened and rearranged?

To begin to answer that question, I suggest the following. Firstly, each location is different and will provide alternative formations enabling different views (as Grossberg would no doubt acknowledge). Secondly, not just the practices, but also the enabling conditions of knowledge production, and the status of knowledge producers, are changing more quickly than Grossberg recognizes. Thirdly, the hegemony of the United States in global knowledge production is very powerful, but its attendant parochialism is also more limiting than many within that system are able to see. Fourthly, the global power of the English language is an important element in that dominance but it could lose its pre-eminence very quickly (Ostler, 2010). Fifthly, some of the global conversations that Grossberg admits are already happening are more accessible than he suggests. Although he implies that his focus on the academy rules out engagement with other knowledge producers from outside the university system, to take such a stance is to ignore the many partnership projects between civil society groups and the universities. These borders are less heavily policed than he suggests. Finally, in his conclusion, Grossberg calls for cultural studies to engage in new conversations with such alternative knowledge-producing groups. Such conversations, he argues, could be 'trans-institutional,' 'trans-epistemic,' 'transnational and trans-regional' and 'trans-disciplinary' (Grossberg, 2010: 291). I endorse such a call, even as I caution against putting too much weight on the power of that word 'trans-'. This chapter suggests some of the transformations that answering his call may entail.

Grossberg notes that 'one cannot be interdisciplinary by oneself, and the collaboration cannot simply reproduce a disciplinary division of labour (e.g. I bring culture, you bring economics)' (2010: 292). As long as we continue to accept the current disciplinary divisions of labour, and the implied autonomy of their concerns, we will not be able to make the connections that globalization increasingly suggests will be essential to survival. The challenge is how to make those connections and keep them productive. Current publications in defence of the humanities, attacking neo-liberalism and written out of an increased sense of the precariousness of their positioning within a changing global higher education regime, may prove counter-productive.

In contrast, Spivak's theorizations of 'transnational literacy' and 'planetarity' offer connected ways of cutting across some of the problems associated with the 'embedded disembeddedness' of current disciplinary terrains and their divisions of responsibility. Each concept is based on respect for the autonomy of others; that is, for their right to make their own kinds of sense of how the world operates and to make their own choices about how to run their lives. This is where autonomy can become quite complex. It is one thing to recognize the value of the autonomy of others, as Grossberg does when he claims that 'it is not my job – as a critical scholar – to tell people what they should be or should desire' (2010: 97). It is another to ask how to adjudicate when competing autonomy claims clash in the politics of knowledge production or the making of public policy, or to ask if it is possible, in theory, for someone to choose, autonomously, to restrict or abdicate his or her own autonomy. That latter question is most often asked in reference to women, children or the cognitively disabled, suggesting that original definitions of autonomy based on the male as norm still trail some of that history with them and have not been as amenable to revision as earlier feminists had hoped. These are questions taking shape around current efforts to legislate the wearing of the *niqab*. Significant work in feminist philosophy, critical race, globalization, postcolonial and multicultural studies wrestles with these challenges. The resolutions of such questions carry material consequences for how we choose to live our lives together. One of the major obstacles to resolving some of these debates is the asymmetrical ways in which culture is understood as operating within different configurations of power.

Versions of planetarity

In this regard it can be helpful to ask what makes the Spivakian turn to 'planetarity' different from theorizations of cosmopolitanism, environmentalism, worldliness or globalization. Spivak is clear she 'cannot offer a formulaic access to planetarity. No one can' (2003: 78). I like the openness to the unforeseen here. Spivak admits she keeps 'feeling that there are connections to be made that I cannot make, that pluralization may allow the imagining of a necessary yet impossible planetarity in ways that neither my reader nor I know yet' (2003: 92). We feel ourselves to be on the cusp of opening horizons, but pluralization alone will not be enough, as she recognizes. Pluralization is so often the default mode of current theorizing, it no longer functions as a viable solution in itself. When she starts to delimit planetarity by clarifying what it is not, and what she hopes it might do, the stakes become clearer. Spivak proposes planetarity as a model to replace both her idea of postcolonialism and what she sees as its investment in 'mere nationalism,' claiming 'I outline this utopian idea [of planetarity] as a task for thinking ground because otherwise a "reformed" comparative literary vision may remain caught within varieties of cultural relativism, specular alterity, and cyber-benevolence' (2003: 81). She continues: '[t]ransnational literacy may remain confined within a politics of recognizing multiculturalism or of international aid, in the interest of a "Development" of which the promise of cyber-literacy is increasingly a part' (2003: 81). These are dangers to guard against as educators rush to embrace the agendas of critical digital and multi-literacies. But when she claims that 'cultural studies is heavily invested in new immigrant groups,' and continues: 'it seems to me that a planetary comparative literature must attempt to move away from this base' (2003: 84), she short-changes the necessary politics of renegotiating the social contract in multicultural nation-states and the potential of critical race studies, in dialogue with indigenous and settler colonial studies, to redefine urban, regional and national imaginaries. She dismisses both cultural and postcolonial studies too quickly in *Death of a Discipline*, equating them with a simplistic form of identity politics, which she labels as 'neither smart nor good' (2003: 84).

In contrast, Paul Gilroy is much more forthright about what he means by planetarity:

The planetary consciousness I am invoking was a precious result of anticolonial conflict. It is now a stimulus to the multi-cultural and a support for anti-racist solidarity. It was linked to a change of scale, a whole re-imagining of the world which had moral and political dimensions. That world became not a limitless globe, but a small, fragile, and finite place [...] It is a critical orientation and an oppositional mood.

(2005: 290)

Gilroy's adoption of the term picks up on its usefulness for forging anti-racist, postcolonial and environmental alliances but at the cost of downplaying radical alterity, which for Spivak is at the heart of the concept. I do not want to give up on the possibility of considering these two versions of 'planetarity' together. This is a project requiring more concentrated attention. Furthermore, if Spivak's planetarity is to grip locally situated imaginations in ways that can take them out of their own inherent biases, then we need to find ways to articulate its premonitions of radical alterity more closely to the histories and modalities of particular places in their specificity.

Ursula Heise (2008) dismisses Spivak's theorization of 'planetarity' as of limited value for eco-criticism due to its lack of attention to more practical issues of how to negotiate within and across currently established boundaries of difference and identity claims. Heise finds the trope of 'planetarity' lacking, because she finds it hard to see how its alternative framing of understanding can have any purchase in our contemporary world, which is structured around the nation-state system and the largely Eurocentric imaginaries that these tropes minimize. But surely this is the point. Spivak is making a utopian argument, less interested in negotiating change on the ground, at least immediately, than in working to rearrange desire through the slower work of teaching and imagining otherwise. She issues a more radical challenge to the imagination, a challenge she sees as necessary if current trends are to be altered. Yet there are dangers in this approach.

The open-endedness of Spivak's advocacy of 'planetarity' has made it vulnerable to co-optation by projects with very different orientations. Wai Chee Dimock (2006) conscripts planetarity to support her analytic shift towards 'deep time.' 'Deep time' highlights 'a set of longitudinal frames, at once projective and recessional, with input going both ways, and binding continents and millennia into many loops of relations, a densely interactive fabric' (Dimock, 2006: 3–4). This introduces an exciting and much broader perspective to literary studies, but there is a real danger that the centrality of unequal power relations gets lost within such a frame. The method becomes a modernist reading-back into history through the key preoccupations of our times: with cosmopolitanism, circulation, intertextualities, hybridities and mobilities organizing the inquiry. What remains is modernity's urge to universalize from an insufficient base and its denial of the power relations distorting its constructions.

In a related move, Susan Stanford Friedman (2010) claims her adoption of 'planetarity,' in opposition to Spivak's utopianism, for the very modernity that Spivak critiques. Friedman concludes her essay 'Planetarity' with the claim: 'Planetarity is not a threat, it is an opportunity. It means leaving the comfort zone for the contact zone' (2010: 494). She offers thirteen ways of looking at planetarity, and none of them involve power disparities. In contrast, Spivak's 'planetarity' *is* a threat. As such, it is the kind of opportunity not everyone will welcome. Friedman and Dimock embrace 'planetarity' as an opportunity to expand modernist studies and American studies, respectively, along what Friedman describes as 'three main axes – the temporal, horizontal, and vertical' (Friedman, 2010: 473). Spivak questions the logic of expansion itself, and the versions of exchange on which it thrives.

Dimock and Friedman show how literary studies are working hard to absorb 'planetarity' into a continuation of the modernist project. Spivak (2011) now regrets using the word 'planet,' given the associations it arouses with custodianship of the earth, which she believes: 'has led to a species of feudality without feudalism coupled with the method of "sustainability", keeping geology safe for good imperialism, emphasizing capital's social productivity but not its irreducible subalternizing tendency' (2011: 101–102). She insists that her use of planetarity 'does not refer to an applicable methodology' (2011: 101), and explains: 'I have given up hope that my counter-intuitive use of "planet" will fly, though many have claimed "planetarity" *a la* Spivak, even Christian theologians' (2011: 101). What she wished to invoke she now describes as 'a sense of the forbidding (non)place of "planetarity"' (2011: 101), a perspective from which liberal humanism, modernist aesthetics and deconstructive theory alike look irrelevant.

Planetarity is valuable, then, for its reminder of a fundamental, grounding precariousness built into the heart of human existence, and a humbling of human pretension, but it is not meant as an excuse for disengaging from immediate issues of injustice or the task of educators to rethink our functions within a changing system. The effort to think beyond contemporary understandings of what is possible is at the heart of what learning through transnational literacy can enable. An engagement with the challenges of Spivak's thinking can help postcolonial, cultural, community and border studies clarify what is at stake within current educational restructuring and maintain our commitment to finding the unexpected openings that Spivak associates with the un-coerced rearrangements of desire within our classrooms and transnational knowledge exchanges. For the range and power of contemporary precarity structures to be understood, more attention will need to be paid to how precarity is gendered, localized and racialized, and how it becomes articulated (made real and realizable), as well as naturalized within particular spaces. That work will need to be accompanied by creative projects that imagine alternative modes of social organization – a project this book begins to undertake.

This chapter has argued that emergent imaginaries of autonomy and planetarity result from the interplay of resurgent indigenous imaginaries and decolonizing initiatives generated from within and outside what is increasingly being seen as the cracking imaginary of 'the cognitive box of imperialism' (Simpson, 2011). That cognitive box creates precarity even as it promises security. Creatives, artists, community activists and academic researchers can come together in reimagining what relational autonomy could look like in multiple forms of practice. When the imagination is understood as a social practice, then the links between cognitive and social justice can begin to be envisioned.

Acknowledgements

The research was conducted, in part, with the support of the Canada Research Chairs program and the Social Sciences and Humanities Research Council of Canada. I am grateful to the Canadian Association of Cultural Studies for the invitation to first share some of these ideas, and for the subsequent audiences who responded to various versions of this thinking – at Linnaeus University in Sweden, at Tromso University in Norway and in the workshops of the Brazil-Canada Knowledge Exchange. Marcelo Milano Falcão Vieira was a valued member of this group who brought inspirational thinking in organizational theory and community cultural initiatives, but who passed away too early for our discussions to find full fruition. I have worked through earlier versions of my analysis of planetarity and transnational literacy in a series of articles, including Brydon (2009, 2010).

References

Alhassen, A. 2007. 'The canonic economy of communication and culture: The centrality of the postcolonial margins', *Canadian Journal of Communication*, 32, 103–118.

Amich, C. 2014. 'From precarity to planetarity: Cecilia Vicuña's kon kon', *The Global South*, 7 (2), 134–152.

Appadurai, A. 2000. 'Grassroots globalization and the research imagination', *Public Culture*, 12 (1), 1–19.

Appadurai, A. 2006. 'The right to research', *Globalization, Societies and Education*, 4 (2), 167–177.

Beck, U. 1992. *Risk Society: Toward a New Modernity*, London: Sage.

Bhambra, G. K. 2007. 'Sociology and postcolonialism: Another "missing" revolution?', *Sociology*, 41 (5), 871–884.

Birns, N. 2010. *Theory after Theory: An Intellectual History of Literary Theory from 1950 to the Early Twenty-First Century*, Peterborough: Broadview.

Boatca, M., Costa, S. and Rodriguez, E. G. 2010. 'Introduction: Decolonizing European sociology: Different paths towards a pending project'. In Boatca, M., Costa, S. and Rodriguez, E. G. (Eds), *Decolonizing European Sociology: Transdisciplinary Approaches*, Farnham: Ashgate, pp. 1–10.

Bongie, C. 2008. *Friends and Enemies: The Scribal Politics of Post/colonial Literature*, Liverpool: Liverpool University Press.

Brydon, D. 2009. 'Competing autonomy claims and the changing grammar of global politics', *Globalizations*, 6 (3), 339–352.

Brydon, D. 2010. 'Critical literacies for globalizing times', *Critical Literacy, Special Issue: Theories and Practices*, 4 (2), 16–28.

Brydon, D. and Coleman, W. D. (Eds) 2008. *Renegotiating Community: Interdisciplinary Perspectives, Global Contexts*, Vancouver: University of British Columbia Press.

Cassin, B., Apter, E., Lezra, J. and Wood, M. 2014. *Dictionary of Untranslatables: A Philosophical Lexicon (Translation/Transnation)*, Princeton, NJ: Princeton University Press.

Castoriadis, C. 1991. *Philosophy, Politics, Autonomy*, ed. D. Ames Curtis, New York, NY: Oxford University Press.

Castoriadis, C. 1998. *The Imaginary Institution of Society*, trans. K. Blamey, Cambridge, MA: The MIT Press.

Cetina, K. K. 2007. 'Culture in global knowledge societies: Knowledge cultures and epistemic cultures', *Interdisciplinary Science Reviews*, 32 (4), 361–375.

Chakrabarty, D. 2000. *Provincializing Europe: Postcolonial Thought and Historical Difference*, Princeton, NJ: Princeton University Press.

Clifford, J. 2007. 'Indigenous articulations'. In Wilson, R. and Connery, C. L. (Eds), *The Worlding Project: Doing Cultural Studies in the Era of Globalization*, Berkeley, CA: North Atlantic Books, pp. 13–38.

Code, L. 2000. 'The perversion of autonomy and the subjection of women: Discourses of social advocacy at century's end'. In Mackenzie, C. and Stoljar, N. (Eds), *Relational Autonomy: Feminist Perspectives on Autonomy, Agency, and the Social Self*, Oxford: Oxford University Press, pp. 181–209.

Dimock, W. C. 2006. *Through Other Continents*, Princeton: Princeton University Press.

Friedman, S. S. 2010. 'Planetarity: Musing modernist studies', *Modernism/modernity*, 17 (3), 471–499.

Gaonkar, D. P. 2002. 'Toward new imaginaries', *Public Culture*, 14 (1), 1–19.

Ghai, Y. 2000. 'Ethnicity and autonomy: A framework for analysis'. In Ghai, Y. (Ed.), *Autonomy and Ethnicity: Negotiating Competing Claims in Multi-Ethnic States*, Cambridge, MA: Cambridge University Press, pp. 415–440.

Giddens, A. 1999. *Runaway World: How Globalization is Reshaping our Lives*, London: Profile.

Gilroy, P. 2005. 'A new cosmopolitanism', *Interventions*, 7 (3), 287–292.

Gluck, C. and Tsing, A. L. (Eds) 2009. *Words in Motion: Toward a Global Lexicon*, Durham, NC: Duke University Press.

Grossberg, L. 2010. *Cultural Studies in the Future Tense*, Durham, NC: Duke University Press.

Gunkel, A. H. 2011. 'On cultural studies in the future tense: Pedagogy and political work in cultural studies', *Communication and Critical/Cultural Studies*, 8 (3), 323–329.

Heise, U. K. 2008. *Sense of Place and Sense of Planet: The Environmental Imagination of the Global*, Oxford: Oxford University Press.

Holborow, M. 2012. 'What is neoliberalism? Discourse, ideology and the real world'. In Block, D., Gray, J. and Holborow, M. (Eds), *Neoliberalism and Allied Linguistics*, London: Routledge.

Lee, E. Y. 2011. 'Globalization, pedagogical imagination, and transnational literacy', *CLC Web: Comparative Literature and Culture*, 13 (1), 1–12, http://docs.lib.purdue.edu/clc/web/vol13/iss1/1. Accessed 6 November 2015.

Luisetti, F., Pickles, J. and Kaiser, W. (Eds) 2015. *The Anomie of the Earth: Philosophy, Politics, and Autonomy in Europe and the Americas,* Durham, NC: Duke University Press.

Mackenzie, C. and Stoljar, N. (Eds) 2000. *Relational Autonomy: Feminist Perspectives on Autonomy, Agency, and the Social Self,* Oxford: Oxford University Press.

Macpherson, C. B. 1962. *The Political Theory of Possessive Individualism: Hobbes to Locke,* Oxford: Oxford University Press.

Malreddy, P. K. 2011. 'Postcolonialism: Interdisciplinary or interdiscursive?' *Third World Quarterly,* 32 (4), 653–672.

Malreddy, P. K. 2015. 'Introduction'. In Malreddy, P. K., Heidemann, B., Laursen, O. B. and Wilson, J. (Eds), *Reworking Postcolonialism: Globalization, Labour and Rights,* London: Palgrave Macmillan, pp. 1–15.

McLeod, N. 2014. 'Cree poetic discourse'. In McLoed, N. (Ed.), *Indigenous Poetics in Canada,* Waterloo: Wilfrid Laurier University Press, pp. 89–103.

Mignolo, W. D. 1995. *The Darker Side of the Renaissance: Literacy, Teritoriality, and Colonization,* Ann Arbor, MI: University of Michigan Press.

Mignolo, W. D. 2000. *Local Histories/Global Designs: Coloniality, Subaltern Knowledges, and Border Thinking,* Princeton, NJ: Princeton University Press.

Mignolo, W. D. 2015. 'Foreword. Anomie, resurgences, and de-noming'. In Luisetti et al. (Eds), *The Anomie of the Earth: Philosophy, Politics, and Autonomy in Europe and the Americas,* Durham, NC: Duke University Press, pp. vii–xvi.

Mignolo, W. D. and Escobar, A. (Eds) 2010. *Globalization and the Decolonial Option,* New York, NY: Routledge.

Mohanty, C. T. 1984. 'Under Western eyes: Feminist scholarship and colonial discourses', *Boundary 2,* 12 (3), 333–358.

Morris, R. C. (Ed.) 2010. *Can the Subaltern Speak? Reflections on an Idea,* New York, NY: Columbia University Press.

Nancy, J. L. 1991. *The Inoperative Community,* trans. P. Connor, L. Garbus, M. Holland and S. Sawhney, Minneapolis, MN: University of Minnesota Press.

Nancy, J. L. 2000. *Being Singular Plural,* trans. R. D. Richardson and A. E. O'Byrne, Stanford, CA: Stanford University Press.

Neilson, B. and Rossiter, N. 2005. 'From precarity to precariousness and back again: labour, life and unstable networks', *The Fibreculture Journal,* 5, http://five.fibreculturejournal.org. Accessed 6 November 2015.

Ostler, N. 2010. *The Last Lingua Franca: English until the Return of Babel,* New York, NY: Walker & Co.

Pauly, L. W. and Coleman, W. D. (Eds) 2008. *Global Ordering: Institutions and Autonomy in a Changing World,* Vancouver: University of British Columbia Press.

Reiss, T. J. 2002. *Against Autonomy: Global Dialectics of Cultural Exchange,* Stanford, CA: Stanford University Press.

Santos, B. S. (Ed.) 2007a. *Another Knowledge is Possible: Beyond Northern Epistemologies,* London: Verso.

Santos, B. S. (Ed.) 2007b. *Cognitive Justice in a Global World: Prudent Knowledges for a Decent Life,* Lanham, MD: Lexington Books.

Simpson, L. 2011. *Dancing on Our Turtle's Back: Stories of Nishnaabeg Re-Creation, Resurgence, and a New Emergence*, Winnipeg: ARP.

Simpson, L. 2013. *Islands of Decolonial Love*, Winnipeg: ARP.

Spivak, G. C. 1988. 'Can the subaltern speak?'. In Nelson, C. and Grossberg, L. (Eds), *Marxism and the Interpretation of Culture*, London: Macmillan, pp. 217–315.

Spivak, G. C. 1990. *The Post-Colonial Critic: Interviews, Strategies, Dialogues*, ed. S. Harasym, New York, NY: Routledge.

Spivak, G. C. 1999. *A Critique of Postcolonial Reason: Toward a History of the Vanishing Present*, Cambridge, MA: Harvard University Press.

Spivak, G. C. 2003. *Death of a Discipline*, New York, NY: Columbia University Press.

Spivak, G. C. 2006. 'World systems and the Creole', *Narrative*, 14 (6), 102–112.

Spivak G. C. 2008. *Other Asias*, Malden, MA: Blackwell.

Spivak, G. C. 2010. *Nationalism and the Imagination*, London: Seagull Books.

Spivak, G. C. 2011. 'Response', *Parallax*, 17 (3), 98–104.

Spivak, G. C. 2012. *An Aesthetic Education in the Era of Globalization*, Cambridge, MA: Harvard University Press.

Staten, H. 2005. 'Tracking the "native informant": Cultural translation as the horizon of literary translation'. In Bermann, S. and Wood, M. (Eds), *Nation, Language, and the Ethics of Translation*, Princeton, NJ: Princeton University Press, pp. 111–126.

Taylor, C. 2004. *Modern Social Imaginaries*, Durham, NC: Duke University Press.

Part II

Emancipating: The Arts and the Possibility of Change

Chapter 3

From the precarious to the hybrid: The case of the *Maré* Complex in Rio de Janeiro

Lilian Fessler Vaz and Claudia Seldin

Introduction

This chapter looks at socio-cultural changes in a region of Rio de Janeiro, Brazil, called *Maré* Complex (*Complexo da Maré*), formed by abandoned industrial areas and expanding slums. In this region, we can observe the emergence of a new territory; an area of resistance, or a hybrid area, where housing, work and culture all mix together and the traditionally formed logic, based on industrialization and slum discourse, has been replaced by new, more complex dynamics – a result of deindustrialization and the multiple uses of urban space.

Maré is formally a wetland area on the Northern Zone of Rio, and is constituted of sixteen different slums. Its growth was parallel to the growth of industrial activities in the region during the 1940s and 1950s, and its population consisted mostly of informal settlements built by nearby industrial workers (Abreu, 2006). Characterized by poverty and a large number of stilt houses, this complex of slums was the target of major urban interventions in the 1980s and 1990s, amongst which we highlight the Rio Project in 1982 that included sanitation and the implementation of social housing, as well as the construction of two new road axes in the 1990s – the Red and Yellow Lines (*Linhas Vermelha e Amarela*).

These major interventions were simultaneous with the process of deindustrialization of the area beginning in the 1980s, which caused several factories to close down, leaving behind abandoned infrastructure and urban voids that pointed to the degradation of *Maré*'s urban landscape. With the reduction of work opportunities and lack of appropriate public policies and social housing options in the region, these empty buildings were subsequently occupied with non-industrial activities. The new mixed occupations, which involved simultaneous cultural, residential and institutional uses, resulted in the formation of a new territory, marked by hybridism.

As part of our attempt to understand the complexity of a hybrid territory in formation, we draw on various fields of knowledge including architecture, urban planning and geography (Bonnemaison, 2002; Haesbaert, 2004; Santos, 1994, 2009); cultural studies (Barker, 2005; Coelho, 2004; Hall, 1992), anthropology and sociology (Canclini, 1997, 2008; Holston, 1996, 2008), as well as urban history (Abreu, 2006; Certeau, 1998). This interdisciplinary approach can help us better comprehend not only the spatial relationships existing in *Maré*, but also the social, cultural and power relations of this territory.

Firstly, we draw on the concept of opaque spaces, as defined by Brazilian geographer Milton Santos (1994, 2009). For Santos, opaque spaces are those connected to poverty, irregularity and informality of settlements, as opposed to the bright spaces, marked by abundance, rationality and formality of design. From the point of view of the opaque, we contextualize the history of *Maré*, presenting the new mixed occupations researched in the area.

Further ahead, we delve into the concept of *Maré* as a unique territory within the city fabric. We draw on the writings of cultural geographer Joël Bonnemaison (2002), for whom a social group, its culture and its territory are inseparable and indispensable elements to understand the interface between space and culture. For Bonnemaison, a place is a lived space, an area to which meanings have been assigned. Following this line of argument, *Maré* territory can be envisaged as a manifestation of the production of meanings in a space.

While addressing territory, we also draw on the concept of hybridization, proposed by Argentinian anthropologist Néstor García Canclini (1997, 2008), which allows us to analyse the blend, retrofits and upgrades that occur in times of globalization, refusing fixation in isolated disciplines and concepts and focusing on the assumptions of heterogeneity. We also use the concept of micro-resistance from Certeau (1998), regarding the tactics and everyday practices used to reutilize objects and spaces and subvert the institutionally imposed references and standards as a means to create fissures in the established relations of power. It could be argued that these practices can be more than silent and subtle forms of resistance, expressed not only through cultural and artistic manifestations, but also through the spaces they are able to create. Through the means of art, culture and space production, these forms of micro-resistance may also be considered as emancipatory movements, or alternative ways to fight for the right to the city, as addressed by Lefebvre (1991).

Precarious spaces vs opaque spaces

When we discuss precarious spaces in Brazil, we automatically think of the 'favelas,' a term that refers to the local slums sprawled either on flat land or on the hillsides of both metropolitan centres and smaller cities across the country. The favelas usually replace former green areas with densely packed constructions, where the poorest sectors of the population live and where low-quality infrastructure prevails.

Over the last century, the favelas in Rio de Janeiro have turned into a significant share of urban reality. In order to understand their proliferation, it is necessary to emphasize the considerable framework of segregation and inequality that characterizes this city. The local disparities are combined with an absence of egalitarian public policies, a lack of social security and a general disregard to the inhabitants of peripheral areas. Furthermore, there is a clear preference for investments (public and private) in the renewal of the most visible and wealthy neighbourhoods. Consequently, the favelas are marginalized and perceived in a derogatory manner – both locally and globally. This perception is largely based on the idea of absence, focusing on what is lacking rather than on what is abundant. As a result, the general discourse surrounding the favelas is linked to negative connotations of violence, misery, ill-health, drugs and the lack of urban infrastructure (such as water supply, electricity, sewage and waste collection). If, for the most part, these problems are indeed real, there is another side to the favelas, frequently ignored by the homogenizing discourse, which deem all favela spaces as poor urban dwellings. We argue here that it is necessary to identify the differing realities of the more than 700 favelas of Rio de Janeiro, acknowledging the diverse and rich culture they produce.

That is why we propose that favelas should be considered not necessarily as precarious, but as 'opaque.' According to the Brazilian geographer Milton Santos (1994, 2009), opaque spaces are those spaces – opposed to the type of spaces considered to be luminous and modernized – that are quick to mobilize, representing an informed city. Whilst luminous spaces, where the wealthiest group of the city population live, would be marked by regularity, restriction, mechanical routines and a lack of surprise, the opaque spaces are organic, spontaneous, filled with social interactions and improvisation. These are spaces marked by proximity, creativity and openness (Santos, 2009: 261).

The opaque spaces would also be the places where the economically non-hegemonic classes inhabit, circulate and survive, 'where times are slow, adapted to the incomplete or inherited infrastructures of the past' (Santos, 1994: 39), representing 'zones of resistance,' particularly cultural resistance. These spaces would be characterized by action, 'beginning with the action of thought' (Santos, 1994: 42). It is in the opaque spaces that we see transformations that could change the homogenous dominant cultural standards of contemporary urban living, thus placing the most disadvantaged groups as actors capable of initiating new debates about the city's future. One such debate concerns cultural access, defending a better distribution of infrastructural facilities throughout the city, as well as generating more visibility and legitimacy to undervalued cultural practices, which emerge in poorer areas. In Rio de Janeiro, such debates materialized in initiatives that altered the homogenous dominant cultural standards of contemporary urban living. Such is the case of the dwellers of the *Maré* Complex. This chapter considers the favela of *Maré* from the perspective of its potential to oppose but simultaneously complement the formal city.

The *Maré* Complex: A brief contextualization

The *Maré* Complex, situated in the Northern Zone of Rio de Janeiro, is formed by sixteen favelas and adjacent spaces, accommodating around 130,000 inhabitants,[1] in an area of approximately 800 km^2. Over the past few decades, *Maré*, as it is known, has been the backdrop for continuous conflicts between different drug trafficking groups. As a result through the media discourse, extreme violence has been associated with this area within the city. Furthermore, in the last demographic Census of 2010, it has also been identified by the Brazilian Institute of Geography and Statistics (IBGE) as one of the districts with

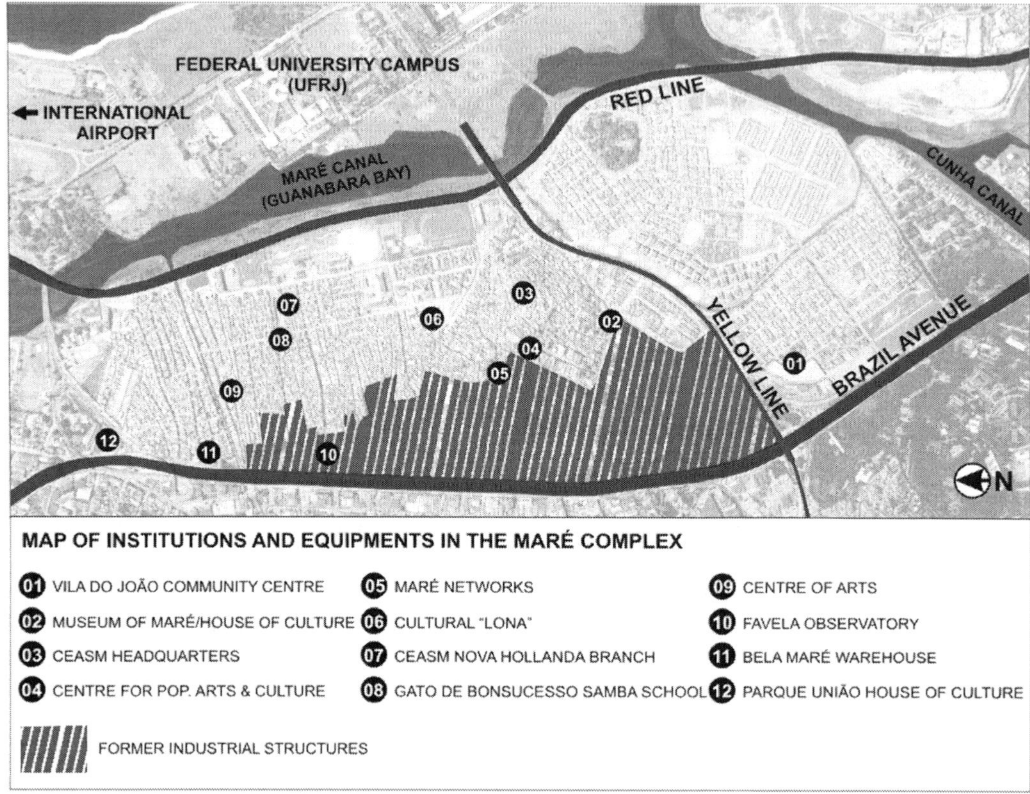

Figure 3.1: Partial schematic map of the *Maré* Complex, highlighting some of its known cultural spaces, 2013. Personal archive. Courtesy of Pereira Passos Institute.

the lowest Human Development Index figures and with the largest concentration of low-income residents.

Despite being recognized as an official district by the local city council since 1994, the region is still considered by many as a transit zone on the periphery of the city. This is mainly due to the fact that the area is located between two of the primary municipal highways – the Brazil Avenue and the Red Line – and is further intersected by a third highway called Yellow Line.[2] Alongside the highway, besides the sixteen clearly defined favela communities, there is a large area of urban fabric, characterized by abandoned industrial warehouses.

The multifaceted scene observed today – defined by a mixture of high-density abandoned areas, overcrowded and unoccupied lots, as well as residential and industrial buildings – started to form in the 1940s, when the occupation of the region intensified. Until then, *Maré* was associated with a bucolic landscape of beaches, mangroves and a fishing village. This intense occupation in the 1940s coincided with the growth of industrial activity in the region, and was greatly influenced by the designation of the area as an Industrial Zone in 1937, and subsequently by the inauguration of the Brazil Avenue in 1946 – for decades the only highway in and out of the city. The spread of factories in surrounding areas attracted a large population, mainly composed of migrants from the northeast of the country. New migrant workers quickly settled in the abundant land of *Maré*, which had escaped property speculation due to the difficulty, or impossibility, of constructing on its marshland, rocky areas and slopes. Due to the mixed landscape of swamps and hills, *Maré* saw two basic types of occupation: the construction of shacks in elevated and dry regions and the construction of shacks on stilts, initially built on swampland close to the highway, and subsequently spread out over the waters of the Guanabara Bay (*Baía de Guanabara*). We could argue that the occupation of each community of the *Maré* Complex occurred in its own particular way, generating a great diversity of urban morphologies and architectural typologies (Vaz, 1994; Seldin, 2008).

Today, this morphological diversity is ever more pronounced, marked by a large number of factories, warehouses and industrial spaces, concentrated in an intermediary strip between the highway and the favelas. Many of these factories have been shut down or abandoned since the 1980s, when the industry sector began to look for more profitable locations, away from the expensive urban centres of the metropolis. Because of this intense process of deindustrialization, countless urban voids were created.[3]

Ways of occupying the *Maré* Complex

Unlike the urban voids located around the historic centre of the city, *Maré*'s outlying industrial voids have not become the target of public policies, nor of private interventions aimed at urban renewal. In the case of *Maré*, as time went by, the former industrial sites began to be occupied once again not for industrial uses this time but by people in search of alternative housing options, local cultural groups and informal service suppliers.

In reference to housing occupations, we have observed a new, different kind of 'intramural favela,' no longer clearly visible on the local landscape. Its growth takes place inside the warehouses and courtyards, hidden by the high factory walls. This residential occupation is often accompanied by the leasing of internal spaces for the development of informal services, car-parking being one of the most common. When not accompanied by services, the residential use is usually followed by a simultaneous cultural use.

The *Maré* Centre for Popular Arts and Culture

A pre-eminent example of mixed residential and cultural occupation refers to the squats growing inside the walls of the former Quartzolit factory, a paint and building material manufacturer, once based in the Timbau Hill favela (*Morro do Timbau*). This particular lot, at one point known as the *Maré* Centre for Popular Arts and Culture (*Centro de Artes e Cultura Popular da Maré*), and more recently as the Portelinha Occupation (*Ocupação Portelinha*), is constituted by a five-storey administration building and equipped with spacious rooms, two vast warehouses and private courtyards. In this case, as with others in *Maré*, there is a territorial dispute over property rights, which involves a diverse range of interests, such as those of dwellers, artists, drug dealers and non-governmental organizations (NGOs).

With the closing of the Quartzolit factory in the early 1990s, its legal owners experienced great difficulties in selling the property, mainly due to a lack of interest by other corporations in acquiring a large building located in an area known for its growing violence, as reported by local and national media throughout the 1990s:

> Residents of the Maré complex, a set of slums in the Northern zone of Rio, clashed with the police on the afternoon of Wednesday, during a protest against the construction of a military police battalion station in the region. [...] In the afternoon, the mood in the complex resembled war. Residents of New Holland (Nova Hollanda), one of the slums in the Maré Complex, occupied lanes of the Brazil Avenue and Red Line in order to protest the construction of the military battalion station. They argue that the battalion will occupy an area of the city that was destined to host the second part of the Olympic Village within the complex. [...] Mário Domingues, president of the Olympic Village of Maré, said that residents would rather have the new battalion built between New Holland and the neighbouring slum of Timbau. [Drug] trafficking in the two communities, separated only by a street, is dominated by rival factions: in New Holland, by the 'Red Command'; in Timbau, by the 'Third Command'.
>
> 'We, of New Holland, cannot use the pool and the court of the Olympic Village, because it is located in the area of Timbau. They will not let us in. That is why we asked for a battalion, but it cannot be built here, nor can it be built in the area reserved for the leisure of the community. If this happens, besides kids getting no activity, we will be trapped', said an annoyed resident identified only as Tereza Cristina.
>
> (Folha de São Paulo, 2001)

The closed building of the former factory in Timbau remained under the watch of private security until 2004, when the site became the target of 'invasions' by people looking to sell remaining industrial material left inside, as well as by families looking for settlement. These invasions culminated in a massive depredation of the building and its structure. After 2005, the residents' association of the Timbau Hill favela attempted to avoid a larger illegal occupation of the site by contacting the building's owners and the local authorities with a proposal for cleaning up the courtyards, in order to convert them into sports courts, initiating a period of coordination and negotiation between different agents. Amongst the parties involved were the squatters, residents of other parts of the *Maré* Complex, leaders of NGOs and cultural organizations that had an interest in occupying the site, the residents association of Timbau, the building's owners, members of public organizations (such as the Federal University of Rio de Janeiro – UFRJ) and even the representatives of drug trafficking gangs. Once the clean-up of the courtyard was completed, the proceeds of the sale of rubble

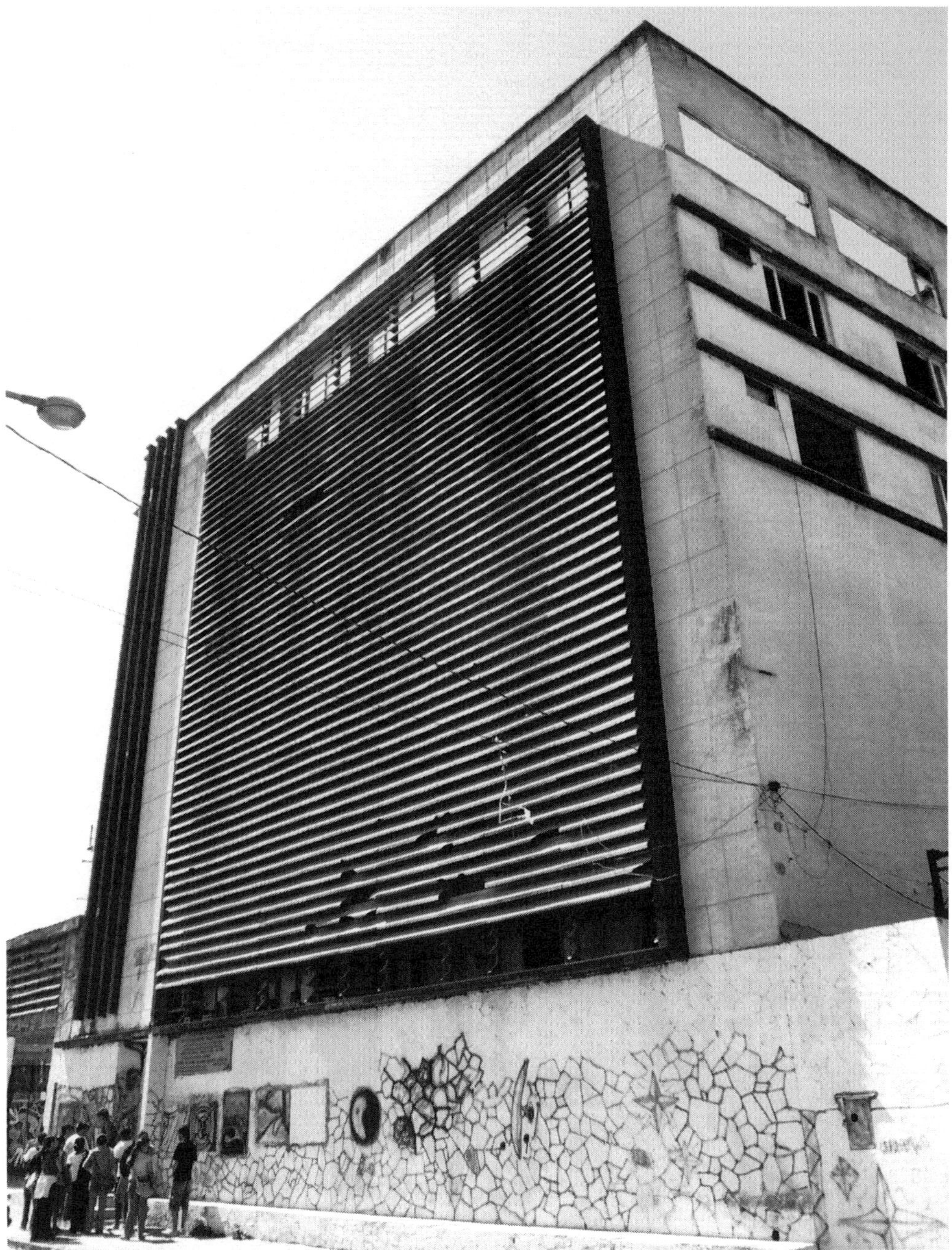

Figure 3.2: Facade of the main building where the *Maré* Centre for Popular Arts and Culture used to be located, 2007. Personal archive. Photograph by Claudia Seldin.

and scrap metal were reverted to the participants. This collective action of tiding up the site encouraged further occupation of the building, as some of the people involved felt entitled to use the spaces they had helped to restore.

It is important to highlight that by 2005, the owners of the building had accumulated large fiscal debts due to evading property taxes. Because of this, they wished to donate the lot to the new occupiers in hopes of a pardon. The city council allowed the transaction; however, the amount of the owner's debts was considered higher than the real estate value, which meant that a full pardon could not be granted. The city council's unwillingness to pardon the amount outstanding, combined with the slow pace of the local government's administration and bureaucracy has resulted in problems with the transfer of property, which to this day remains unresolved.

In the subsequent years, the confusion surrounding the ownership of the lot, along with a lack of resources from the initial occupying groups, led to further invasions. Soon, a new residential occupation took hold of the internal courtyards and one of the warehouses. The squatters were mainly former *Maré* residents, evicted from nearby favelas. Their settlement triggered the aforementioned process of 'intramural favelalization,' hidden by the factory walls, and invisible to the outside.

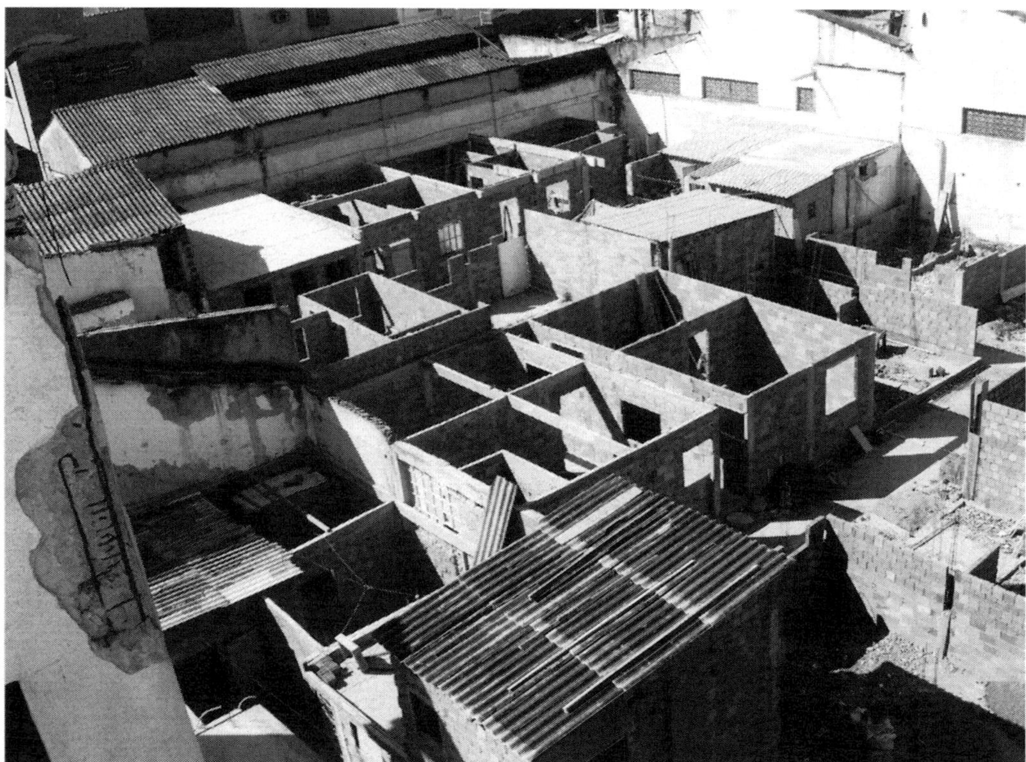

Figure 3.3: View from the terrace of the *Maré* Centre for Popular Arts and Culture to one of the internal courtyards, 2007. Personal archive. Photograph by Lilian Fessler Vaz.

In 2006, a cultural group entitled Capoeira Angola Ypiranga de Pastinha (GCAYP) occupied the ground floor of the administration building with the intention of securing the space, preventing later invasions. This artistic collective focused on the practice of *capoeira*, teaching its history and emphasizing its roots with the purpose of raising cultural and social awareness. *Capoeira* is a practice that mixes sports, martial arts, music and dance, and was brought to Brazil by Bantu slaves from Africa (Vaz and Seldin, 2007). Requiring great flexibility, speed and muscular effort, the *capoeira* player can attack or defend himself against the opponent within a circle composed of other participants, who sing songs to the sound of specific musical instruments particular to the *capoeira* practice, such as the *berimbáu*. *Capoeira* mixes sports and artistic elements, but also requires the player to have attitudes and take initiatives based on reasoning, intuition and improvisation as responses to the misleading movements of the opponent. This art form is seen by many as a means to prepare for life, to cope with everyday situations and with struggle. The type of *capoeira* practiced by the GCAYP is known as *Capoeira Angola* and follows the school of Master Pastinha, a defender of slave traditions and of the original philosophy behind this art form. Inside the old Quartzolit factory building, the GCAYP group also offered African dance classes and provided extra school tutoring in partnership with four municipal public schools in *Maré*. In doing so, the organization crossed the boundaries of mere cultural practice, transforming the space into an alternative social facility with a 'bottom-up' discourse, responding to real local needs.

After the GCAYP's successful installation in the building, other musical, martial arts and educational collectives showed an interest in the former factory's large empty rooms. These smaller groups, who also suffered with the scarcity of spaces for the development of their own activities, sought to form a partnership with the GCAYP, bringing about the creation of an alternative cultural facility under the name of *Maré* Centre for Popular Arts and Culture.[4]

The creation of the *Maré* Centre for Popular Arts and Culture can be perceived as a direct result of the lack of accessible formal cultural facilities in Rio de Janeiro, as well as of the unequal distribution of cultural experience in the city. History proves that the dwellers of marginalized areas are able to overcome certain obstacles because they possess the necessary endurance and creativity to 'invent' solutions to experienced problems. In this case, the solution was the creation of a new, alternative cultural space. The former factory, once marked by mechanical activities, line production, control and regularity was substituted by improvisation, artistic practices, dialogue and spontaneity. We highlight that the *Maré* Centre for Popular Arts and Culture, which remained open for over six years, is only one of the several alternative cultural spaces that emerged and continue to emerge in old industrial warehouses in the *Maré* Complex, denoting the stark contrast between the process of deindustrialization and the proliferation of cultural activities in the region.

After 2010, the residential squatters of the former Quartzolit factory began to organize more systematically, holding meetings in partnership with local NGOs and academic institutions in order to become better informed on the issues of ownership of the property and understand their legal rights. As the housing occupation of this site gained strength, many of the cultural projects located inside the building opted to move to other parts of the *Maré* Complex and of the city.[5] Nowadays the site is better known as the Portelinha Occupation, a name that refers to the story of a Brazilian soap opera of 2007 entitled *Duas Caras*. The residential occupation of Portelinha still holds an uncertain future due to the lack of clarification of the legal issues surrounding the land.

The Museum of *Maré*

Despite the transitory character of the cultural occupations in *Maré*, the complex is still home to one of the city's most important cultural facilities located in a favela and officially recognized by the Brazilian Ministry of Culture:[6] the Museum of *Maré*. Also situated in the Timbau Hill, the museum was developed by one of the most significant local associative movements, the *Maré* Centre for Studies and Solidarity Actions (CEASM), a non-profit civil association conceived in 1997 by a group of local and former residents with the aim of widening the local residents' access to culture. Inaugurated in 2006,

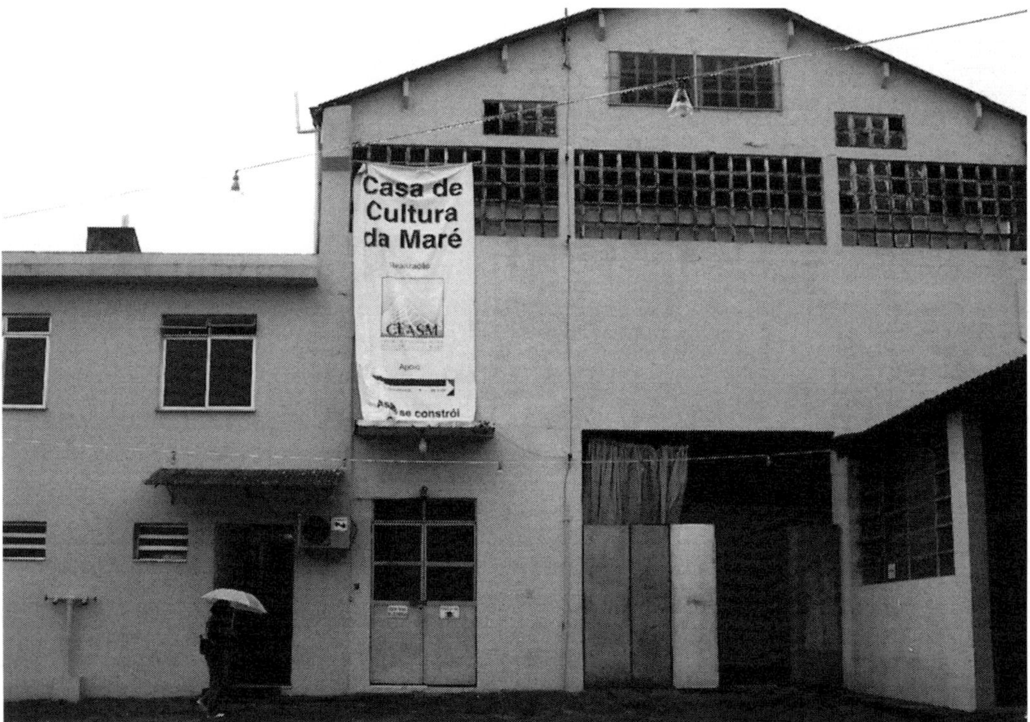

Figure 3.4: Facade of the Museum of *Maré*, 2007. Personal archive. Photograph by Claudia Seldin.

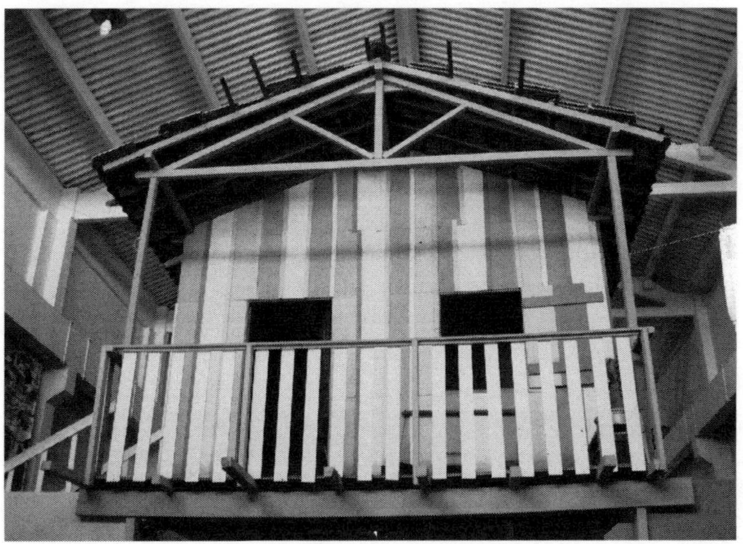

Figure 3.5: Reproduction of the Stilt House at the Museum of *Maré*, outside, 2007. Personal archive. Photograph by Lilian Fessler Vaz.

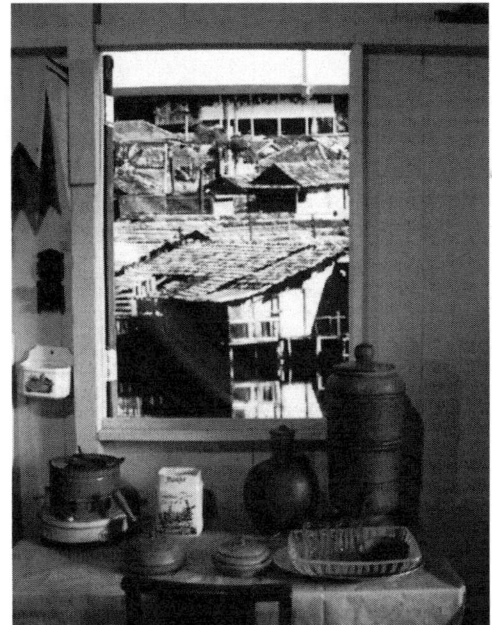

Figure 3.6: Reproduction of the Stilt House at the Museum of *Maré*, inside, 2007. Personal archive. Photograph by Lilian Fessler Vaz.

the museum is part of an 800 m² site where, until the beginning of the 1990s, was a boat repair yard.

The Museum's archive is composed almost entirely of objects donated by residents of *Maré*. The museum focuses the exhibition around the history of the community from a local point of view. The permanent exhibition, named *Times of Maré*, is divided into twelve installations, each focused on one important aspect of life in *Maré*, such as: *Times of Immigration, Times of Water, Times of the Home, Times of the Everyday, Times of Resistance, Times of the Festivity, Times of Street Markets, Times of Faith, Times of Children, Times of Fear, Times of the Future*. This way, the curators highlighted the importance of immigrants from the northeast of Brazil coming to Rio de Janeiro in order to build the favelas in *Maré*, their struggles to build the stilt houses on the water terrain and the cultural and religious practices of different settler groups. The central element of the museum is the installation called *Times of the Home*, represented by a tall stilt house that reproduces the typical dwelling of the region. The stilt house has a small veranda, and is an independent structure, supported by wooden stakes, inside the warehouse. Internally, the house has only one room furnished and decorated with various objects donated by the community.

The museum's emphasis is placed as much on the physical aspects of the area as on the identities that make up the region. The replica house embodies the meanings and symbols that exist therein, and also denotes the act of dwelling as a right. The centrality of the stilt house within the museum makes clear the importance given by the community to the urban components of *Maré*, particularly the act of dwelling – the house as a symbol for one of the most significant material forms of preserving local history. The replica house evokes memories and fragments of the lives of its residents. The central position given to the house serves as a form of community self-affirmation: despite the eradication of the old favela and its precarious living conditions, the stilt house represents memories of its inhabitants. We here witness a reversal of meanings, a redefinition; the despised symbol of national misery is transformed into a symbol of cultural resistance.

According to Chagas and Abreu (2007), the Museum of *Maré* distinguishes itself from other museums because the principal interest is not the act of preservation, but the social life of the residents. The museum appears different from the other cultural centres that have spread throughout the city because its set-up is not the product of a generic policy. The differentiating element of the Museum of *Maré* is its intention to put residents in touch with their own origins, raising awareness about their history and suggesting that the memory of the favela can be found through the stories of those that lived and still live there. We add that the Museum of *Maré* is also different because it is not the product of a generic urban renewal project nor is it devoid of content to offer a spectacular experience for the public. The very existence of the museum denotes a resistance to the concentration of cultural facilities in the urban centres. It affirms the favela as a place of culture and memory, recognizing the differences among its many communities and positioning the favela as a diverse and heterogeneous space.

The Favela Observatory

Another example of an occupation of a former industrial warehouse in *Maré*, this time for educational and research purposes, refers to the Favela Observatory (Observatório de Favelas), an institution that was also initially linked to the CEASM group. The project for the observatory was created in 2000, as one of the actions that made up the CEASM association. It was set up under the label of Social Observatory Network, with the purpose to assist in the research for the first internal demographic Census of *Maré* Complex in 2000. The *Maré* 2000 Census was developed by the local dwellers as a way to overcome the scarcity of information related to the complex and allow the inhabitants of *Maré* to have a better knowledge over their own reality. Once completed, the funds for this network were cut and CEASM was forced to terminate the program. The team responsible for the census transformed it into a new initiative, changing their name to Favelas Observatory.

In subsequent years, the program began to develop its own projects responding to the specific demands revealed by the 2000 Census. The Favela Observatory became an independent institution in 2003, with its own identity and clear political principles – fruits of reflections of their creators, geographers Jorge Luiz Barbosa and Jailson de Souza e Silva, professors at the Fluminense Federal University and also dwellers of *Maré*. Their main goals were:

> training of grassroots leaders with technical profiles and political engagement; the organization, production, analysis and dissemination of popular interpretations of spaces, urban violence and human rights; and the provision of assistance to local community groups, in the field of diagnosis and social communication.
>
> (Silva and Barbosa, 2005: 227)

Until 2005, the observatory functioned in the House of Culture of *Maré*, on the same site where the Museum of *Maré* is located today. However, with the establishment of these new premises, it was thought necessary to establish headquarters at a new place, where the work would not be limited to the *Maré* Complex, thus including other favelas of Rio de Janeiro.

For the past decade, the Favela Observatory has been located inside a former industrial warehouse, situated in close proximity to Brazil Avenue. As in previous cases, the occupied land was abandoned for years. It is, therefore, a similar process of occupation in an area also affected by deindustrialization. The most interesting point regarding this occupation relates to its location. While both the Portelinha Occupation and the Museum of *Maré* are situated on the Timbau Hill, the Favela Observatory is situated on the Teixeira Ribeiro Street, the main access to the favela known as New Holland (*Nova Hollanda*). This particular street delimits the area segregated by different drug trafficking gangs, therefore being constantly portrayed by the media as one of the most dangerous and violent places in the city. That is why the installation of the group in this particular site acquires a symbolic character, as one of its objectives is to promote the integration of different slums, opening bridges of dialogue between their communities.

More recently, the Favela Observatory gained attention in the midst of the wave of protests taking place in Rio de Janeiro and in many cities across Brazil in 2013. The government's decision to raise the fares of public transportation in eleven state capitals of Brazil led to large protests in many metropolitan centres such as São Paulo and Rio de Janeiro. These protests were met with violence from the local military police forces, leading to perplexity and massive discontent of both lower and middle classes. On 20 June, 2013, over 1 million people took to the streets in several cities of the country (Folha de São Paulo, 2013), an event that led to other demonstrations in the months following. While initially setting out to protest against the raise in transportation fares, the demonstrations began to incorporate different demands, reflecting the level of dissatisfaction of the Brazilian population regarding its national politics. Aside from the lack of proper urban transportation, claims were made on the subjects of political corruption, urban violence and police brutality, poor urban infrastructure, access to health care, excessive public funds spent on mega events (such as the 2014 World Cup and the 2016 Olympic Games) as well as deficiency in advancing human rights-driven policies.

On 24 June, 2013, after a demonstration on Brazil Avenue, a police operation was conducted in the *Maré* Complex, in the favela of New Holland, leading to the death of thirteen people. While the police claimed they were in search for criminals carrying out mass robberies throughout the demonstration, the Favela Observatory had a key role in speaking up for the residents and denouncing serious human rights violations that took place at that time, leading to the killing of innocent people in *Maré*:

Since last night the New Holland favela, Maré, is occupied by agents of [the elite squad] BOPE, the Shock Troops and the National Guard. The action supposedly took place in response to a mass robbery in [the neighbourhood of] Bonsucesso moments before. During the raid, at about 19:00, tear gas bombs were thrown at the residents, one of which reached the outer courtyard of the headquarters of the Observatory, startling the people who were in the institution. This was followed by intense gunfire, which lasted through the night, when the power was cut off from the community.

This morning, the favela was still occupied, still without power, its commerce closed and the presence of the police was visible. According to reports from residents, the operation, which has so far resulted in thirteen deaths, also had a large number of human rights violations, such as home invasions followed by vandalism, looting and intimidation of residents by police. [...]

In addition to the raids and depredations, residents denounced the illegal confiscation of money and documents.

(Observatório de Favelas, 2013)

The killings in *Maré* soon led to further demonstrations. The Favelas Observatory has become another example of an occupation that surpasses its initial purposes to play a bigger role within the local socio-political reality of city regeneration and development.

The examples presented in this chapter are all recent initiatives aimed at altering the negative perception of *Maré*; a move from a discourse tied to 'an immense group of favelas' to a new 'hub' for cultural and social development in the city. Several other collectives, organizations and civic initiatives can be found in the many favelas that make up the complex.[7] These micro-organizations constitute a range of mobile activities, very often interconnected. It is not uncommon to see resident associations using the facilities of religious organizations, and cultural groups using public spaces or associations' offices for their temporary activities and workshops. What can be observed is a consolidation of partnerships, which revolve around the spaces and morph to function under the logic of networks.

In short, the examples presented in this chapter lead us to believe that the *Maré* Complex is more than a collection of favelas in the peripheral area of Rio de Janeiro. Owing to the complexity of the region, we suggest that the *Maré* Complex is better conceptualized as a complex territory characterized by cultural and social multiplicity.

Maré: A hybrid territory

In order to understand the idea of a complex of favelas as one single territory, we briefly discuss the notion of territoriality. Drawing on the writings of social and cultural geographers Joël Bonnemaison (2002) and Rogério Haesbaert (2004), we consider that a territory is a region of complexity, marked by diverse identities, uncertainty and power struggles. Haesbaert (2004) presents the territory as a system composed of distinct spheres, referencing, in particular, the political, economic, natural and cultural spheres. The cultural sphere is of most interest to us here, as it implies the vision of space derived from the symbolic appropriations of a group. Other writers have adopted the analysis of the cultural dimension of territory and place. Within the field of cultural studies, Brazilian author Teixeira Coelho (2004) defines territory as the construction of identities and day-to-day relationships of individuals in their place of origin, similarly highlighting the cultural domain. The socio-cultural dimension of territory is also defended by the social scientist Chris Barker (2005), who points out that territories are socially constructed locations, wherein the production of meaning for the space occurs. And, finally, Bonnemaison (2002) presents territories formed as results of the relationship between culture and space, emphasizing the inseparable and complementary link between a social group, its culture and its territory. Bonnemaison also associates the concept of territory to the concept of networks, conceptualizing it through a hierarchy of places connected through the practices of certain social groups.

We note that contemporary discussions about territory bear upon its permanency, questioning transformations that result from the intensification of globalization, and the allied compression of notions of space and time, to the shortening of distances and the weakening of borders. Regarding the paradigm of de-territorialization, Haesbaert (2004) asserts that we live in a moment of transition from a more palpable and material reality to one of constant mobility that is increasingly symbolic and subjective:

Under the impact of globalization, processes that have 'compressed' space and time, eradicating the distances through instant communication and promoting the influence of faraway places on one another, the weakening of all types of border and the dominant crisis of territoriality of the State-nation, our actions being governed more by the images and representations that we create than by the material reality that involves us, our lives immersed in a constant mobility, concrete and symbolic, what is left of our 'territories', of our 'geography'?

(Haesbaert, 2004: 19–20)

The traditional territories to which we are accustomed – fixed, stable, continuous, contiguous and homogenous – guided by a defined and exclusive spatial logic (which rarely permits overlapping due to its exact limitations and well-marked boundaries) have begun to give way to a new configuration. This new configuration appears to be more fluid, dynamic and mobile – simultaneously divisible and connectible. The new territories possess properties that are increasingly immaterial, intangible and heterogeneous, resembling networks. In this sense, the current concept of territoriality should mix multiple spatial appropriations, from the fixed to the fluid. Haesbaert claims that we are not exactly experiencing a moment of de-territorialization nor the end of the territories as a concept; instead, we are undergoing a phenomenon of multi-territorialization, or rather that we are currently living the simultaneous experience of various territories. Unavoidably, we are also living through consequent processes of re-territorialization, meaning that we can observe a constant redefinition of territories through the transformation of their uses, and the relationships and social agents present in them.

Based upon Coelho's, Barker's, Bonnemaison's and Haesbaert's works, as well as upon our observation of the *Maré* case study, we have come to understand territories as hubs, where groups meet and where their culture is condensed into symbolic form: materially through their architectures, or immaterially through the practices performed in them, and the meanings that remain embedded within the places (Vaz, 2010). In view of the different forms of occupation and connections presented in the *Maré* Complex, we believe that this area of Rio de Janeiro corresponds to the description of multi-territorialization proposed by Haesbaert. In *Maré*, we can observe multiple micro-territories within one larger territory, where different social actors co-exist and appropriate space. More than that, the discussed examples point at the web of interaction that identifies various initiatives inside and outside of *Maré* as networks of collaboration. For instance, the *Maré* Museum has worked closely with state universities located in other neighbourhoods and the *capoeira* group from the Timbau Hill performs frequently on the streets and squares of the downtown area. The networks formed between these groups and the territories that they facilitate to morph are not fixed, expanding the limits of the favela complex, decentralizing action in order to take the symbolic territory of *Maré* to the rest of the city of Rio de Janeiro.

In this sense, the established connections can be considered as 'seams' between an area of residential slums and a previously industrial zone, as well as between this 'zone' and the rest of the city. We speak here of 'seams' because, in a way, our examples function as a means for symbolically sewing back together places that were never linked or no longer connected. It is important to point out that, because these examples refer to the fringes of the favelas (being located at their edges) and because they maintain strong ties with each other, they end up transposing boundaries and merging different territories. Inside *Maré*, the 'seams' suggest the reinforcement of a local dialogue, outside *Maré* they suggest an approximation between the informal city and the formal city.

The projects, networks and relationships created by the aforementioned groups have contributed to transforming the existing dynamics of *Maré* by creating new local experiences and also by taking these experiences to other parts of the city. The continuous construction of the *Maré* territory is, therefore, a process of exchange, in which space is used in different and multiple ways, serving the purpose of uniting and not of fragmenting, as was once typical of early modernity, when every activity had its own place in the sectored city. Within the post-modern context, dwelling, working, leisure and circulation are activities not necessarily set apart, as suggested by modernist theory, but can co-exist within a single, space. They are ever-changing and hybrid.

Argentinean social scientist Néstor García Canclini (1997, 2008) claims that in Latin America there is a long history of constructing hybrid cultures, often seen through the plurality that merges hegemonic and subaltern relations – traditional and modern, cult, popular and mass. The practice of *capoeira* itself constitutes a good example of hybridization; until the mid-twentieth century, the *capoeira* players were persecuted because *capoeira* was seen as a threat, having been considered a criminal act. Having moved from the rural areas to the streets in the twentieth century, it gathered a strong urban character and eventually became an important expression of Brazilian culture. Today, *capoeira* is practiced freely and has spread to several countries, experiencing adaptations and transformation.

According to Canclini, hybridization is a set of 'socio-cultural processes in which discreet structures and practices, that exist in a separate form are combined to generate new structures, objects and practices' (2008: 19). The author also recognizes the impossibility of establishing totalities in the contemporary city, claiming that there is a tendency towards fragmentation and decentralization in social mobilization, as well as in the structure of the city. He believes that today's urban life transgresses the rational order imposed by modernist thought, which tried to distribute objects and signs in specific locations and to classify them via a systematic organization of the social spaces in which they should be consumed.

The idea of analysing contemporary spaces through the concept of hybridity with a focus on social-cultural relationships is also mentioned by Stuart Hall, who treats the concept of hybridism from the perspective of the cultural sphere, claiming that: 'the hybrid cultures constitute one of the various types of new distinct identities produced in the late modern era' (1992: 89). For Hall, to live in hybrid cultures implies the need to practice translation, or rather, learn to co-exist with different logics simultaneously, to inhabit, speak and cope with multiple identities and various cultural languages. We argue that this is precisely what happens in the *Maré* Complex today, where different urban morphologies, groups and actions are mixed together in order to form a diverse and dynamic territory.

Final comments on territory and resistance

What can be observed in the case of the *Maré* Centre for Popular Arts and Culture is the emergence of a new typology within the urban landscape, characterized by shacks built within the old factory walls. We also observe attempts at cooperation between different agents working towards a common goal of retaining a building that was once abandoned, ensuring its positive contribution to the life of the local community.

The Museum of *Maré* validates the marginalized favela culture through the recuperation of its roots, memory and history. It proves that the local community is able to create a successful facility that serves as a local landmark despite the very little attention and funding from the governmental agencies. The Museum of *Maré* represents how the favela community can reaffirm itself as a valid part of the city, endowed with rich culture in this part of Rio de Janeiro's urban history.

The Favela Observatory, with its focus on education and research, has an important role in making the *Maré's* voice heard. By providing accurate data and statistical backing, the Observatory contributes to the production of research that informs city policy development with regard to the improvement of the quality of life across the favelas of Rio de Janeiro. In the context of protests across Brazil in 2013 and 2014, this institution attracted international and national attention to the violation of human rights in *Maré* and beyond, paving the way for protests against police brutality in the peripheral areas of Rio de Janeiro and other locations.

The examples presented in this chapter, where cultural actions merge with educational projects and alternative housing, all contributed new facilities in areas that are usually perceived as being deprived of basic services. The new organizational forms represent the marginalized population's struggle to be heard and considered as a significant part of the city development. According to Lefebvre (1985), the city is a product of social construction and relations that should be perceived within their material and symbolic dimensions that are both past and present. In this sense, it is necessary to acknowledge that the spaces that evolve in response to cultural and artistic actions as well as from alternative appropriations represent another reality to the formal city. This idea leads us to draw on Lefebvre's *The Right to the City* (1991) and his argument that all citizens should, in theory, be allowed equal access to collective goods and services, but are, in practice, denied this access due to urban segregation. For Lefebvre, the right to the city is a right to urban living, to human conditions and to a renewed democracy. In opaque areas, such as *Maré*, this right has been frequently denied and continues to be fought for, often through insurgent manners, which challenge the dynamics imposed by globalization, while presenting alternative urban solutions of temporary occupation that do not necessarily follow the patterns of the traditional urban planning.

The right to the city, in this case, is achieved through the instances of micro-resistance, contributing to reconfiguration of territory of resistance in *Maré*. In order to speak of resistance, we draw on Certeau (1998), who advocates the understanding of spaces from the perspective of the small daily activities and the social practices of those who inhabit them. Certeau considers these practices as 'the art of doing' – typically dispersed and not particularly evident, although revealing in terms of their progressive ways of re-appropriating the territory. The *Maré* cultural occupations are manifestations of micro-resistance to the hegemonic forces prevailing in the Rio's city council. We connect the concept of micro-resistances and territory of resistance observed in *Maré*, with the concept of insurgent citizenship, suggested by Holston (2008), who carried out extensive research about the Brazilian peripheries. According to Holston, spaces of insurgent citizenship are built environments where social affirmation exists, resulting from an 'action against.' In the case of *Maré*, the 'action against' can be perceived as the action against urban invisibility, and its success comes with the ability to overcome the negligence of the state policies through the creation of the community's own means to survive. In this region, what stands out is not only the territorial multiplicity and hybridization of the different categories (activities, artistic practices and architecture), but, principally, the endurance of the local population in escaping the logic of formal planning. It is the results of these practices that give meaning to these spaces and change the existing urban dynamics, allowing for new sociability and relationships to emerge, integrating the precarious to the formal city.

References

Abreu, M. A. 2006. *Evolução Urbana do Rio de Janeiro*, Rio de Janeiro: IPP.

Barker, C. 2005. *Cultural Studies: Theory and Practice*, London: Sage Publications.

Bonnemaison, J. 2002. 'Viagem em Torno do Território'. In Correa, R. L. and Rosendahl, L. (Eds), *Geografia Cultural: Um Século*, Rio de Janeiro: Editora UERJ, pp. 83–131.

Canclini, N. G. 1997. 'El Malestar en los Estudios Culturales', *Fractal* 6, 2 (2), 45–60, http://www.fractal.com.mx/F6cancli.html. Accessed 21 June 2013.

Canclini, N. G. 2008. *Culturas Híbridas: Estrategias para Entrar y Salir de la Modernidad*, São Paulo: EDUSP.

Certeau, M. de. 1998. *L'Invention du Quotidien, Tome 1: Arts de Faire*, Pétropolis: Vozes.

Chagas, M. S. and Abreu, R. 2007. 'Museu da Maré: Memórias e Narrativas a Favor da Dignidade Social', *Revista Musas*, 3 (3), 130–152.

Coelho, T. 2004. *Dicionário Crítico de Política Cultural*, São Paulo: Editora Iluminuras.

Folha de São Paulo. 2001. *Protesto de Moradores de Favela no Rio Interdita Av. Brasil*, São Paulo: Folha de São Paulo, http://www1.folha.uol.com.br/folha/cotidiano/ult95u35980.shtml. Accessed 29 August 2001.

Folha de São Paulo. 2013. *Manifestações Levam 1 Milhão de Pessoas às Ruas em Todo País*, São Paulo: Folha de São Paulo, http://www1.folha.uol.com.br/cotidiano/2013/06/1298755-manifestacoes-levam-1-milhao-de-pessoas-as-ruas-em-todo-pais.shtml. Accessed 21 June 2013.

Haesbaert, R. 2004. *O Mito da Desterritorialização: do 'Fim dos Territórios' à Multiterritorialidade*, Rio de Janeiro: Editora Bertrand.

Hall, S. 1992. 'The question of cultural identity'. In Hall, S., Held, D. and McGrew, T. (Eds), *Modernity and Its Futures*, Oxford: Polity Press/Open University Press.

Holston, J. 1996. 'Espaços de Cidadania Insurgente', *Revista do Patrimônio Histórico e Artístico Nacional*, 24, 243–253.

Holston, J. 2008. *Insurgent Citizenship: Dysfunctions of Democracy and Modernity in Brazil*, Princeton/Oxford: Princeton University Press.

Lefebvre, H. 1985. *La Production de l'Espace*, Paris: Éditions Anthropos.

Lefebvre, H. 1991. *O Direito à Cidade/The Right to the City*, São Paulo: Editora Moraes.

Observatório de Favelas. 2013. 'Ação violenta da polícia chega a 13 mortos na maré', http://observatoriodefavelas.org.br/noticias-analises/acao-violenta-da-policia-chega-a-13-mortos-na-mare/. Accessed 25 June 2013.

Prefeitura da Cidade do Rio de Janeiro. 2010. *Indicadores Ambientais Da Cidade Do Rio De Janeiro*, Rio de Janeiro: IPP.

Santos, M. 1994. *Técnica Espaço Tempo. Globalização e Meio Técnico-Científico Informacional*, São Paulo: HUCITEC.

Santos, M. 2009. *A Natureza do Espaço. Técnica e Tempo. Razão e Emoção*, São Paulo: EDUSP.

Seldin, C. 2008. 'As ações culturais e o espaço urbano: o caso do Complexo da Maré no Rio de Janeiro', MA dissertation, Rio de Janeiro: PROURB/FAU-UFRJ.

Silva, J. S. and Barbosa, J. L. 2005. *Favela: Alegria e Dor na Cidade*, Rio de Janeiro: Senac Rio/X Brasil.

Vaz, L. F. 1994. *História dos Bairros da Maré: Espaço, Tempo e Vida Cotidiana no Complexo da Maré*, Rio de Janeiro: SR-5/UFRJ and CNPq.

Vaz, L. F. 2010. 'Um território híbrido na Maré, RJ. Novo território cultural?', paper presented at *The International Seminar of Cultural Policy: Theory and Praxis*, Rio de Janeiro, Fundação Casa de Rui Barbosa.

Vaz, L. F. and Jacques, P. B. 2004. 'Morphological diversity in the squatter settlements of Rio de Janeiro'. In Stanilov, K. and Scheer, B. C. (Eds), *Suburban Form, An International Perspective*, New York and London: Routledge, pp. 61–72.

Vaz, L. F. and Seldin, C. 2007. 'Nova forma de relação entre espaço e cultura no Rio de Janeiro contemporâneo – o caso do quilombo das artes', paper presented at the *Latin American Symposium City and Culture: Contemporary Dimensions*, São Carlos, EESC/USP.

Notes

1   According to the official data provided by the Census from the Brazilian Institute of Geography and Statistics (IBGE) 2010. In reality, this number is likely to be larger.

2   *Avenida Brasil* – Brazil Avenue; *Linha Vermelha* – Red Line; *Linha Amarela* – Yellow Line.

3   The proliferation of urban voids in Rio de Janeiro is not limited to this region, and can be observed in various other parts of the city. Since the 1990s, many of these spaces – especially around the historic centre – have become targets for projects and public and private urban regeneration initiatives. This is because they are believed to be endowed with the potential to positively affirm the image of the city, with potential for economic growth, attracting tourism, investment and profitable businesses. A recent example of these projects

is the urban operation 'Marvelous Port' (*Porto Maravilha*), aimed at creating facilities and infrastructure for the 2016 Olympic Games in Rio de Janeiro's formerly degraded port area.

4   Inside the former factory building, the following organizations were located: the *capoeira* group; a martial arts gym; a recording studio attending around fifteen local bands; the NGO Latin American University Association (AULA); and an institute called Staumbor – a musical project responsible for the local orchestra *Maréimbau*. The top floor of the building was reserved for community activities; however, it remained covered with debris and was left unutilized.

5   Today, the founder of the *capoeira* group, Master Manoel, travels around the world conducting workshops; the Staumbor Institute operates in the Timbau Hill residents' association building, as well as in the *Providência* favela in the centre of Rio, in the Cabritos as well as Tabajaras Hill in the neighbourhood of Copacabana.

6   The Museum of *Maré* was, at one point, considered by the Brazilian Ministry of Culture as the first museum located in a favela in Brazil.

7   Examples of such initiatives include the *Maré Redes* (*Maré* Networks) collective, the Gato de Bonsucesso samba school, the Favelas Observatory, the *Bela Maré* Warehouse and the Parque União House of Culture, just to mention a few.

Chapter 4

Painting free from gentrification: Participatory arts-based interventions in the favelas of Rio de Janeiro

Katarzyna Kosmala

Introduction

This chapter examines examples of arts-based projects that produce interventions in socio-economically disadvantaged urban spaces. This type of artistic practice – aside of criticisms concerning the artist's positioning, constructed power structures, durability or sustainability of the intervention itself – can be perceived as functional in offering a possibility of alteration of the space in which interventions arise and providing tools for critical reflection about the uses of space and possible change.

Dutch-born and based Jeroen Koolhaas and Dre Urhahn are an artistic collaboration initiated in 2005, known as Haas&Hahn. They have adopted a working methodology of action within the built environment, located at the socio-economic and cultural peripheries. Their flagship project 'Favela Painting' was born out of the idea to create public artworks, using the favelas of Rio de Janeiro, self-built and self-organized constructions, as a space of intervention. Favelas are organically grown neighbourhoods that are constructed outside official governmental regulation by the residents themselves with an objective to satisfy their housing needs. Currently, several of them face gentrification, evictions and few even risk demolition.

Haas&Hahn's interdisciplinary ways of working, situated at the intersection of land art, design and urban intervention, encompass predominantly short-term, community-focused creative projects that have been realized at relatively low costs. Such a method of working is at the essence of the tactical urbanism movement (Lyndon and Garcia, 2015). Such projects have now become an adaptable tool for urban activists as well as for policy-makers in facilitating lasting improvements in urban milieus and beyond. Addressing the question of functionality of art in the 'Favela Painting' projects, the chapter reflects on the critical potential of arts-based interventions and their impact in the context of ongoing land developments and city planning politics.

Miwon Kwon argues that much of site-specific projects or public art interventions lack criticality and despite their critical potential are always opened for co-option by the market forces and institutional structures (2002: 1–2). Jane Rendell, introducing critical spatial practice in her *Art and Architecture: A Place Between,* draws on Kwon (2002) and her reference to Homi Bhabha's concept of 'relational specificity' as a way to underline the importance and particularity of the relationships created through the intervention between people, objects and spaces (2006: 16). Analysing the examples of individual projects under the 'Favela Painting' flagship, I will reflect upon the specificity of relationships created

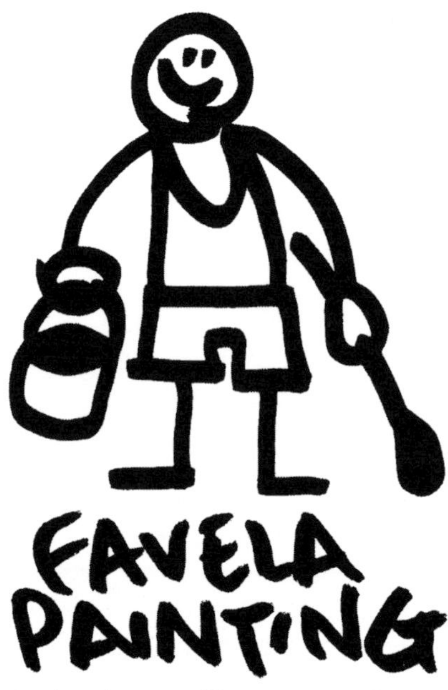

Figure 4.1: 'Favela Painting' logo. Courtesy of Haas&Hahn.

between people and objects in the space where the intervention has taken place, as well as in relation to space of the intervention itself.

'Favela Painting': Arts-based methodology of action

Favelas in Rio de Janeiro are low-rise and highly dense, organically grown neighbourhoods that started as squatters' settlements around 115 years ago. These settlements have grown over time, continuously evolving and morphing, depending on the access to resources and occupational proximity for residents. Today, nearly a quarter of Rio's population lives in favelas. Currently, there are around 600 favelas across Rio de Janeiro, which are the examples of sustainable and low-cost housing, built by residents, shaped by generations of kinship ties, and grounded in a sense of identity and connection with a place and its people. Yet, favelas have been socially marginalized for a long time and their residents continue to be largely excluded from the city's life and the city's services (e.g. Perlman, 2010).

'Favela Painting' and the Haas&Hahn artistic collaboration started in 2005 when Jeroen Koolhaas and Dre Urhahn came to Rio de Janeiro to make a documentary film about the culture of hip-hop in favelas. They were inspired by both the architecture of the self-built environment and the vibrancy of local culture. They were also shocked by the social and economic divide in the city and its class-specific spatial distribution. During their first visit to Rio's favelas, their creative 'dream' was born: 'Wow, imagine if you could paint that.' Initially, for them it was a crazy, cool idea to realize, coming from the outside, from the 'padded' ordered world. And at that point, the idea was based solely on a dream. The activism mind came later:

> 'At first we just wanted to paint, but then our responsibilities changed,' Koolhaas said, 'and before you can work in a neighborhood which has had 30 years of decline, downfall and broken promises there is more talking to be done than painting.' Urhahn explained: 'The neighborhood has to respect you, and that is not something you can buy or force. You really have to earn that by moving there, shopping there, partying there and having your birthday there.'
>
> (Koolhaas and Urhahn retrospectively in Williams, 2013)

The underlying objective of this Dutch artistic collaboration, Haas&Hahn, is to seek possibilities for improving the look of a place as well as for creating a dialogue with the local surroundings. Historically, due to limited resources, favelas' residents worked together to provide much needed services for the community, such as child care. A strong community-based ethos continues today across Rio's favelas. Can art become an encounter for new kinds of relationships to function there between people and objects? And more so, can newly formed encounters enable long-term constructive interactions?

For 'Favela Painting', Urhahn manages the projects and public relations. Koolhaas is the graphic designer and illustrator. He also makes films about the projects. Currently, Haas&Hahn are involved in a new large-scale community-centred project with an objective to paint an entire favela with local residents. Initially, in 2005, they thought that it would be great to enable local people to paint their own houses in order to improve the look of the rather dilapidated neighbourhoods, simultaneously sending a positive message to the world, and subsequently, challenging the negative perceptions concerning the local communities. Their initial dream has quickly transformed into a strategy informed by the tactical urbanism movement – in facilitating lasting improvements across Rio's urban milieus and beyond. Their working method has been referred to as painting urbanism (Franch i Gilabert, 2011). Urban designs for projects are constructed based on collective action; action that expands throughout the city (and in particular across favelas) whereby built environment is used as:

> A continuous territory beyond notions of public and private; it activates the urban fabric introducing new spaces of intensity and collectivity beyond spatial conditions and denounces the underutilization of residual spaces of design and action within the city.
>
> (Franch i Gilabert, 2011)

The site-specific and location-specific first interventions of Haas&Hahn were small-scale pilot-type projects, located in one of the most deprived favelas in Rio de Janeiro, Vila Cruzeiro. These projects were aimed at testing the possibilities for larger realizations, and exploring how the future projects could possibly work, by reflecting upon the evidence of how local people react to

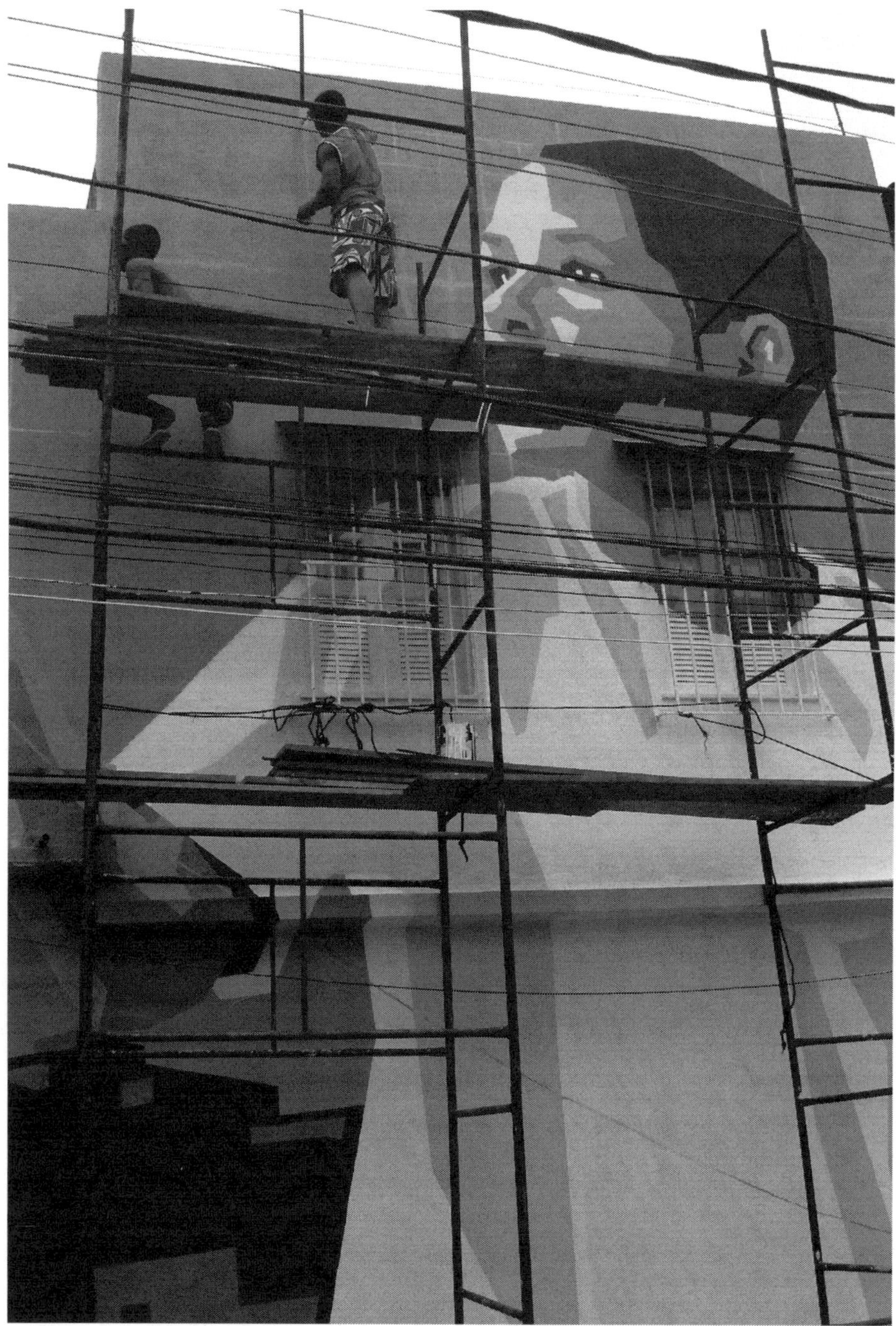

Figure 4.2: *Boy with the Kite*, 'Favela Painting', 2007. Courtesy of Haas&Hahn.

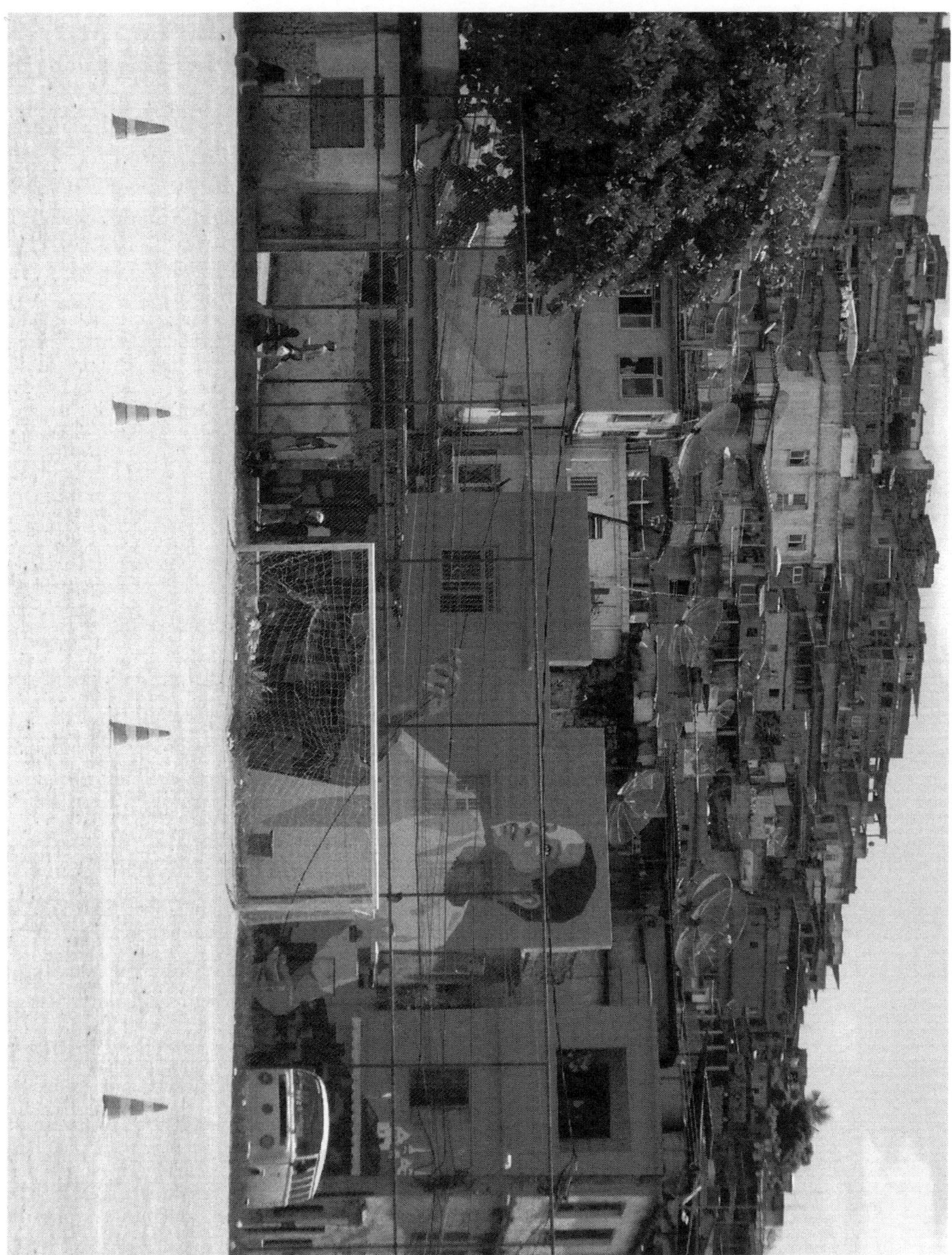

Figure 4.3: *Boy with the Kite*, full view, 'Favela Painting', 2007. Courtesy of Haas&Hahn.

and engage with their works. The design for the first project, a 150 m^2 wall mural entitled *Boy with the Kite* (2006), was chosen together with the local people. It depicts a boy playing with a kite against an intensive blue sky, a symbol of favelas' children. It took two months to create the mural, which was painted together with two local boys. Before the work could start, Haas&Hahn had to network in order to gain access to the neighbourhoods. And indeed, the networking in this instance was facilitated by being aligned with cultural and business elites in Holland and beyond. It was the founder and executive director of Brazilian Institute of Innovations of Social Health (Ibiss), a non-profit organization that works in the favelas, who introduced Haas&Hahn to Vila Cruzeiro's community and helped to negotiate the access:

> We first went to Vila Cruzeiro with fellow Dutchman Nanko van Buuren of Ibiss […] His organization helped set up a social center in the heart of the favela. As the community was getting very, very bad press at that time, he challenged us: 'If your project works here, it will work anywhere.'
>
> (Dre Urhahn in Gray, 2013)

Without an established network from the outset, negotiated access and a back-up of like-minded individuals, the realization of this project would be much more complicated to execute.

Two years later, another project was realized in the same neighbourhood. *Rio Cruzeiro* (2008) is a mural covering a drainage ditch. The project involved painting the concrete slabs of a 2000 m^2 drainage ditch, featuring a Japanese-style design – a colourful river with koi carp in vibrant oranges, greens and blues. Resembling a gigantic tattoo, the stairs on Rua Santa Helena were transformed into a funky colourful 'bridge-passage' over the drainage ditch 'filled' with running water. The design was created by Amsterdam-based tattoo artist Rob Admiral who previously designed a dragon tattoo on Urhahn's back. The project also employed the help of local youths and involved training and preparatory work. *Rio Cruzeiro* took almost a year to complete.

These two projects, according to Haas&Hahn, resulted in the overall gratitude of the local community across Vila Cruzeiro and also caught the attention of the international media, which somewhat stirred the stigmatized public opinion about the place. Indeed, these first two projects of 'Favela Painting' were realized in the neighbourhood that has been perceived as one of the most violent in Rio de Janeiro. Dutch documentary maker Patricia Maresch who produced a film about Vila Cruzeiro a few years earlier in 2008, together with local youths, argued: 'The truth is, 99 percent of the people living in the favela have no part in the trafficking of drugs and arms […] and people are desperate for peace' (Maresch retrospectively in Hestbæk, 2010). The community of Vila Cruzeiro has existed now around 45 years, and is located in Penha in Rio's North Zone, near Complexo de Alemao, which occupies around 40 favelas in total. The area has an estimate of between 40,000 and 70,000 inhabitants and all the houses – in contrast with some newer favelas – have key amenities, including water supply, gas and electricity.

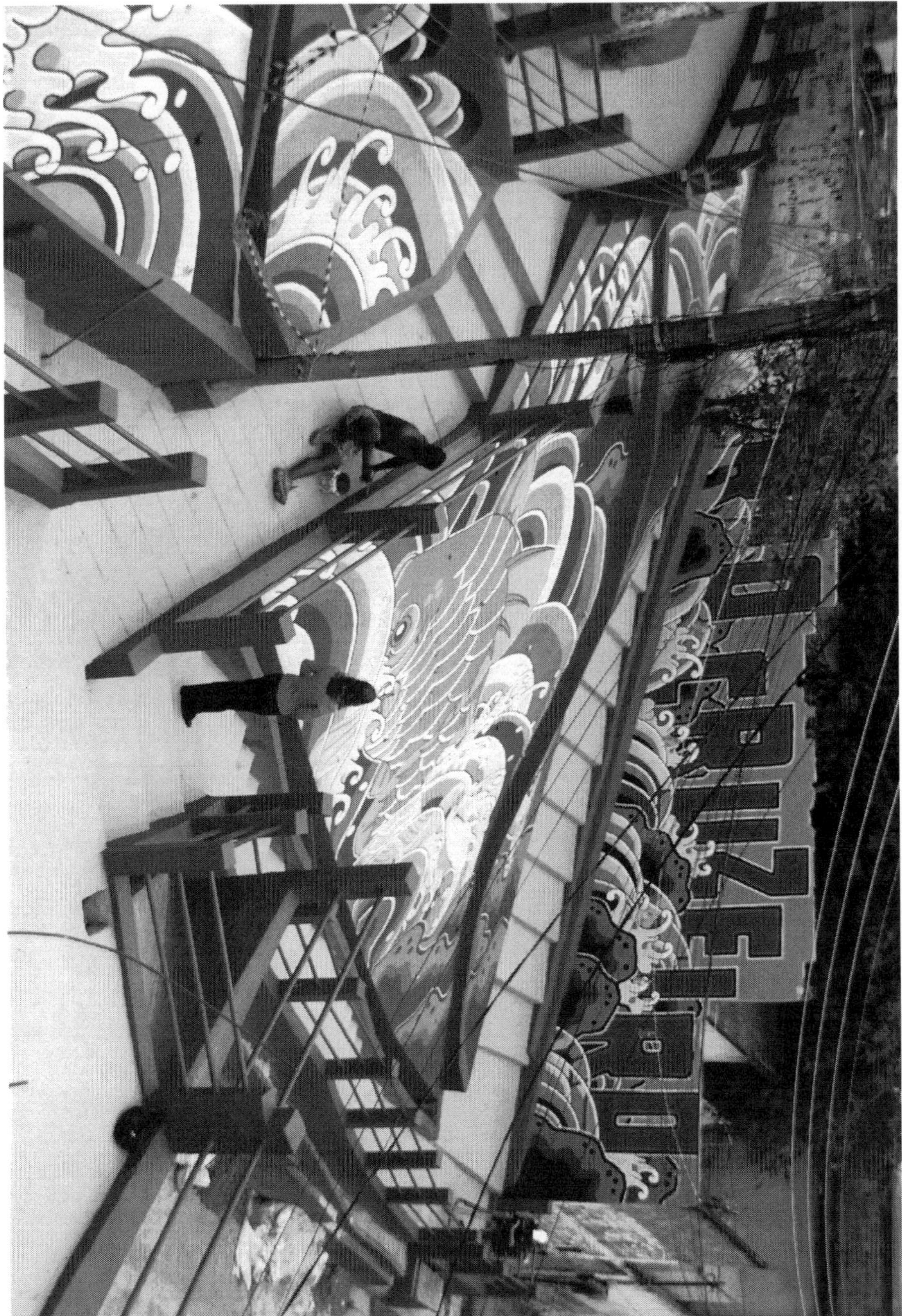

Figure 4.4: *Rio Cruzeiro*, street view, 'Favela Painting', 2009. Courtesy of Haas&Hahn.

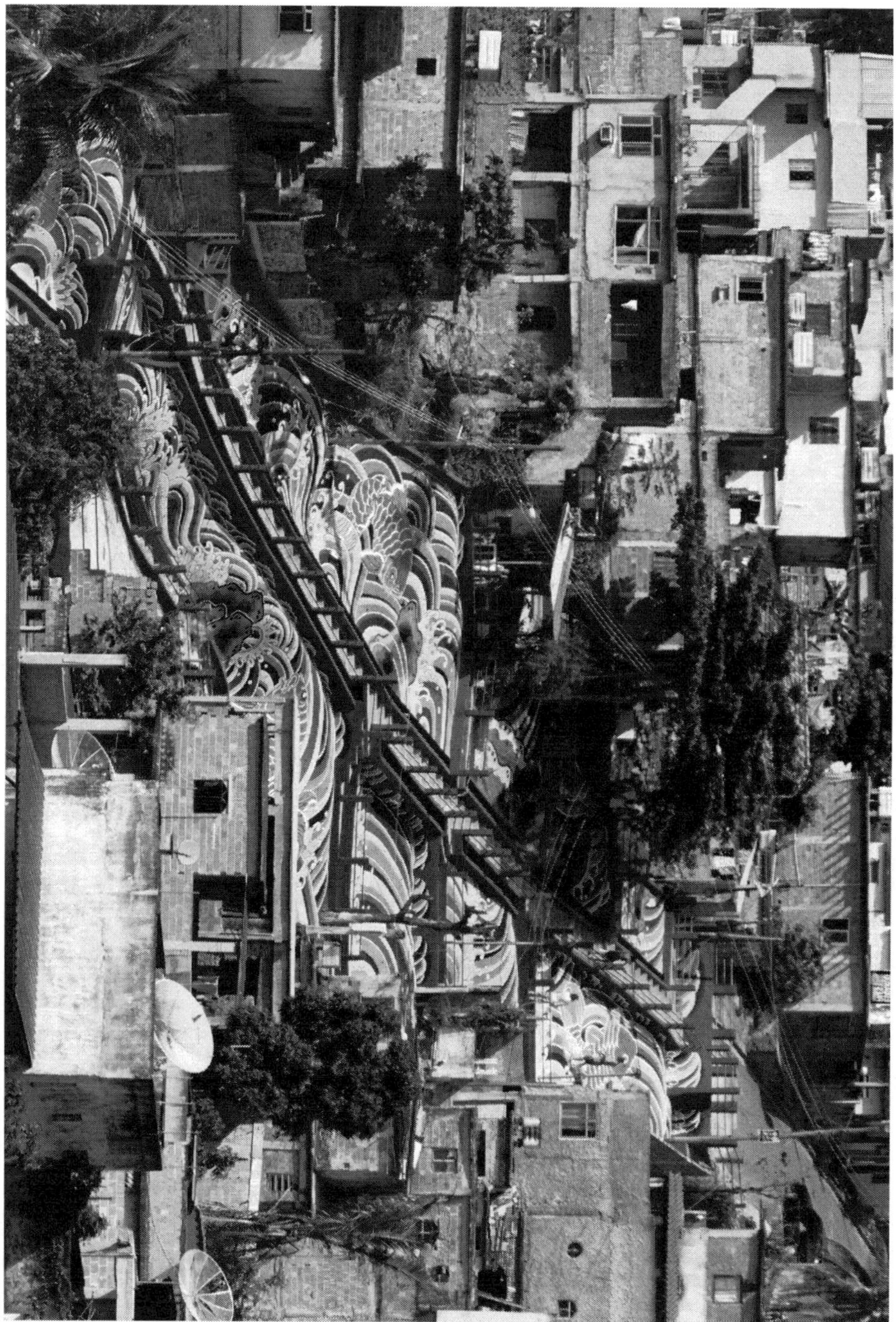

Figure 4.5: *Rio Cruzeiro,* full view, 'Favela Painting', 2009. Courtesy of Haas&Hahn.

In 2010, Haas&Hahn returned to Rio to realize a larger project in the centrally located favela in Botofogo area, Santa Marta, thanks to the sponsorship they received. The project was realized after the favela was 'pacified' and required a simpler design as it involved painting over 34 houses, covering an area of 7000 m² at a central square of Praça Cantão in an explosion of pastel rays of sunshine. The project involved training the local youth in painting and employed 25 local people to complete the project within a month. Overall, the focus of the first pilot-type projects on the neighbourhood's concerns and its daily routines within a fabric of the city – such as improvements to pedestrian access or children's playgrounds – situates the 'Favela Painting' initiative broadly within a paradigm of everyday urbanism (Chase et al., 1999/2008).

The image of a central square in Santa Marta favela, painted in a design with colourful glowing pastels, attracted worldwide attention and media exposure. For instance, CNN coverage pointed out how the 'Favela Painting' project realized in Praça Cantão has put Rio de Janeiro in the top 10 in a league table of 'the world's most colourful places.' Such coverage made fundraising for subsequent Haas&Hahn's projects much easier.

The new Back to Rio project under the 'Favela Painting' banner is under construction. Preparatory work for the project commenced in 2014. The objective now is to paint a section in the community of Vila Cruzeiro, part of Complexo de Penha in the North Zone of Rio. The funds to enable preparation work, organization of initial training for local youth and to commence the project were raised via Kickstarter, a Brooklyn-based, private, company-run online platform for fundraising to support the realization of creative projects across the world. Thanks to their good connections; support of home-grown back-up and international support, especially across the United States; through their connections established with the Mural Arts Programme in Philadelphia; as well as extensive PR campaigns across social media and the press, Haas&Hahn succeeded in raising 116,000 USD to enable them to return to Rio and start the project. During the fundraising campaign in 2013, they raised the monetary minimum required for the project to commence, with an expectation that funds would continue to flow in during the project's realization:

Our goal is to raise at least USD 100,000. With this money we will be able to build the base, train the first team and pay for wages and materials to paint the first houses. Every additional dollar will let the project grow in scale and duration. The more money we raise, the longer we can go on and the more houses can be painted. If the whole hill is painted, there is always another hill.

(Dre Urhahn in Gray, 2013)

The Back to Rio project required setting up a local head office and training of the production team. Simultaneously, the neighbourhood-based approval process has commenced, whereby the design plans for each house were to be discussed with residents, and approvals gathered from all the households (Haas&Hahn, 2013). During the first year, the site for work was set up – a small square in a community – with repairs and wall plastering completed by local

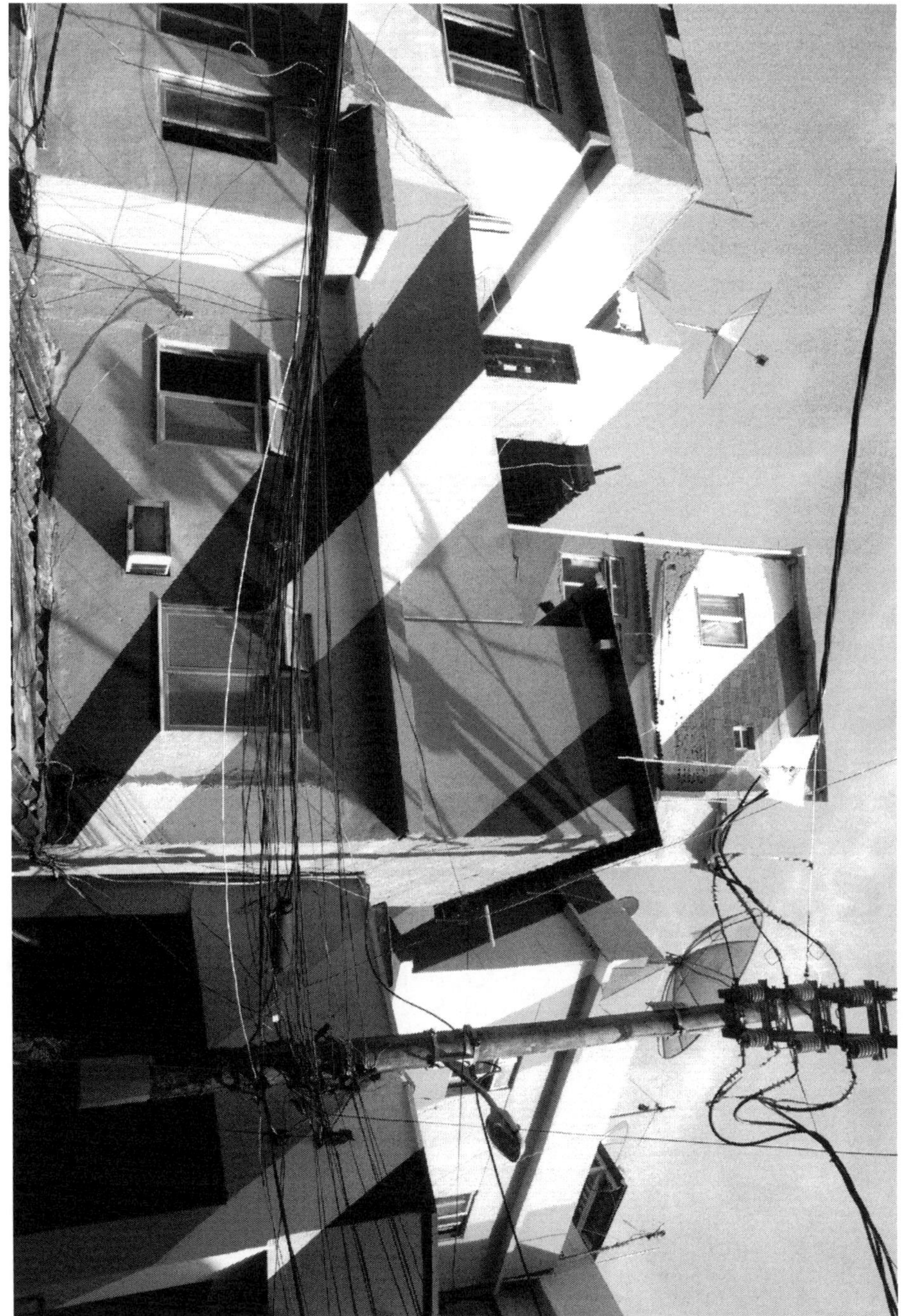

Figure 4.6: *Praça Cantão*, 'Favela Painting', 2010. Courtesy of Haas&Hahn.

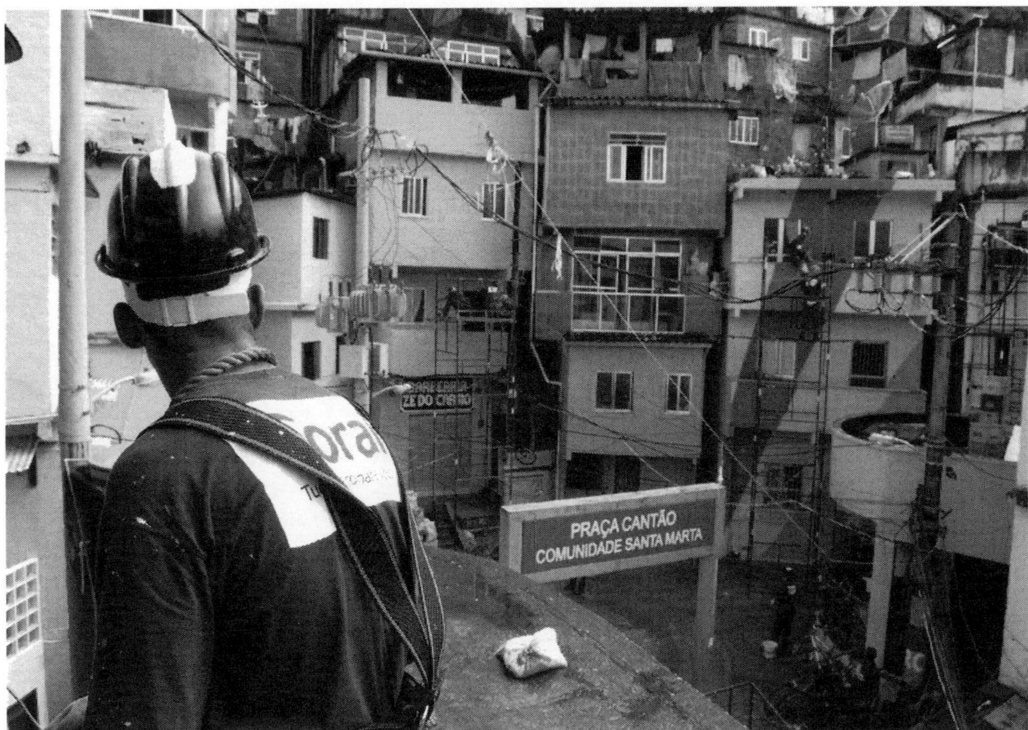

Figure 4.7: *Praça Cantão* in progress, Santa Marta, 'Favela Painting', 2010. Courtesy of Haas&Hahn.

masons. After several months, the site had to be relocated to the main avenue that cuts through the community for safety reasons – as it was reported 'due to conflicts between police and drug gangs.' At the main avenue, the work commenced with priming of the walls, paint application and design testing, while a local team was trained in the process. A decision was also made to paint the houses already plastered in order to concentrate efforts on creating a 'catalogue of design possibilities' and to learn on-site what can work. After few weeks, the local crew took over from Haas&Hahn the production process with a functioning design and the system in place.

The Back to Rio project's overarching objective is to establish the operating system that can be taken over locally, allowing the community to continue on its own, but facilitated by Haas&Hahn's multiple returns to Rio, enabled via Kickstarter continuous PR fundraising campaign, and depended on the levels of the funding obtained. It is yet to be seen how the Vila Cruzeiro's neighbourhood-based approval process will work, and how the community will respond to the set up and take ownership over this ambitious project's realization. In the meantime, Haas&Hahn's continue to expand geographically with their interventions, exporting their working method and community-focused participatory approach to other parts of the world.[1]

Timing with the World Cup 2014 and Summer Olympics 2016 hosted in Brazil, the follow-up fundraising campaign is now in place, with an objective to raise 1 million USD to enable to paint, as Haas&Hahn claim, 'every home in every favela in Rio' (Murray, 2014), a somewhat unrealistic aim, yet catchy marketing strategy for attracting the funding and private sponsors.

Sustainable projects, maintenance issues

One can easily acknowledge the visual impact of the design of the first 'Favela Painting' projects, but the sustainability of such projects and their long-term impact, necessary for the potential socio-economic transformation that could arise from such initiatives, pose a challenging question about the established relationships and well-being of favelas' residents. The communities, in which these projects were realized, continue to be poor and disadvantaged, still situated at the social margins, in the midst of a battleground with the government over threatened evictions and the disputed tenure rights.

Sally Williams in her feature for the *Telegraph* on 'Favela Painting' pointed out that painting patterns on houses, when the entire neighbourhood is on the verge of socio-economic collapse, might seem pointless. But she cited Haas&Hahn's words, arguing for an impetus for change: 'Our projects bring hope, positivity, beauty, job opportunities and stability,' Urhahn says. 'You know, we are actually offering quite a nice package' (Urhahn retrospectively in Williams, 2013).

It is undeniable that Haas&Hahn's works deliver a durable aesthetic experience for local inhabitants and an upgrade of the infrastructure in the sites, as well as – in the case of the Santa Marta project – an improvement of housing for inhabitants of the central square. Furthermore, the process of co-production with the community's youth impacts positively on confidence building and skill development. Nanko van Buuren, cited in Williams (2013), argues that Haas&Hahn's projects gave the inhabitants of Vila Cruzeiro a kind of self-esteem, that they feel valued by the artwork's presence in the favela. In my view, Haas&Hahn's realized projects are small in scale, and their participatory effect and social impact in relation to the local community are limited to those individuals who were lucky to be selected to work for these projects' realization. But the scale issue does not necessarily diminish their value; it highlights its outreach capacity.

Van Buuren, who introduced Haas&Hahn to the drug lords and their networks in Vila Cruzeiro to 'guarantee their safety' during realization of the projects, pointed out that the murals have also become something of a tourist attraction, with Ibiss setting up a tourist agency that runs tours of the sites by *ex-soldados* bringing some extra income to the community (Williams, 2013). However, the favela tourism that now flourishes in Rio de Janeiro, partly a direct result of pacification that undermined the power of gangs, and the discourse it promotes, only reinforce the existing stereotypes and reproduce favela myths based on a mix of prejudice and 'exoticizing' of the other (Kruschewsky, 2014). The media's negative coverage of the neighbourhoods, the use of particular imagery and language that emphasizes terror, violence and victimization, only increases the already deeply rooted social and economic divide in the city. The same goes for favela-based tourism. Now, tourists use a funicular to go and see *pico de* Santa Marta or travel in a cable car over Complexo do Alemão built in 2011, photographing the communities from above, as if on safari.

There is a question of longer-term sustainability of the projects realized under 'Favela Painting', and specifically, concerning the maintenance of the executed work. The mural *Boy with the Kite* (2006) had to be completely restored in 2012, as over time the paint had faded by the sun and the wall was covered in bullet holes from the ongoing conflicts between drug gangs and the police. In 2010, BEPE Special Forces and the Brazilian navy took over the favela to capture drug dealers but most of them escaped. Subsequently, between 2010 and 2012 special 'pacifying' police units UPP were placed within various favelas around Rio de Janeiro, including Compelxo Alemão and Vila Cruzeiro. For several years, during the police actions across Rio's favelas, there was parallel negative media coverage of them, again including Vila Cruzeiro.

The idea for repair was born in the community. Repairs were not envisaged in Haas&Hahn's plans as by that time they had moved to North Philadelphia, US to paint houses of one section of Germantown Avenue under a one-year Mural Arts residency program. The 'Philly Painting' project involved hiring and training a group of local people to paint 50 storefront buildings and was completed in 2012. After the favelas' resident-based campaign to restore the mural, and in particular, correspondence between young boys who painted the mural and Haas&Hahn, they returned temporarily to Rio de Janeiro to help to restore the mural. As a result, now there are general plans to set up maintenance for their new project, involving the painting of houses in Vila Cruzeiro. The question is, how will work be maintained, and in what ways?

The politics of pacification across Rio's neighbourhoods: Facilitating gentrification?

The current politics of pacification-driven urban planning and development strategy in Rio de Janeiro is strongly tinted by a discourse of security. The city needs to be seen as being able to deliver security for hosting of mega events, such as the recent FIFA World Cup 2014, which proved controversial with a number of protests organized by local communities in response to city planning policy. With the Summer Olympics 2016, the city needs to represent to the world that it is capable of delivering security. The 2013–2016 Strategic Plan of the City, announced during Rio's Mayor Eduardo Paes' campaign for re-election, includes a 5 per cent reduction of favelas and the elimination of residential areas in – as it has been framed – environmentally protected zones, or so-called 'risk' areas (Heck, 2013). Favela removals is thus immanently on 'the cards', a rather controversial dimension of urban development in Rio de Janeiro.[2]

The politics of pacification has been translated into evictions and gentrification initiatives; incentives that run the risk of moving people from their homes and modifying the locations into 'elite areas.' In several instances, evictions already have resulted in residents losing their jobs and capital they have invested in their residences, adding to community fragmentation and the distress, experienced by displacement and joblessness. Home ownership is highly valued in Brazilian culture, especially among favela residents and lower income groups. Penglase (2014a), reflecting on security in Rio de Janeiro in the context of the World Cup 2014, pointed out, drawing on his own research, Cummings (2012), Williamson (2013) and others, that it remains to be seen if the pacifying policies are able to transform favelas into more 'regular' neighbourhoods where residents would lose some of the benefits associated with their 'informal' status.

It is important to emphasize that favelas can no longer defined by their strictly 'illegal' status, as currently their legal status is in limbo and several favelas have a form of de facto tenure (Perlman, 2010: 30). Many residents already have to pay for utilities, such as water or electricity, and it is harder for people to stay. In the context of recent developments and pacification processes, it seems that the residents will soon be also obliged to pay property taxes and local businesses operating as informal economy will be phased out.

The pacification processes so far have resulted in perceived improvements to security across the city, and such views are projected via the media. As a consequence, in the past years housing prices of properties across the city significantly rose up. The urban developments for hosting of mega events and a demand for properties have resulted in a current property boom (*O Globo* report cited in Cummings, 2012). There is now a flourishing real estate market, with prices in the well-located favelas in South of Rio and in central areas rivalling those of legitimate neighbourhoods. This includes Santa Marta, where Haas&Hahn executed a project in 2010 that resulted in painting 34 houses around the central square. The value of Santa Marta houses around the central square increased even more. At the same time, families who have lived for over three generations in the houses at the heights of the Santa Marta are now threatened with eviction because favela residences that are mapped within high-risk areas are subject to removal or resettlement programs as per the 2013–2016 Strategic Plan of the City. Santa Marta, as well as other favelas due to their geo-location – occupying hills across the city – has been subjected to several landslides in the past and its top area is marked as 'at risk'. Heck (2013), in his analysis of recent favela resettlements, pointed out that in case residents do not agree to the resettlement options that are dictated to them, the amount offered for their homes by the city is never going to be enough to purchase a residence anywhere in the community from which they came, particularly in the upscale South Zone of Rio where Santa Marta is located.

Cummings (2012) argues that expanding issuance of title deeds and subsequent access to the property markets can be of great benefit to many of favela residents, yet he also warns against subjecting these communities to purely market forces and economic gentrification. There is a risk that, in effect, the neighbourhoods may be transformed into urban territory but affordable only to the middle and upper classes, particularly the hillside neighbourhoods in South Zone. Community awareness campaigns aimed at offering alternatives to economic gentrification are organized. One such solution could be the introduction of community-based land trusts (CLTs) as a model for sustainable and affordable housing. CLTs are non-profit entities that are run by the community residents, possibly offering a balance between the private and collective ownership. Cummings (2012) also points out that a CLTs model developed for Rio's favelas could lead to the empowerment of land tenure without the risk associated with trappings of individual titles that could damage the community's fabric and force majority of residents to the fringes.

Haas&Hahn's project in Santa Marta that resulted in an improvement of housing at the central square, at the very bottom of the favela, in a peculiar way seemed to contribute to a deepening of the already existing social segregation within the community (the poorest housing at the top), based on a differentiation of their property value. Cultural theorist Malcolm Miles (1997) has pointed out two main pitfalls of publically engaged arts-based projects, arguing that such initiatives are potentially used either as a wallpaper to cover social conflicts or as a monumental type of realization, aimed at promoting aspirations and 'good will' of corporate sponsors and underlying dominant ideologies.

Would it be naïve to think that painting over this dilapidated self-built housing can do anything more than mask the social and economic problems as highlighted above? The danger is that 'Favela Painting' interventions could be viewed by some as a 'feel-good' approach that is passed off as an economic development initiative. On the other hand, if the economic gentrification is seen as a way forward for 'integrating' favelas into Rio's formal socio-political structures, and if that strategy prevails and succeeds among local politicians, without proper participatory process and community engagement, then increased security in Rio de Janeiro may be associated with an increasingly precarious daily life for many of its residents.

In the context of the recent property boom and economic gentrification, the challenge for local politicians is associated with the connectivity issue. How to 'regularize', or in other words, how to incorporate favelas and their residents into the city's political, urban and economic infrastructure? At what price? In such a challenging reality, focusing all efforts on a participatory potential and long-term sustainability during realization of the new project under 'Favela Painting' banner would be of an immense benefit to both local neighbourhoods and the city authorities, showcasing a blueprint for a success story of co-producing with the community. Painting the whole favela with the help of residents can become an example of a good practice in the grassroots-grown strategy for socio-economic regeneration, an alternative to urban development under the 2013–2016 Strategic Plan for the City. And indeed, the strategy Haas&Hahn propose appears to reflect a strong ethos of community:

We are working on ideas to make the project self-sustainable, by creating merchandise and even our own paint. A local paint factory would not only supply extra jobs, but could also create income, that could support the project.

(Haas&Hahn, 2013)

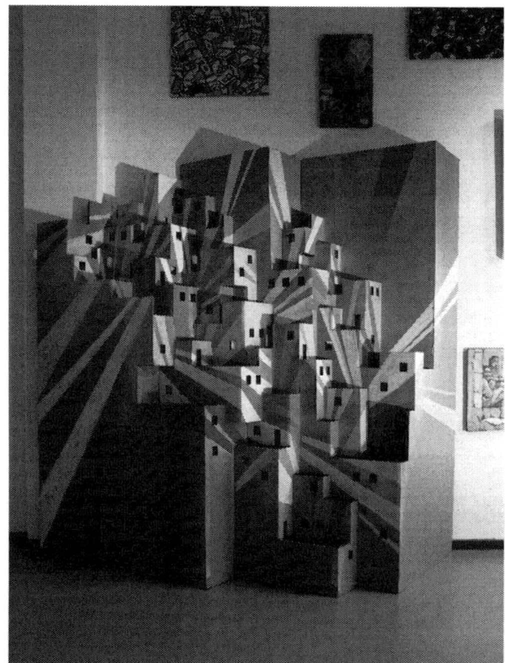

Figure 4.8: *O morro* model, 'Favela Painting'. Courtesy of Haas&Hahn.

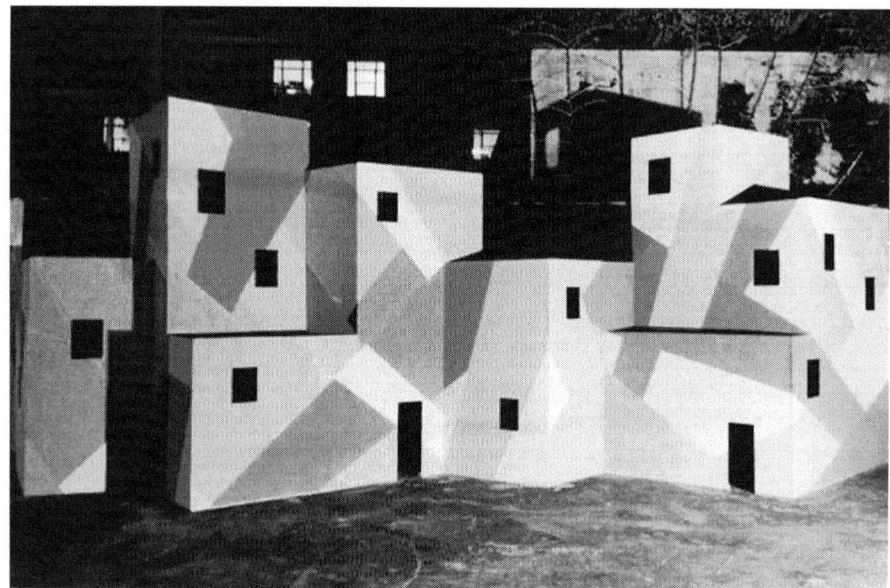

Figure 4.9: 'Favela Painting', Miami Art Basel, 2013. Courtesy of Haas&Hahn.

Haas&Hahn's alternative strategy of working, largely based on community empowerment discourse, is aimed at improving the living conditions for residents and by residents, employing locals in plastering and painting their own houses, and setting up the factory for producing the paint on situ for further work, with an objective of creating even more new jobs in the community. A work of art, as a finished object, as installation, typically provokes a response based on the viewer's aesthetic experience. Yet, in the 'Favela Painting' projects, articulated within a set of arts-based interventions, drawing on terminology of relational practices (Kester, 1999, 2004; Bourriaud, 1998/2002), its criticality lies in an exchange of knowledge, learning and skills transfer that forms an integral part of the work itself and determines its durability.

Networked realities of Haas&Hahn: How to balance the books?

Although living a quasi-traveller life, a life of in-between for over ten years now, of what could be summed up a nomadic existence in order to realize their projects, Haas&Hahn belong to and benefit from being a part of Dutch artistic circles and affluent international

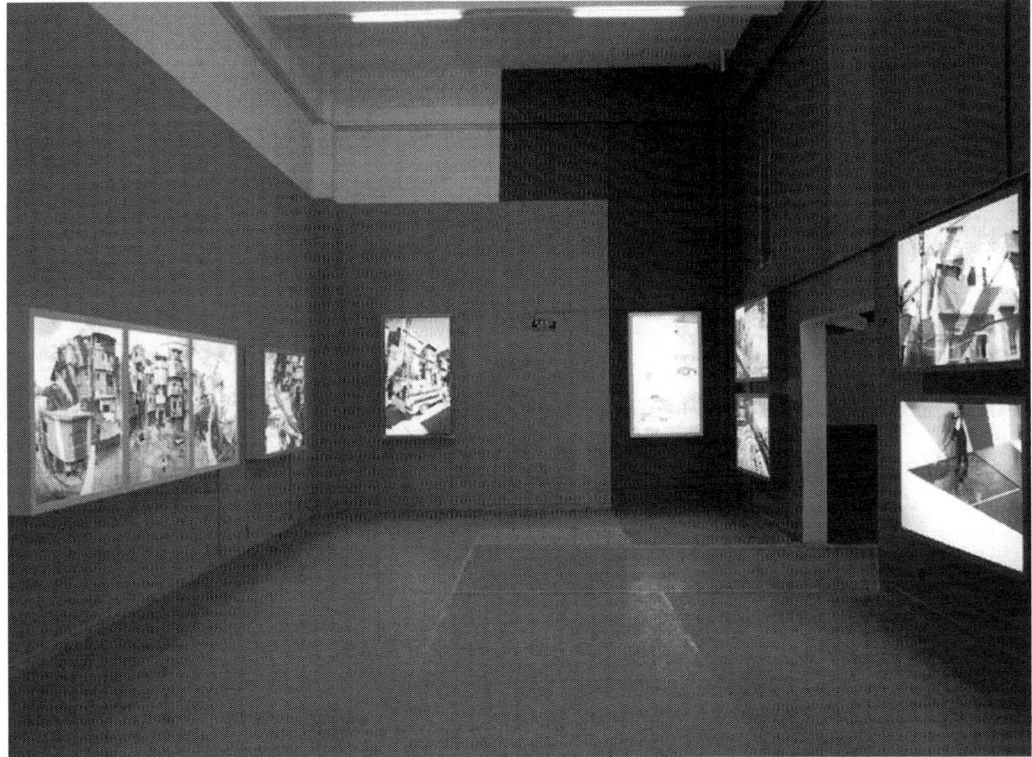

Figure 4.10: 'Favela Painting' project exhibition, Shenzhen Hong Kong Biennale, 2011. Courtesy of Haas&Hahn.

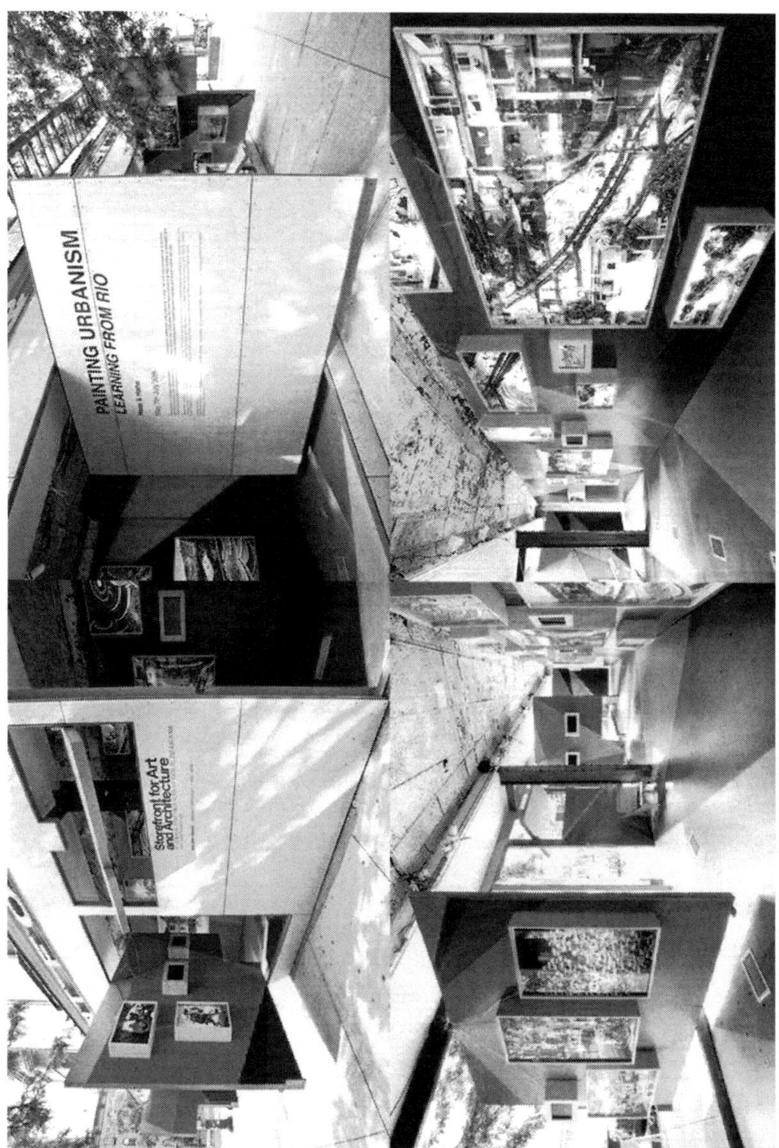

Figure 4.11: *Painting Urbanism: Learning from Rio*, Storefront for Art and Architecture, New York, 2011. Courtesy of Haas&Hahn.

networks. The types of projects they realize rely on an imaginary community of sponsors and activists, backed up by the existing elite-based network, building spaces of engagement and virtual forums of like-minded individuals, interested in change or supporting the socio-economic transformation of the perceived precarious condition associated with the favela-based living from the inside. On the 'Favela Painting' website, Haas&Hahn give examples of fundraising help they received, in addition to funds raised via the Kickstarter platform. 'Favela Painting' features regularly at international exhibitions and art events, such as Art Basel in Miami in 2013 and Shenzhen Biennale in 2012. Fundraising is realized through direct sales of 'Favela Painting' documentation as well as produced merchandise, such as T-shirts, at exhibitions and through website-based campaigns. Also, several organizations including restaurants, schools, bars and churches have mobilized their networks to raise funds for 'Favela Painting' projects via various initiatives, such as organized painting days, collected tips or hosting parties and social events.

Koolhaas combines working for 'Favela Painting' with his freelance work for big designer labels, for instance designing projections for Prada fashion shows and creating illustrations for the *New Yorker* magazine. The fashion house is a client of the OMA, the Office for Metropolitan Architecture, the firm founded by Jeroen Koolhaas' uncle, the world-celebrated architect Rem Koolhaas, for whom Jeroen Koolhaas is a freelance graphic designer. Urhahn grew up in Amsterdam as a son of an urban planner and an artist; Koolhaas grew up in Rotterdam, the son of a professor at the Delft University of Technology and an art historian. Urhahn studied Chinese language and culture and has no formal art training. Previously, he worked as an artistic director, copy writer and journalist (Williams, 2013). Haas&Hahn became a team almost by accident. It was a hip-hop film project that brought them together. Koolhaas was awarded €5000 to make a documentary after winning a prize for his graduation work, a short animation. After a short visit to São Paulo and Rio de Janeiro on a student exchange, Koolhaas decided to make a film about hip-hop in the favelas. He proposed collaboration on the film project to Urhahn. They have worked together on 'Favela Painting' ever since. It seems appropriate, therefore, to emphasize the importance of class, elite-centred power-bases and positionality-based influence in the success of Haas&Hahn's tactical urbanist interventions.

Initially, the €5000 was just enough to cover accommodation, travel and living expenses. Based on the interview with Haas&Hahn, Williams (2013) pointed out that since 2006 they have been living a 'hand-to-mouth' nomadic existence. For instance, Dulux provided 136,000 USD for the favela paints, and they managed to raise 34,000 USD themselves. Yet, with time their circumstances have changed from being two single enthusiastic young artists experimenting with sites and medium to family men with obligations and responsibilities. Both now fathers, they need to balance family lifestyle with the project realizations.[3] These new circumstances require a new organizational structure for 'Favela Painting.' An increasing number of people manage the day-to-day business, marketing and communication and execution – perhaps this is the only way forward. Under the new structure, Haas&Hahn enterprise has a potential for attracting funding for larger projects, via like-minded networks, no doubt supported through their connections.

Beyond painting the houses? Working within a paradigm of relational art

Haas&Hahn's site-specific art interventions, drawing on notion of 'space as a practiced placed' (Certeau, 1988), are based on working in specific places, and simultaneously, on producing critical spaces. Grant Kester in his *Conversation Pieces* provides a definition of dialogical aesthetics as a process that is being 'based on the generation of local consensual knowledge that is only provisionally binding and that is grounded at the level of collective interaction' (2004: 112). Within a set of art practices that aspire to dialogic aesthetics, as defined above, arts-based intervention embraces the importance of a dialogue, as an integral component to an engaged practice, resulting in a participatory process. Despite the obvious politics of capital circulation, 'Favela Painting' works do have a social function, and provide tools for reflection on the appropriateness of working method. The projects embrace criticality through the executed process of work and offer a possibility for a social change.

Artists intervene in a particular locality, in a specific context and its spatiality.[4] Santos defined space as 'an indivisible, integral and also a contradictory set of systems of objects and systems of actions, not taken in isolation but as a unique scenario in which history unfolds' (2006: 63). In this sense, each change arises from and generates new changes, because 'the spatial forms also oblige other social structures to transform themselves, striving for adaptation, whenever they cannot create new forms' (Santos, 2008: 45). Critical and resisting potential, associated with the method of working that defines spatial realm as transformational, can acquire a more pragmatic form. Haas&Hahn seem to be concerned with the specific effects produced by exchanges of communication in the context of the favelas' built environment. Their art-centred inquiry also embraces a movement and expands into virtual spaces. The focus is, therefore, on a process that challenges or shakes various stereotypes associated with favela life, fixed meanings, official discourses and media representation, associated with what can be perceived and represented as 'precarious' places.

Art practice, in Haas&Hahn's tactical urbanism-based interventions, becomes a performative medium, creating a platform for a discussion on change, and engagement with a social reality through the multiple registers of meanings. In other words, it is by participating and re-writing the stories of everyday life in favelas that this process becomes art.

Nicolas Bourriaud pointed out that the ways of working for some contemporary artists today are governed by a concern to 'give everyone their chance,' through forms that do not establish any precedence, a priori, of the producer [the artist] over the beholder, but rather negotiate more open-based relationships with it (1998/2002: 58). Representational conventions of the arts and aesthetics, therefore, may be challenged by the creative facilitation of knowledge exchange and/or a possible dialogue formation and research. It is also site-specificity, such as the favelas of Rio in the case of Haas&Hahn's tactical urbanism, that can become a space of encounter.

Conclusions

Urhahn and Koolhaas' projects epitomize an alternative creative way upon which the objective is to realize community-based work in collaboration with local inhabitants. I would argue that the 'Favela Painting' murals realised in Rio de Janeiro seem to have brought a sense of impetus for change. The projects invited local inhabitants to co-create and co-represent much more constructively and positively the life of their neighbourhood. 'Favela Painting' collaborations succeeded in articulating a different discourse of social change – that of engagement – and encouraged local people to embrace the potential for an improvement of living conditions around them.

These interventions have a potential to achieve long-term sustainability, especially under the current climate of city's urban development planning and the politics around pacification. The city's development plan for favelas, as it seems, with its emphasis on developing cable cars and focusing on ecological aesthetics, demonstrates a priority for tourism rather than building durable infrastructure that would integrate favelas into the city (for instance, improving the sewage system in Santa Marta, investing in the public transportation network across the city to reduce congestion).

A sustainability potential in Haas&Hahn's tactical urbanism-based interventions is related to the process of co-production with the community and timing of the projects, punctuated by multiple visits. Their multiple returns strengthen the established relationships, as 'coming back visits are most appreciated by the community,' Urhahn explained, 'people are always happy to see us back everywhere we have painted.' Indeed, the successful realization of such projects requires flexibility, openness and multiple role taking. Haas&Hahn are the creators, wanting to 'realise their artistic dreams and do something amazing.' At the same time, 'they consult with community and listen to everyone – as anthropologists, social explorers, social mediators and humble observers of an unfolding political situation' (Urhahn in interview with Kosmala, June 2015, unpublished).

A sustainability potential coincides with esteem-building, which occurs on a small scale, indirectly and incrementally. Esteem-building may prove significant in the fight against poverty in the long term, highlighting the exclusion of favelas communities. These projects are in effect co-productions built on the community's feel. The inhabitants of favelas are an integral part of community-driven action, capitalizing on its identity and a sense of pride.

The new project Back to Rio currently being realized – painting the whole favela with the help of the residents – offers a blueprint for social and organizational co-existence for local neighbourhoods of Rio, a longer term strategic design that could also result in balancing the books, if the established networks and Haas&Hahn's positionality could persuade potential funders of the success in the philanthropic frame of 'everybody contributes.'

In my view, Haas&Hahn's projects, based on collaboration with the local neighbourhoods, have succeeded in altering, temporarily and possibly for the long term, the media discourse that stigmatizes favelas. The negativity attached to favela-based communities is predominantly imposed from the outside, without real knowledge of favela life. Conflation of negative connotations attached by references made to, for instance, 'slum' or 'violence' discourse negates the range of community-based qualities and undermines favelas' historic role in development of Rio de Janeiro and cities across Brazil (Kosmala, 2011). These negative perceptions influence exclusionary urban planning policies and politics behind urban development. For certain, by attracting the media coverage and utilization of social networks for documenting, information sharing and fundraising, Haas&Hahn's 'Favela Painting' projects challenge the status quo. Beyond pure painting, the projects have opened the door to global networks and campaigning via social platforms. Haas&Hahn's collaborative action has already contributed to an alteration of the discourse of stigmatization.

'Favela Painting' seems to affect the aesthetic order of how favelas are perceived from within and from outside. The colours used express a positive ambience and housing is upgraded, but we also learn about the risk of evictions in the context of ongoing struggle for the housing rights' formal recognitions and precariousness of daily living associated with pacification politics. In my view, Haas&Hahn flagged up the potenial for 'Favela Painting' to contribute to a sustainable ecological model of urban development in the future, capitalizing on dynamics created between local people, objects and spaces of the intervention itself.

References

Bhabha, H. 1994. *The Location of Culture*, London: Routledge.

Bourriaud, N. 1998/2002. *Relational Aesthetics*, Dijon: Les Presses du Reel.

Certeau, M. de. 1988. *The Practice of Everyday Life*, Berkeley, CA: University of California Press.

Chase, J., Crawford, M. and Kaliski, J. (Eds) 1999/2008. *Everyday Urbanism: Expanded*, New York, NY: The Monacelli Press.

Cummings, J. 2012. 'Favela community land trusts?', *Rio on Watch*, 16 March, http://www.rioonwatch.org/?p=3148. Accessed 17 April 2014.

Franch i Gilabert, E. 2011. 'About *Painting Urbanism: Learning from Rio*: Curatorial statement', New York, NY: Storefront for Art and Architecture.

Gray D. 2013. '"Favela Painting" project returns to Rio', *The Rio Times*, 23 October, http://riotimesonline.com/brazil-news/rio-business/favela-painting-project-returns-to-rio/. Accessed 17 April 2014.

Haas&Hahn 2013. 'Back to Rio', Favela Painting, http://www.favelapainting.com/page/backtorio. Accessed 24 November 2014.

Heck, C. 2013. 'The area of risk justification for favela removals: The case of Santa Marta', *Rio on Watch*, 29 October, http://www.rioonwatch.org/?p=11410. Accessed 12 December 2014.

Hestbæk, C. 2010. 'Vila Cruzeiro. Life in a warzone', *The Rio Times*, 30 November.

Kester, G. 2004. *Conversation Pieces: Community, Communication in Modern Art*, Berkeley, CA and London: University of California Press.

Kosmala, K. 2011. 'Temporality and alteration of social boundaries in the making of an art installation', *Creative Industries Journal*, 4 (1), 53–69.

Kruschewsky, G. 2014. 'One step forward, ten steps back: On exoticization of Rio's favelas', *Huffington Post*, 9 March, http://www.huffingtonpost.com/gabrielakruschewsky/exoticization-of-rios-favelas_b_4972573.html. Accessed 16 January 2015.

Kwon, M. 2002. *One Place after Another: Site Specific Art and Locational Identity*, Cambridge, MA: The MIT Press.

Lyndon, M. and Garcia, A. 2015. *Tactical Urbanism*, Washington, DC: Island Press.

Miles, M. 1997. *Art, Space and the City*, London: Routledge.

Murray, R. 2014. 'Painting a favela: The kickstarter aiming for a million dollars', *The Chromologist*, 11 June, http://thechromologist.com/painting-favela-kickstarter-aiming-million-dollars/. Accessed 16 January 2015.

Penglase, B. 2014a. 'Pacifying Rio's favelas: Innovation, adaptation or continuity?', Security in Brazil: World Cup 2014 and Beyond forum, *Anthropoliteia: Critical Perspectives on Police, Security, Crime, Law and Punishment around the World*, 16 May, http://anthropoliteia.net/2014/05/16/pacifying-rios-favelas-innovation-adaptation-or-continuity/. Accessed 5 December 2014.

Penglase, B. 2014b. *Living with Insecurity in a Brazilian Favela: Urban Violence and Daily Life*, New Brunswick, NJ and London: Rutgers University Press.

Perlman, J. 2010. *Favela: Four Decades of Living on the Edge in Rio de Janeiro*, New York, NY: Oxford University Press.

Rendell, J. 2006. *Art and Architecture: A Place Between*, London and New York, NY: I.B. Tauris.

Santos, M. 2006. *A Natureza do Espaço: Técnica e Tempo. Razão e Emoção*, São Paulo: Editora da Universidade de São Paulo.

Santos, M. 2008. *Da Totalidade ao Lugar*, São Paulo: Editora da Universidade de São Paulo.

Williams, S. 2013. 'Ghetto fabulous: The murals of Haas&Hahn', *Telegraph*, 5 March, http://www.telegraph.co.uk/culture/art/art-features/9899749/Ghetto-fabulous-the-murals-of-Haas-and-Hahn.html. Accessed 26 November 2014.

Williamson, T. 2013. 'Land tenure and urban planning in Rio de Janeiro's favelas', *Rio on Watch*, 19 September, http://www.rioonwatch.org/?p=11075. Accessed 15 March 2014.

Notes

1   Information obtained from the 'Favela Painting' website 2015 and the author's interview with Dre Urhahn in June 2015.

2   Risk discourse frames the current policy development in Brazil. The area of risk designation, as a legal tool, links a policy of favela reduction to a policy of conservation and reforestation, all buzzwords for related issues for environmentalists in Brazil and

international NGOs. This framing of the evictions seem to obscure international criticism of the removals and seems to delegitimize more grassroots-organized activism by favela residents. For more see Heck (2013).

3   Information obtained from the author's interview with Dre Urhahn in June 2015.

4   As Bourriaud explains in *Relational Aesthetics*, art is the place that produces a specific sociability (1998/2002: 16); it is a state of encounter. The artistic process also involves mapping and documenting of what happens. Multiple registers of meanings are results of such practice.

Chapter 5

Beyond aesthetics: Poetics of *Autoconstrucción* in Mexico City

Benjamin Parry

Introduction

This chapter discusses the multidisciplinary project *Autoconstrucción* by Mexican artist Abraham Cruzvillegas, which relates the story of the artist's childhood through the self-build construction of his family home on the uninhabited and inhospitable volcanic lands of the *Pedregales de Coyoacan* outside Mexico City. The first in a series of realizations for *Autoconstrucción* began far from the precarious spaces of Mexico City, when Cruzvillegas took up a six-month residency at Cove Park and the Centre for Contemporary Arts in Glasgow in 2008. During that time, he created his customary sculptures of found objects, produced a book documenting his experiences growing up on the squatted lands of the Ajusco, and wrote the lyrics for eighteen songs that were then offered to a diverse range of local Glaswegian bands.

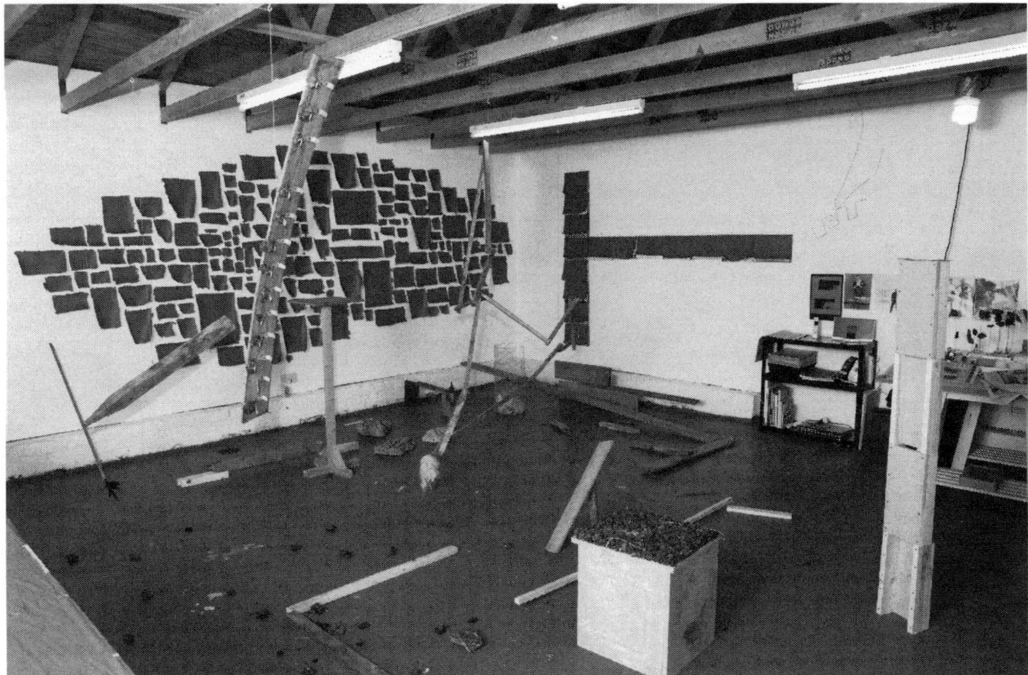

Figure 5.1: *Autoconstrucción* exhibition, CCA Glasgow, 2008. Photograph: Ruth Clark.

I fell apart when you said goodbye to me
I didn't understand why you left
When we were just building the house
Our own place made with our own hands
Without money, without plans
Without everything, but love

(Cruzvillegas, 2008: 83, lines 1–6)

These are lyrics from the song 'With or Without You' (2012) by Abraham Cruzvilleges, which narrates the stories of Ajusco and the ongoing self-construction of his family home. In an unlikely meeting of cultures, these lyrics were sung and put to music by a variety of Scottish bands in the city of Glasgow. The songs were then heard through Glasgow streets from a mobile sound system mounted upon a homemade bicycle, reminiscent of the *Sonidero* tradition of Mexico City.

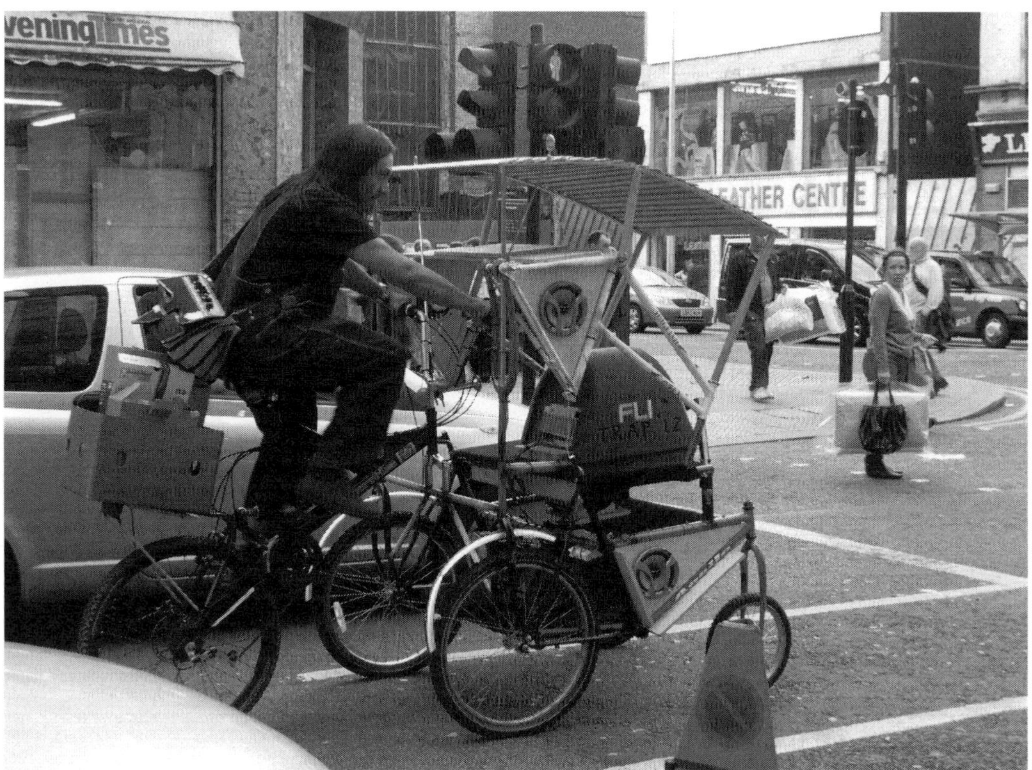

Figure 5.2: Abraham Cruzvillegas with sound system mobile sculpture on the streets of Glasgow as part of *Autocon-struccion*, CCA, 2008. Photograph: Francis Mckee.

With or without you, I'll finish the house
My own place made with my own hands

(Cruzvillegas, 2008: 83, lines 11 and 12)

Of the many dynamic and hybrid forms the *Autoconstrucción* project takes, this social sculpture, part street cart, part autobiography in a mix of local sounds and collaborations, is a compelling communicative instrument for narrating the traditions and disjuncture of his childhood. What follows is an in-depth analysis of this particular aspect of the project, which extends into a broader discussion about the wider contribution of social art practice in the critical discourses around urban informality and user-generated urbanisms. I also explore how the personal experiences of self-build, self-organized communities have formed the methodology of Cruzvillegas' social practice, artistic sensibility, aesthetics, poetics and politics that raise critical challenges to current debates around precariousness in art.

Autoconstrucción

The *Autoconstrucción* project begins with the story of Cruzvillegas' childhood, growing up in a squatter settlement on the then-vacant periphery of Mexico City, in the so-called 'unofficial zone' of Ajusco. Throughout the 1960s and 1970s Cruzvillegas watched the lone squatter settlements grow from simple one-room dwellings to eventual houses built from the volcanic rock, as residents came together forming self-organized communities to build streets and schools and install basic services. With the City's expanding periphery came the besiegement of opportunistic developers constructing new, well-planned and serviced districts such as the *Romero de Torreros* and *Pedregal del San Angel* built for the 'economically privileged.' At the same time, improved access and new supply chains gave way to shops, the establishment of a public square, a local market and schools, and eventually, the supermarkets and the highways with the walls dividing the rich from the poor.

In September 1971, the largest ever single land invasion in the history of Latin America took place in a barren area of the Pedregales that would later become the official zone of *Pedregal de Santo Domingo*. In response to a presidential address by Luís Echeverría Álvarez, in which he acknowledged the huge housing shortage by promising to legalize de facto tenancy of public lands, '*Hay Tierra!* (there's land)' rang out. Overnight as many as 5000 families invaded Santo Domingo (Gutmann, 2007: 312), 'joining the older barrios of resistance' (Esteva and Prakesh, 1998: 85). In a counter-response to rapid growth, walls were then built across Mexico City to separate the squatter zones from the well-planned districts, as in the *Pedregales*, where the locally named Berlin Wall divided *Santo Domingo* from *Romero de Torreros*. Like other marginal areas of the city, the writing on the walls 'marking frontiers or personal experiences' carried manifestos, images and slogans. These were a response to the rising divisions and inequality that brought with it a period of gang activities and civil unrest. Cruzvillegas reflected upon these developments:

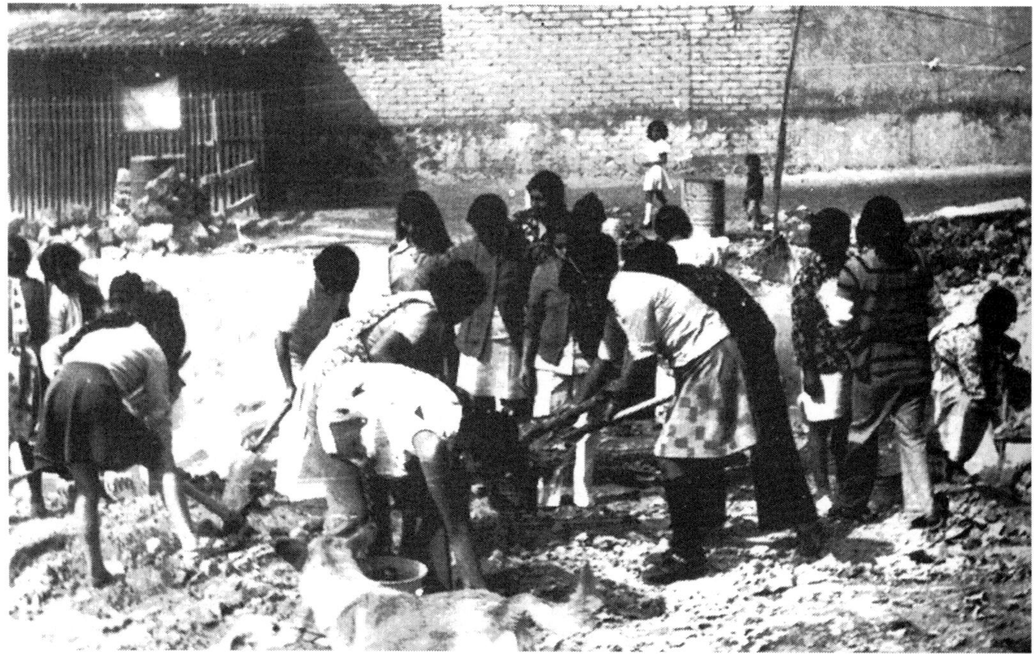

Figure 5.3: Image from *Las mil y una historias del Pedregal de Santo Domingo* by Fernnano Diaz Enciso (2002) published by the Delegacion Coyoacan y la Direccion General de Culuras Populares e Indigenas / Habitat ONU in Mexico.

In a reaction to the lack of opportunities, of access to education, work or housing, a territorial spirit began to assert itself which aspired to define that harsh territory as its own [...].

(2008: 50)

In the book *Autoconstrucción,* which accompanied the exhibition, Cruzvillegas recalls the details of his house and brings to life the characters, events, social struggles and community solidarity that formed his identity; that, like the peculiarities of his house, remains unfinished. He argues that the story of the Coyoacan Pedregales is also a story of resistance. Without land titles, families of the Pedregales, encircled by rising land values, were faced with evictions and during the height of the urban struggle of Ajusco, men, women and children worked together taking shifts to occupy the land. As the lyrics of the song 'Razzia' describe, '*We stayed there / All night long / And for the rest of the days* [...] *We made fire outside* [...] *We sang songs and drank / We told tales and jokes / Of a humour very dark / And we laughed so loud / Until the police arrived*' (lines 5–7, 11, 13–17).

By the mid-1970s, many neighbourhood groups had formed into social movements in a front to claim back the land they occupied. '*While many men were working / At Factories, Offices, Schools*', or building their homes, the women held meetings, organized demonstrations and marched on the Zocalo Square, '*The land belongs to those who work it.*'

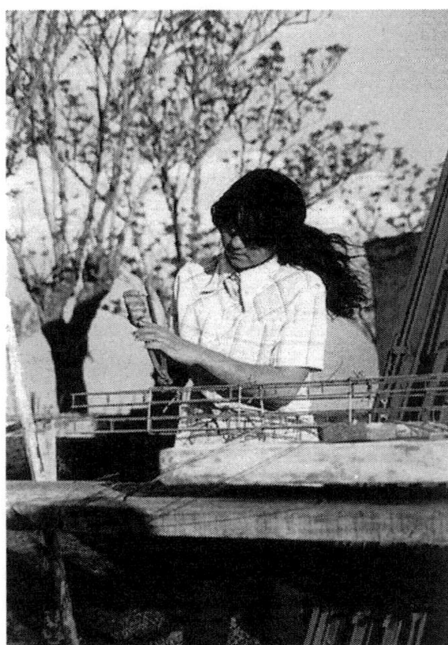

Figure 5.4: The Ajusco District, Mexico City. Photograph taken by the Cruzvillegas Fuentes family, Ajusco, Mexico City. Courtesy of Abraham Cruzvillegas.

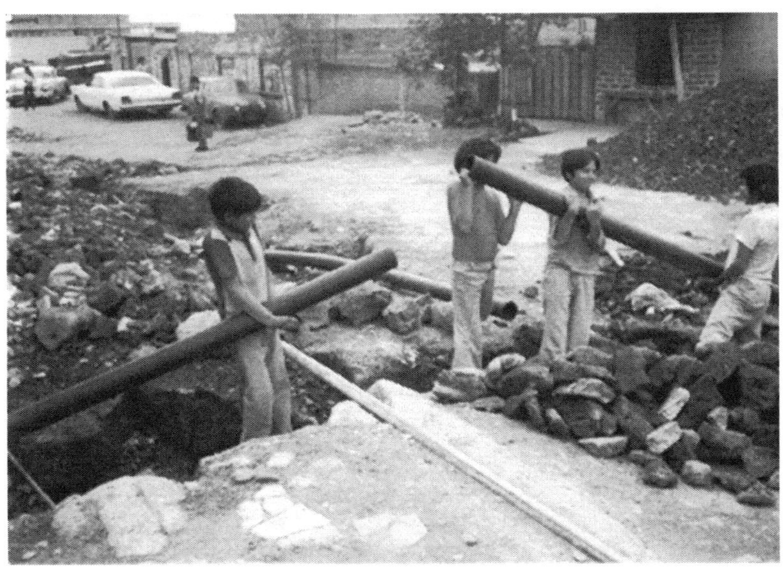

Figure 5.5: The Ajusco District, Mexico City. Photograph taken by the Cruzvillegas Fuentes family, Ajusco, Mexico City. Courtesy of Abraham Cruzvillegas.

They went there with their children
To the government offices
Screaming, yelling, claiming
The right to their lands

('Aprons', Cruzvillegas, 2008: 182, lines 7–10)

Women played a crucial role in establishing these social movements and in the self-organizing process as a whole: 'we are not all men but we are many.' Local resident and one of the leaders of the 1971 invasion, Fernando Díaz Enciso made a recent and important intervention – in the form of a book collecting oral histories from residents of Santo Domingo, *Las mil y una historias del Pedregal de Santo Domingo* (2002), which attests to the instrumental position women played in the community. In the words of Eulogia Hernández:

Since we began to raise the community we, the women, have always worked the most because we are all day at home: if a roof falls, we raise it; if there is a ditch to fill, we fill it; just like we attend to the houses, we attend to our husbands and children. The men have to go to work, and the women cannot wait until they return in order to resolve the problems that arise; all we need are our hands and our will to do the same as the men. [...] Women with their children worked in the construction of the whole community every day of the week; what's more, to the women fell the responsibility of the children, the education, the family economy, and, above all, dealing with facing the constant fear of eviction.[1]

(Encisco, 2002)

The specific participation of women in grassroots mobilization of the Pedregales, Mexico's popular movements and feminist groups later morphed into NGOs (Monk, 2010). This is evidenced in the roles performed by Cruzvillegas' mother who was not only active in the social movements of the district, but also helped found the first market, established the local traders organization and owned her own clothes stall.

My mother used to sell pants
School uniforms, shirts, socks
Brassieres, panties and thongs
But she also sold aprons
Many women wore them at home
But also at big demonstrations.

('Aprons', Cruzvillegas, 2008: 182, lines 1–6)

When the supermarkets finally arrived, forcing the local market into decline, his mother sold her business and joined an NGO defending human rights.

Like many other women, my mother became an intermediary between community and the institutions; faced with the slippery demagoguery of the politicians and the stubborn

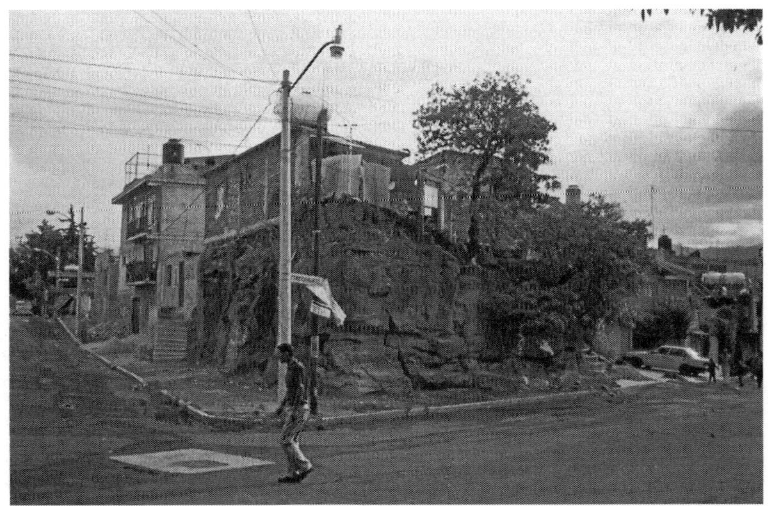

Figure 5.6: The Ajusco District, Mexico City. Photograph taken by the Cruzvillegas Fuentes family, Ajusco, Mexico City. Courtesy of Abraham Cruzvillegas.

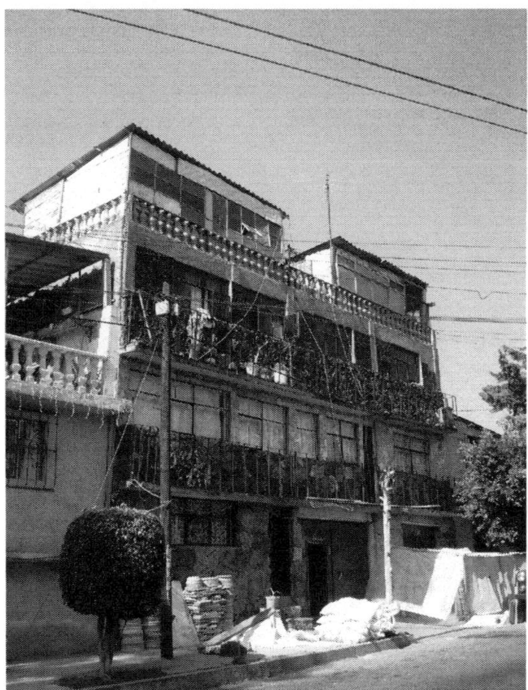

Figure 5.7: The Ajusco District, Mexico City. Photograph taken by the Cruzvillegas Fuentes family, Ajusco, Mexico City. Courtesy of Abraham Cruzvillegas.

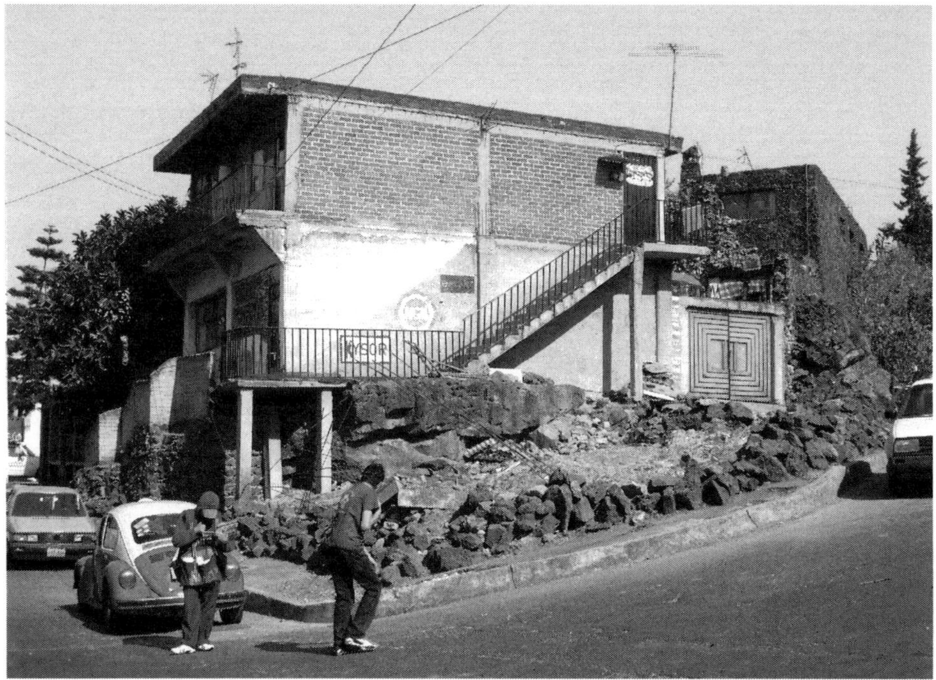

Figure 5.8: The Ajusco District, Mexico City. Photograph taken by the Cruzvillegas Fuentes family, Ajusco, Mexico City. Courtesy of Abraham Cruzvillegas.

invasions of the bureaucrats, she wrote letters, documents and manifestos, confronted candidates and leaders of the street sellers and was sometimes rewarded with threats and offered corruption of every sort.

(Cruzvillegas, 2008: 50)

Cruzvillegas notes that despite pressures and involvement of numerous political parties who attempted to control the land movements, and thus credit victories for electoral purposes, the popular organizations defended their activities and their autonomy without aligning to a particular party or the state. This autonomy was most important in enabling women to take a more central role in organizational change and introduced an immanent space for the creation of a feminist voice within social movements (Stephen, 1997). In *Women and Social Movements in Latin America* (1997), Lynn Stephen notes how women's political mobilisation in defence of their lands, demand for child education, housing, food and medical care integrated a commitment to the challenge of subordination of women and women's rights.

The turbulent succession of events and early life experience of Cruzvillegas are charted through the creation and transformation of an unofficial urban zone. The social and political realities wrought by the rapid growth of Mexico City, combined with the urban struggles and formation of social movements – including those such as the National Coordinating

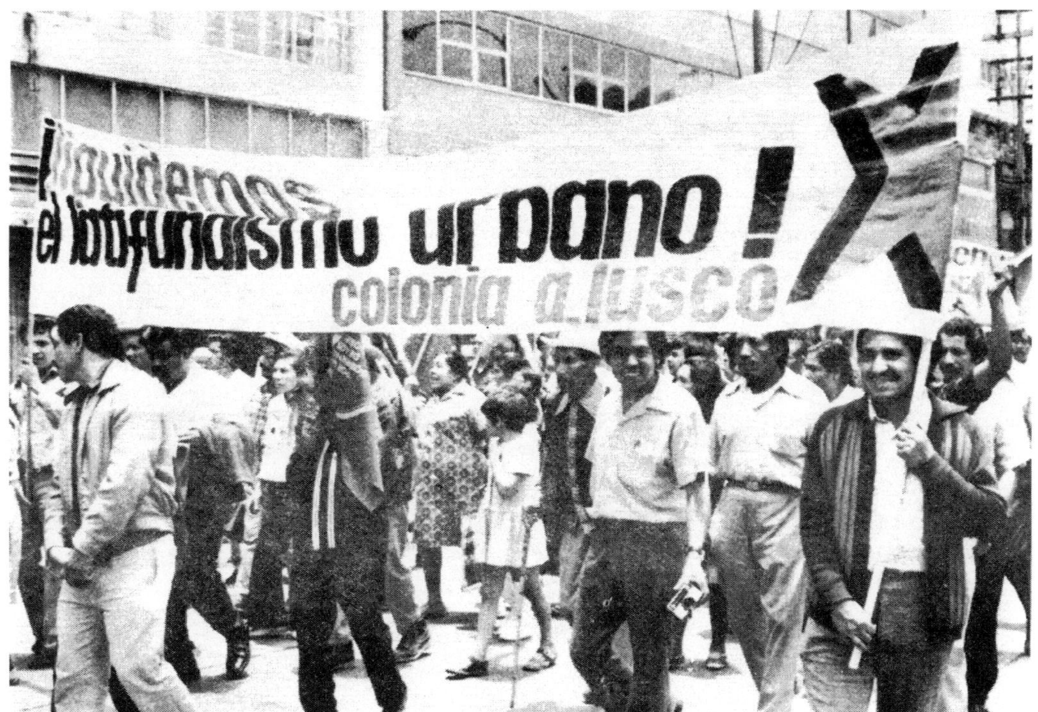

Figure 5.9: Protest in Ajusco, Mexico. Image from 'Revista Palabras del pueblo', *Fomento Cultural AC*, 3 (October), 1975. Courtesy of the rights holder.

Committee of the Popular Urban Movement (CONAMUP) – inform methodology for the construction of Cruzvillegas' identity and artistic process.

> One of the most powerful and moving moments of those times, for me, was the huge CONAMUP march to Mexico City at the beginning of the 80s. It was an endless stream of urban and rural families demanding recognition of the rights that they had already assumed for themselves.
>
> (Cruzvillegas, 2008: 37)

These aspects of Cruzvillegas' life in Ajusco and the construction of his family home are implied in the title *Autoconstrucción*, meaning the self-build techniques and self-organized processes, particular to informal housing settlements. In relation to the artist's visual forms and aesthetics of precarity, *Autoconstrucción* describes how collaboration and the sharing of skills combine education and self-awareness in the construction of community and solidarity. Writing about the squatter *barriadas* in Lima around the same period, architect John Turner made a similar observation: the *barriada*-builder who invests everything 'in an environment he creates, forms himself in the process.' He writes:

The person as a member of a family and of a local community, finds in the responsibilities and activities of home-building and local improvement the creative dialogue essential for self-discovery and growth.

(Turner, 1968)

The advantages Turner observed in the freedom to manipulate one's own living space and construct one's identity in the process stemmed from the adaptability of spaces and structures to the changing needs and behaviour patterns of the family, and the intense dialogue that took place. The particularities of auto-construction drawn from Cruzvillegas' experience and applied to his artistic practice are adaptability, improvisation, dialogue, collaboration, human agency, recycling and experimentation, which highlight the reciprocity between creativity and social change. However, it should be noted that this human creativity is manifest in the self-build process, and its collaborative deployment in the construction of community took place without the so-called community art or a formalized notion of an artistic practice.

In revisiting *Autoconstrucción* as an art project through the conventions of gallery display and modes of public reception, it is important to consider which aspects of the self-build process – intense dialogue, self-discovery, formation of political subjectivity and/or personal growth – might be available to the viewer. And how might we read such social exchange and encounter under the rubric of dialogical aesthetics?

Songs of resistance

By inviting local musicians to interpret his lyrics about personal stories of life in Ajusco into new songs played on the streets of Glasgow from a bicycle-mounted mobile sound-system, Cruzvillegas created new narratives of emancipation that broke down the psycho-social barriers of the 'Other' of the Third-World precarious situation. These 'songs of resistance,' in turn, formed a collision of the informal to reveal contradictions of the formal city, so that, citing Michel de Certeau: 'the struggles and inequalities hidden under the established order may be perceived' (1988: 18).

The mobile sound system that broadcasted the songs through the streets of Glasgow was built in collaboration with Common Wheel, a charity that provides meaningful activity for people with mental illness through working with bicycles and music.[2] John O'Hara, who worked on the project with Cruzvillegas, noted: '… what is beneficial is the social contact of the workplace and the creation of another self-identity as a bicycle repairman or women, instead of just a "mental patient."'

Cruzvillegas' mobile sculpture also references the *Sonidero* sound system culture of creating street parties in Mexico City, in which local residents transport their mobile sound system, often on a home-fashioned bicycle. Unique to *Sonidero* is the participation of the crowd who pass written messages or poems to be read out by the MCs who typically talk over the music, as an address to friends and family. These greetings and music performed in the streets of the capital are recorded and then handed out at the end of the night so that the protagonists can send their stories directly to family and friends across Mexico. The *Sonidero* movement originating from the marginalized neighbourhoods of Mexico City has carried over to the Mexican communities of New York and Los Angeles, where the tradition functions as a way of sending messages back home; 'it's like a long-distance telephone call, set to the rhythm of *cumbia*.'[3]

The sound system created by Cruzvillegas is a peculiar hybrid of transnational storytelling, in which he borrows from the *Sonidero*, the participatory tool in the creation of temporary communities, and inserts himself in the music culture of Glasgow. The communicative feedback loops, essential to the *Sonidero*, highlight forms of storytelling invisible or absent in the gallery presentation of the work. The new songs have potential to live on through the musicians, in other forms at other times, and indeed will have done so – each time generating new stories and encounters. Meanwhile, the process of collaboration and intense creative dialogue among the musicians and artists is sorely missing. And it spikes the imagination to think: what value might these sonic interpretations have if they found their way home, played in the streets of the Pedregales? Reflecting upon how such work might circulate and generate discourse – be that in the process of negotiating the work into existence, the performative intervention in public space or as documentation presented in the gallery – raises critical questions about where value resides.

The participatory aspects of *Autoconstrucción* certainly fulfil the 'transformatory potential' of human consciousness through 'collaborative' and 'collective art practices,' as expounded by art historian Grant Kester (2011). The inter-subjective exchange between local Glasgow-based musicians and a visual artist from Mexico indeed substantiates Kester's confidence that collaborative art practice of this nature involves a 'compassionate recognition of difference' (Kester, 2011: 185), and through new modes of social interaction mobilized by the work, occurs a 'dual consciousness of both local and global implications and interconnections of a given site and situation' (Kester, 2011: 225). Cruzvillegas explains this further:

> Very important parts of this project are collaboration and creation in a 'contaminated' cultural environment, which means shifting something very personal and subjective, from my own experience, to a very local platform and circumstance. For example the appropriation of lyrics by the bands into their own subjectivity is central to the collaboration. It means that all opinions are welcome and useful.
>
> (Cruzvillegas, 2008: 12)

The creative dialogue, the negotiation of the collaborators response and their necessary willingness to enter into a co-authored work that accepted an undetermined outcome, remains both the wisdom and the agency of this project. The collaborative production of music, though only the first stage in the many modes and forms that the *Autoconstrucción* project continues to take, is perhaps the most significant in its method of inter-subjective exchange. One that was able to transcend class difference and geopolitical boundaries because it negated passivity in favour of a compassionate negotiation of the Other, in what, for Cruzvillegas are 'hybrid marriages.' This process offers fresh insights into how we might not only negotiate difference, but also foster an awareness of difference and similitude in the appropriation and reformation of someone else's world. If the surreal juxtaposition of Cruzvillegas with a Glaswegian band – singing a song about eating tortillas three times a day just to glimpse through the blouse, *'those black round enormous nipples'* of the lady at the Tortilleria – is immediately a humorous story of a global Other, then the childhood vision of the boy is universal, just as the borrowed lyrics of Zapata, *'it is better to die standing than live on your knees'* echoes in struggles for land, freedom and justice everywhere. In a sense these unwitting encounters, which become hybrid marriages, can only produce extension, not reduction in meaning. Instead the dreamlike songs become less exotic (of a distant foreign country) as 'some place else' becomes closer to home, as the conviviality and solidarity *'under the avocado tree, in the shade'* of hot Mexican skies, or *'the girl next door, she's a guerrilla girl,'* become personalized and are recast and embodied in new topologies of place. Rich stories of resistance, of loss and endurance and of the strange discoveries of childhood echo just as strongly under a menacing and blustery Glasgow sky. This is not just an encounter with cultural difference but a dialogic process, a challenge not merely to respond to an invitation but to take the stories and make them one's own.

But which of these relational and inter-subjective aspects of the collaborators are put forward as essential aspects of the work – how are these negotiated in the gallery? The traces though not explicit nor given specific treatment are there if you look closely enough, and as we become more visually literate to the nuance of cultural difference through the mash-up and *detournement* there is much to be found through a critical interpretation in the combination of music, sculpture, intervention and collaboration offered by the project. To be sure, the background to Cruzvillegas' subjectivity in the form of narrative storytelling is a critical dimension of the *Autoconstrucción* project, well documented in the book, song lyrics and filmed interviews with the artist's parents that appear in later iterations of the project. By contrast, Cruzvillegas' sculptural praxis of working with found objects in the gallery space does not immediately carry a sense of the self-construction of squatter settlements. Whilst his art is rooted in the practice of *Autoconstrucción*, the meaning derived from his sculptural works using found materials available in the locality of production, be it Glasgow or elsewhere, seems less about the politic of urban informality or 'evidence of a social clash and uneven wealth distribution' and more about 'the ingenuity and wisdom' that are part of self-build process of urgent and specific needs (Cruzvillegas, 2009). This frames some of the prescient concerns in art discourse around the instrumentality and agency of art in the context of precarity and urban informality. This discrepancy if you will between different artistic forms of similar concern is mediated by the space of the gallery towards a precariousness in art, whereas beyond the gallery the contingent and contaminated social spaces of everyday life fulfil a different set of concerns around art and social change. The questions *Autoconstrucción* poses to architecture and urbanism and emergent interdisciplinary discourses around user-generated cities though apparent in my critical reading is very much underplayed and all but lost to the more self-referential concerns of gallery practice. How Cruzvillegas implements his artistic process in a western European context, outlined in his collaborative and itinerant interventions in the streets of Glasgow, is also an enquiry into the growing interest among artists and curators around informal urban practices, linking these to the fields of 'socially engaged art,' 'relational art,' 'participatory art,' 'interventionist art' and 'social practice.' This is evidenced in the work and associated discourse of artists such as Francis Alÿs, Santiago Sierra, Marijetica Potrc and leading voices of art historians and critics such as Claire Bishop, Grant Kester, Nicolas Bourriaud and Shannon Jackson.

The art of precariousness

In order to outline the broader concerns and agency of *Autoconstrucción*, I shall highlight some of the work of artists engaged in the practices and theory of informal urbanism. Anna Dezeuze (2006) refers to artist's encounters with the informal city through the 'art of precariousness,' highlighting a growing interest in the precarious existence of the urban poor. In surveying a number of key works by artists and curators at major exhibitions around the world, Dezeuze looks at how they theorized this trend and what it might contribute to a discourse on precarity. She cites several shows by Argentinean curator Carlos Basualdo that have 'contributed to the growing celebration of contemporary practices relating to adversity and crisis.' The exhibition, *On Adversity we Thrive*, at the Musée d'Art Moderne de la Ville de Paris, and the exhibition that followed, *The Structure of Survival* at the 50th Venice Biennale in 2003, in which 'favela' was the show's guiding principle. These titles alone suggest a romanticization of adversity in which ingenuity and creative resourcefulness characterise precariousness and survival that should be celebrated. From this stems the legitimate concerns of an 'aestheticization of poverty' that masks the complexities of survival in a creative and dynamic world of 'making do.' Whilst Cruzvillegas' work at no point attempts to aestheticize poverty, I would caution that in the context of major international art exhibitions it does follow a romanticized notion of creativity in the face of adversity in which the true causes of struggle are superseded. It is for this reason that I focus on the street-based collaborative aspects of the *Autoconstrucción* project, compelling in their ability to tell another story. The politics of urban struggle, solidarity and land rights are present in the song lyrics but seem to disappear in the aesthetic dimensions of Cruzvillegas' sculptural works as celebration of ingenuity and creative adaptation, which gnaws away at expectations of how the work might have engaged wider debates around self-organization, user-generated urbanisms and community empowerment in the locality of Glasgow and beyond.

The art of precariousness (representations of Latin American precarious situation in Western context) mirrors the persistent dialectic around informal urban practices, between our own implication in, and the neglect of, the conditions of poverty on the one hand, and a celebration of ingenuity and creative problem-solving on the other. This stems from what Mike Davis in *Planet of Slums* refers as the allusion of the aided 'self-help' policies of the World Bank that first emerged in the 1970s, whose then-advisor was the English activist architect John Turner. His experience of working in the squatter settlements of Peru, from 1957 to 1965, left him 'mesmerized by the creative genius' of squatter housing and the 'capacities for communal self-organization and clever construction' (Davis, 2006: 17).

In his groundbreaking work, *Housing by People: Towards Autonomy in Building Environments, Ideas in Progress*, John Turner (1976) asserted that the Global North had much to learn from the rapidly developing Global South, establishing the idea within architectural and urban research that self-built, self-organized neighbourhoods, developed and improved incrementally, were a better solution than housing project imposed by government-led development since residents were experts in their own needs (Awan, Schneider and Till, 2011). Despite this paradigmatic shift towards an 'enabling approach' to housing – marked by the first Habitat conference in Vancouver (1976) – policies of self-help and slum upgrading have for the most part given way to demolitions and evictions. As elsewhere, diminished official social support and neglect of basic services demanded the creation of autonomous organizations in the Pedregales and elsewhere to sustain self-building and resist evictions.

In conjunction with the rapid growth of cities across the globe and subsequent explosion of slums and informal settlements is a significant revival within academic, professional and policy circles interested in the spatial dimension of the informal city. In *Urban Informality: Transnational Perspectives on Space and Place*, Alsayyad and Ananya Roy suggest that the discourse and investigations into future cities are best observed in places like Rio, Cairo, Istanbul and Mumbai, where 'new forms of urban informality' may be emerging as a 'new paradigm for understanding urban culture' (Roy and Alsayyad, 2004). The role of social art practice in unpicking the formal–informal urban context is much less defined than the fields of spatial planning, architecture and urbanism. Instead urban informality within art discourse manifests in notions of precariousness. This is likely a result of art retaining its autonomy from the spatial practices of the built environment to engage primarily within the critical space of cultural production and consumption. Precariousness rather than urban informality is a social condition of the built world and thus can more readily create a space of contemplation through aesthetics and relational processes. Furthermore, the accepted realities of a precarious existence bound to the effects of capitalist globalization are no longer the preserve of the urban poor (as those working in the informal unregulated economies as marginal or invisible citizens), rather a living reality of the twenty-first century, neo-liberal city. The precarious condition recently associated with art and public space, as discussed in Chapters 1 and 2 in the volume, has become a political issue of the 'creative class,' finding agency within social movements and political philosophy by theorists such as Paolo Virno, Gerald Raunig, Chantal Mouffe and Jacques Ranciere among others (Seijdel, 2009). In the edited volume, *A Precarious Existence: Vulnerability in the Public Domain*, Seijdel writes, 'precarity refers to the relationship between temporary and flexible labour arrangements and a "precarious" existence – an everyday life without predictability and security – which is determining the living conditions of ever larger groups of society.' The obvious attraction to the art world is its own identification within the precarious narrative, which is no longer associated solely with migrant workers, black economy workers, shift workers and so on, but the 'creative class' themselves (Seijdel, 2009).

Perhaps to this end we have begun to identify with a do-it-yourself aesthetic as many people within the global city begin their journeys towards self-reliance. In replace of a job held for life is the anxiety of the precarious worker, subject to job instability and types of employment that demand ever broader skill sets in which adaptability, creativity and reinvention become the conditions for survival in an entrepreneurial society. And so, the extremes of precarious living often associated with the informal city – the slum, favela or shanty, whose defined borders divide and contain informal urbanity from those regulated spaces of comparative privilege – are very much a condition of the regulated city: they are found in the interstices of the formal city. This is tested by Cruzvillegas in offering stories of a precarious life through a process of rapid informal urbanization, to a place and public appearing far removed. In doing so he prompts questions of precariousness in an urban context like Glasgow and its own stories of struggle, collapsing differentiation towards shared understanding.

Part of the re-conceptualization of globalizing trends of the formal–informal relation in both economic and social terms is a recalibration of our interdependence: 'the role of squatter colonies is fundamental rather than marginal: The urban economy is heavily subsidized by their existence, and cannot function-much less be competitive-without this subsidy' (Berner, 2000). This tendency of ignoring what appears marginal to the functioning of socio-economic systems is in fact fundamental in maintaining it, a key theme explored in art discourse on precarity. Artist Santiago Sierra extends this interdependence to one of implication, participation even complicity in the complex systems of economic exploitation. This is emphasized in such works as *8 People Paid to Remain inside Cardboard Boxes* (1991), which first took place in the G&T building in Guatemala city, in which low-paid workers were hired to remain hidden inside cardboard boxes as a representation of their social and economic invisibility. In this and many other contested works about economic exploitation, Kester suggests Sierra aims for 'a therapeutic "dislocation" in which the viewer is brought to recognize their own contingency and implication in the suffering of the other' (2011: 167).

Another useful example of a precarious situation that expresses the formal–informal relation can be found in the work of Slovenian artist Marjetica Potrč (born Ljubljana 1953). Also an architect, Potrč manages to create convenient art–architecture crossovers in which her mock constructions of shanty town houses and shelters, encountered in cities and rural communities across the world, are relocated in a gallery context as 'architectural case studies.' The *hybrid house* (2004) as Potrč refers to it can be observed in various urban contexts as the project suggests: the artist juxtaposes the community-based structures of Caracas, the West Bank and West Palm Beach, Florida, together in the gallery space (MIT List Visual Arts Center, Cambridge) showing how they form their own architectural language. This is very much an 'art of precariousness' and an aestheticization of the hybrid styles of the non-architect architecture that Potrč celebrates. In the Balkans, Potrč made extensive research after the political changes in the 1990s left a development vacuum filled by self-organized, self-building that, without planning permission, took on a 'multiplicity of personal architectural styles.' The 'beautiful-ugly' of these inventive styles are what architect Srdjan Jovanovic Weiss – in a negative positivization – calls a 'Balkanisation of architecture.' Weiss writes:

> As the republics of the former Yugoslavia split from each other, many displaced people marched in desperation from enclaves towards homeland states. There, life had to be started anew. Many were prompted to build their own homes and businesses rather than wait for the nationalist systems to help out.
>
> (Weiss in Ferguson, 2006: 125)

And so in the haphazard, unexpected nature of construction that saw buildings appear on rooftops, over alleyways, on top of each other, 'buildings started to speak about where they were coming from' (Ferguson, 2006: 126). Self-build hybridizations of the Balkans echoed the same informality of the gecekondus of Istanbul, the favelas of Rio or the slums of Mumbai. In the gallery space, however, the forces behind this 'building by necessity' are largely divorced from the realities of an 'architecture of politics' (Ferguson, 2006: 126) and a 'politics of precariousness,' favouring instead an optimistic aestheticization of precariousness and informality. The multiplicity of styles and bricolage mask a homogenizing tendency towards the multiplicity and complexity of factors causing marginalization in which people must fend for themselves. Whether or not Potrč's celebration extends its agency to Weiss' claim that 'Balkanisation is optimal because it is an architecture of conflict that shifts the results of war to city building,' able to turn 'Balkanisation into a tool for catalysing difference,' remains up for debate (Ferguson, 2006: 126). It raises then the important question: can art in this form (stripped of its real-world context) be a valid tool for catalysing an appreciation of difference in the minds of gallery spectators? To be sure this murky territory is only partially charted, and in art discourse would ideally include interventionist, art activist and other practices aligned to social movements that stretch further back than the emergence of a precarious world in academic and political discourse.

I have attempted to divert a discourse on precarity in art, which for Bourriaud 'cannot be reduced to the use of fragile materials or short durations, […] because precariousness now impregnates the whole of contemporary aesthetics, with its negative as well as positive versions,' (Bourriaud in Seijdel 2009) towards an informal urbanism, in particular, the narratives of self-build, self-organized communities where artists like Cruzvillegas and Potrč's apparent (perhaps legitimate) failings towards instrumentality and political agency in art, are however a genuine challenge to, and critique of conformist architecture, neoliberal planning and development policies. Any critique levied at Potrč's gallery exhibits, however, should take account of her long-standing pedagogic research into informal urbanism and socially driven architecture that extends beyond the gallery to include the implementation of participatory design projects and sustainable solutions in the field. Despite the paradoxical nature of representation in the gallery space, Potrč's concerns are less with the art world and more with a shift in attitude and focus in urbanism, providing a platform for reflection upon 'unregulated city surfaces like urban voids and shanty towns' usually overlooked and 'thought of as revitalization and not as urban quality' (2004).

In a different way, the autobiographical narratives of precariousness in the work of Cruzvillegas transcend a discourse on precarity from art into urbanism, which questions its value in a Western context. Throughout *Autoconstrucción* the individual works speak more directly to the formal–informal relation in which notions of precariousness are always implicit but not always explicit, since the unfinished auto-construction remains non-determined and open-ended, allowing for multiple readings to unfold. What is particularly strong in the appropriation of Cruzvillegas' songs is a negotiation through dialogue of possible representation and collective authorship. The precarious situation of the distant non-European 'Other', now present, must be translated, reformed and relayed through new interpretations in a series of relations with real-life experiences of precariousness in a Glasgow context such as worklessness, living in areas of mass deprivation, poor social bonds and lack of social mobility.

This text began with an investigation into how the life of Cruzvillegas, growing up in a squatter settlement in Mexico City, had formed the methodology of his art practice, and became the metaphor for self-build practices that underscore his artistic sensibility, aesthetics, poetics and politics. At the same time, and by contrast, other artists and self-organized communities are looking to (not coming from) precarious spaces and the spatial practices of the informal city, as site, situation, form and material in new experimental art practices. From those mentioned, Francis Alÿs remains the most celebrated artist in this field in the West, whose scope and breadth, ingenuity and brevity have created a poetics of precariousness that provides us a rich and unique reading of complexities of the formal–informal relation, and of the exigent needs and socio-political conditions of contested urban places. Alÿs, who trained as an architect and engineer, left his native Belgium for Mexico City in 1986 as part of a French Assistance program and has continued to live there ever since. It is not without Mexico City, the protagonist, the source of the script and co-author of so many of his works, that such an achievement could be possible. A city 'that always offers the perfect setting for accidents to happen' (Alÿs in Godfrey and Biesenbach, 2010: 37), Mexico City is Alÿs' muse, like Paris in Breton's *Nadja*, 'this always inspired and inspiring creature who enjoyed being nowhere but in the streets, the only valid field of experience' (1960: 113). Writes Alÿs: 'Mexico City forces you to respond to its reality, it requires you to resituate your presence all the time, to reposition yourself in the face of this inacceptable urban entity' (Alÿs in Godfrey and Biesenback, 2010: 37). It is perhaps unsurprising then, that the fourteen years Santiago Sierra lived in Mexico City had a major influence on his critical art practice. When asked in various interviews about his choice to move there, Sierra responds: 'Mexico is a catalog of situations. It's a miniature planet Earth [...] Mexico is an immense city that summarizes the world's social conditions' (Santiago Sierra interview by Ross Birrell in Yuill and Mey, 2004: 109).

If in Mexico City informal urbanism and precariousness are the common denominators, what can the work of Sierra and Alÿs offer the reading of Cruzvillegas? In particular, how does each artist utilize and describe the role of collaborator and/or co-author in the production of meaning and politics of representation? Sierra often comments on the extreme divisions and disparities between social classes and labour relations in which workers are remunerated to 'play themselves' as commodity objects in the service of the artist, and the economic systems that make their presence as art possible. Birrell writes:

> Sierra's remuneration actions position his workers as de-humanised objects, functioning on the level of commodities rather than as active human subjects. Whether this is a critical action against the dehumanization of global capitalism, or a situation which merely reiterates and conserves the relations of capital, has to be negotiated by each viewer for themselves.
>
> (Santiago Sierra interview by Ross Birrell in Yuill and Mey, 2004: 109)

For Sierra, the only 'inter-social dialogue' possible is confrontation. There is no dialogue for the workers (participants) beyond the remunerative transaction. What remains is only the social implication of art, to appeal an art discourse over any idea of social change, as Sierra explains, 'we artists fabricate luxury products and we are distanced from the social praxis that would at least validate our commentaries' (Margelles, 2004). Bishop makes a necessary correction to this art of living labour:

> Where inter-social dialogue would imply interactivity, the passive spectator in this scenario, is merely replicating the dominant mode of capitalist inter-passivity. In other words, inter-passivity is the secret language of the market, which degrades bodies into objects, *and it is also* the language that artists use to reflect this degradation.
>
> (2012: 235, original emphasis)

By contrast, works by Alÿs such as *Barrenderos*, 2004, in their use of 'people as medium' are not simply participants, they are also active collaborators. In *Barrenderos* street sweepers form a line pushing rubbish through the streets of Mexico City, collecting ever more as they move forward until they are stopped by an immovable mass of garbage. In this social allegory the living labour performs its original role in the space and time assigned in the correct economic cycle, the object of rubbish becomes the economic signifier, and 'one of its most revealing social indices' (Alÿs cited in Godfrey and Biesenbach, 2010). In a poetic *detournement*, Alÿs' reclaims the time of Capitalist labour to create a moment of conviviality and sociability that also contains the impossibility of social mobilization in the face of economic subjugation. The original event – the first iteration of the work – becomes a representation through a documentary video in its final iteration as commodity-object in the gallery. Speaking in an interview Alÿs foregrounds this aspect in the following terms: 'It's really two different moments. Two different consecutive lives of a single: the events and the transmission of the events.' Or as Samual Steinberg, writing about the 500 participants in Alÿs' *When Faith Moves Mountains*, questions whether such work exists to 'document an action':

The work as such exists as the contingent moment of collective experience; it cannot be housed in a museum, but is lived and told (documented). That is, in such projects persists the question regarding whether the work is located in the documentary record, or something else -the experience, even the thing that is not recorded.

(2012)

From Alÿs' own response to *When Faith Moves Mountains* we know the artist finds it difficult to say whether the work belonged to himself, or the participants; he is, however, in no doubt that the film *event-as-image*, belongs clearly to Alÿs.[4]

And so we are left with the difficult duality: is the original event of *Barrenderos* for those invisible workers subjugated by the dark forces of labour in a moment of conviviality; or, like Sierra, are the works made only to serve the interests of the privileged art world and its viewers (by way of critique), and upholding a poetico-political aesthetic autonomy? Are we talking about the participants' agency or the viewers' agency? These questions are important because, although Cruzvillegas' work occupies the narrative space of a precarious situation in Mexico City presented in the gallery space, his work also exists beyond it in the social relations and collaborative exchange with Glasgow communities. His work is immediately complicated in this regard for the artist creates rich participatory and multi-author forms, utilizing both in situ interventions and later employing the documentation of these works in multimedia gallery installations. These exchanges have not been used in the conventional methods of dialogical practice to exhibit process or the social relations of collaboration. Instead we have the original sound-system bicycle on which is mounted a monitor showing a video of the performance by the artist cycling through Glasgow streets (on an object made in collaboration with people with mental illness), broadcasting songs (made by local musicians). Elsewhere, Cruzvillegas' sculptural practice creates the commodity artefacts that accrue social capital in the contemporary art world and advance his career as an artist.

Towards the end of her essay on an art of precariousness, Anna Dezeuze (2006) poses a similar question on the positioning of such work in the gallery. She asks: 'Can the rarefied conditions of display and reception in the contemporary art world really provide a platform for the exploration of political alternatives?' Dezueze holds an interesting position on the art world's interest in precariousness, seeing the artist and the art world as a possible site of a 'revolutionary coalition' between slum dwellers and the 'progressive' part of the symbolic class (i.e. the precarious labour of the creative class). Whether or not artists are able to forge such a coalition in the arena of art and discourse – notwithstanding its recuperation by the art world – Dezeuze suggests 'it can nevertheless contain the seeds of a globalised discourse of protest.' By celebrating ingenuity in this context however, the idea of a discourse of protest (in art) seems distant from attempts by activists, architects and advocacy planning to find meaningful and workable solutions to the problems of poverty, exclusion and reclaiming rights to the city.

I would suggest that with each presentation, the agency of such work is frequently at risk of being lost through recuperation by 'a conservative discourse of passivity and conformism.' The artists, already discussed here, are indeed the obvious international-circuit artists who present at Biennials, museum shows and art festivals around the world, forging a discourse that must primarily uphold its relevance to art, not other fields. As Dezeuze's comment clearly demonstrates, the interest of art discourse is that art generates discourse rather than bringing about change in the world it investigates, and at best might implement change by insertions into a discourse on protest. In defence of these practices, I would also argue that the poetics of a precarious art have something to offer the insurgent imagination of activism and social movements who are increasingly adopting the tools, tactics and poetics of these artists.

Conclusions

Out from the concerns of dialogical aesthetics, Cruzvillegas' authenticity, his unique position and his subjectivity present another reading of the art of precariousness that explores familiar territory from an unfamiliar path. Like Sierra and Alÿs, as discussed in this chapter, his methodology is derived from both creative ingenuities of informal urbanism and the socio-political conditions of their subjugation to neo-liberal globalization. However, where such methods are normally employed in the invited locations of a globalized art world, Cruzvillegas offers the possibility for hybrid formations in a negotiation of difference, through inter-subjective exchange based on agency that originates and resides beyond the gallery. *Autoconstrucción* creates its own alchemy in which the ways of operating and representations of self-build and self-organization becomes fuel for the engine of agency. As a collaborative social practice it carries the seeds of self-reliance and possesses the possibility of emancipation through self-discovery towards self-commitment. We have established that Sierra has little concern for the emancipation of his subjects, preferring the potential awakening of the art world spectator, meanwhile Alÿs' *Barrenderos* adds a clever subversion of the time of Capitalist labour, reassigned to an affective labour of resistance, in which the participants enact the possibilities of collective empowerment.

In encounters with the art of Cruzvillegas, the contested urban politics of auto-construction seem muted, as the artist chooses not to place the demands of social change upon his multi-disciplinary participatory projects, nor challenge directly the assumptions of dialogical aesthetics in exhibition or beyond the gallery. The possible clues as to the socio-economic and political ambiguity in the art of Cruzvillegas are found in the relationships between art and process of auto-construction in an unusual narrative-twist. In the case of Ajusco, art was not directly employed in a socio-political capacity by virtue of the fact that Cruzvillegas grew up with social-self-organizational change in which creativity (not art) was a naturally occurring thing. In other words, the political and emancipatory force of self-build and self-organized squatter settlements had never used art per se as a tool of activism. For the Pedregales, art was not at the numerous scenes of collision with the forces of gentrification and the subjugating powers of Capitalism. What Cruzvillegas can however invoke and engender through art is the appropriation of that naturally occurring creativity, implied in a user-generated urbanism and its necessary elements – adaptability, dialogue, collaboration, recycling and experimentation – the ingredients that help build the muscles of self-reliance needed for social change. It exists through the possibility of participation in the way Cruzvillegas has enabled it, whereas for the spectator such a possibility likely collapses back into the self-serving sphere of the art world.

Perhaps then, the question we should be asking is where should the discourse of these works take place? Cruzvillegas' practice does not represent the underlying conditions but embodies and employs the processes of urban informality, not so much through a language of critique but rather as a suggestion of self-discovery and emancipation of the self. And so, finally, Cruzvillegas is not part of the referred discourse on protest, nor so much a discourse on precarity, but rather a discourse around social change in the context of informal urbanism that, through the possibility of collaboration and the practice of *Autoconstrucción,* creates new forms of living and social relations, political subjectivities and solidarity amongst diverse groups. An appraisal of the role that the participatory art practice of Cruzvillegas can play in an evolving urbanism seeks to extend its agency into a discourse on self-organizing systems, micro-politics and environmental solutions, taking place in the fields of architecture, planning, critical urbanism, urban and cultural geography.

And yet, there is another question as to where the discourse might take place, and it is arguably the most radical. The benefits of having produced a book that describes and documents intimately the mechanisms of auto-construction, the formation of self-organized communities and how self-building translates and organizes both acts of resistance and solidarity movements cannot be underestimated. In *Autoconstrucción,* through the written word, sculpture and song, Cruzvillegas narrated and documented his family history and that of his community, reflecting on its influence in forming the metaphor and methodology of his practice. What is not evident in the gallery presentation, however, is its importance as a form of storytelling to the people of the Pedregales themselves. Earlier, I referred to a book *A Thousand Stories of the Pedregale de Santo Domingo* (2002) by Fernando Diaz Encisco, a community activist and cultural organizer who spent a decade collecting stories from people in the neighbourhood who 'tell of their experiences of struggling for land – against the rocks, as well as against the authorities' (Esteva and Prakesh, 1998: 82). The intention behind this project was to return history to the community since those fundamental problems had been solved in a transformation that came from below, from the community itself. Through this and other cultural projects (Campbell, 2009), Encisco continues to advance the educational and cultural development of Santo Domingo through reflection of its own history. He notes:

> the central idea of the book is to recover collective history of the community, and return it to the community so they can reflect on their own work and life. The transformation has been done with men, women, children, young and old through collective work.
>
> (Jimenez, 2002)

This reflection by the community on its own history is enabled through the book, delivered free to all the families and the founders of the colony, so that the transformation benefits those below. In the mid-1990s the first theatre emerged in Santo Domingo, then a cultural centre, and more recently the first library and now a bookstore.

What Cruzvillegas has achieved in *Autoconstrucción*, reflecting on his own history with the participants and spectators (including Western art context), is in fact an essential tool for the community (from which it is derived) to also reflect. Here then is the exigent site of discourse, in this case the Pedregales as the place transformed through self-build and self-organizational processes. The answer to the prescient question posed by Dezeuze in the case of *Autoconstrucción* seems clear. It could be argued that nurturing the energies of transformation in a place of empowered political alternatives outweighs the possible conversion through a presupposed 'agency of the viewer' in a privileged space of contemplation and reflection. We should perhaps envy Cruzvillegas as he does not have to worry too much about such questions, for this artist gets to gracefully play inside and outside, creating compelling works of authenticity for the art world, problematizing collaborative practice discourse, and giving back the results of his labour to the communities that provide metaphor and meaning to the *Autoconstrucción* project.

References

Awan, N., Schneider, T. and Till, J. 2011. *Spatial Agency: Other Ways of Doing Architecture,* London: Routledge.

Berner, E. 2000. 'Learning from informal markets: Innovative approaches to land and housing provision', paper presented at ESF/N-AERUS and UNRISD Workshop Cities of the South: Sustainable for Whom?, Geneva, 3–6 May, http://www.ucl.ac.uk/dpu-projects/drivers_urb_change/urb_economy/pdf_infor_econo/ESF_NAERUS_Berner_informal.pdf. Accessed 25 June 2013.

Bishop, C. 2012. *Artificial Hells: Participatory Art and the Politics of Spectatorship,* London: Verso.

Breton, A. 1960. *Nadja,* New York, NY: Grove Press.

Campbell, B. 2009. *Viva La Historieta; Mexican Comics, NAFTA and the Politics of Globalisation,* Jackson: University Press of Mississippi.

Certeau, M. de. 1988. *Practice of Everyday Life,* Oakland: University of California Press.

Cruzvillegas, A. 2008. *Autoconstrucción,* Glasgow: Centre for Contemporary Arts.

Cruzvillegas, A. 2009. Interview by A. Decker-Parks, *Museo Magazine,* http://www.museomagazine.com/ABRAHAM-CRUZVILLEGAS. Accessed 1 February 2014.

Davis, M. 2006. *Planet of Slums,* London: Verso.

Dezeuze, A. 2006. 'Thriving on adversity: The art of precariousness', *Mute* 2 (3), http://www.metamute.org/editorial/articles/thriving-adversity-art-precariuossness. Accessed 24 June, 2014.

Enciso, F. D. 2002. *A Thousand Stories of the Pedregale de Santo Domingo - Las mil y una historias del Pedregal de Santo Domingo,* Mexico City: Direccion General de Culturas Populares e Indigenas del Consejo Nacional para la Cultura y las Artes.

Esteva, G. and Prakesh, M. S. 1998. *Grassroots Postmodernism: Remaking the Soil of Culture,* New York, NY: Palgrave.

Ferguson, F. (Ed.) 2006. *Talking Cities: The Micropolitics of Urban Space,* Switzerland: Birkhauser.

Godfrey, M. and Biesenbach, K. 2010. *Francis Alÿs: A Story of Deception*, London: Tate Publishing.

Gutmann, M. 2007. *The Meanings of Macho: Being a Man in Mexico City (Men and Masculinity)*, Oakland: University of California Press.

Jimenez, A. 2002. 'En un libro, el Coyoacán negro recobra su identidad', *La journada*, Mexico City, 18 November, http://www.jornada.unam.mx/2002/11/18/05an1cul.php?origen=cultura. html. Accessed 14 October 2013.

Kester, G. 2011. *The One and the Many*, London: Duke University Press.

Laguerre, M. S. 2010. *The Informal City*, New York, NY: St Martin's Press.

Margelles, T. 2004. 'Interview with Santiago Sierra', *BOMB*, 86 (Winter), http://bombsite.com/articles/author?issue=86&who=Margolles%2C+Teresa. Accessed 7 October 2013.

Monk, H. D. 2010. 'Mexican Women – Now and Then', *International View Point*, http://internationalviewpoint.org/spip.php?article1922. Accessed 5 February 2014.

Pascolo, E. 2010. *Informal City*, Course module, Architectural School of Architecture, London, Available at: http://informalcity.ac.uk/?page_id+4. Accessed 18 August 2013.

Potrč, M. 2004. 'Public space in contemporary city'. In Matsner, F. (Ed.), *Public Art*, Germany: Hatje Cantz Verlag.

Roy, A. and Alsayyad, N. 2004. *Urban Informality, National Perspectives from the Middle East, Latin America, and South Asia*, Oxford: Lexington Books.

Seijdel, J. 2009. 'A precarious existence: Vulnerability in the public domain', *SKOR*, 17, 1-2.

Spatial Agency, http://www.spatialagency.net/database/john.turner. Accessed 15 March 2016.

Steinberg, S. 2012. 'Politics of the line', *Politica Comun*, 12, Denison University, http://quod.lib.umich.edu/p/pc/12322227.0002.005?view=text;rgn=main. Accessed 15 March 2016.

Stephen, L. 1997. *Women & Social Movements in Latin America*, Texas, FL: University of Texas Press.

Turner, J. 1976. *Housing by People: Towards Autonomy in Building Environments, Ideas in Progress*, London: Marion Boyers.

Turner, J. 1968. 'The squatter settlement: An architecture that works', *The Architecture of Democracy*, *Architectural Design*, 8, 357–360, http://www.communityplanning.net/JohnTurnerArchive/pdfs/ADAug1968SquatterSettlement.pdf. Accessed 15 March 2016.

Weiss, S. J. 2006. 'Balkanisation is architecture'. In Ferguson (Ed.), *Talking Cities: The Micropolitics of Urban Space*, Switzerland: Birkhauser, pp. 125–127.

Yuill, S. and Mey, K. 2004. *Cross-Wired*, transcript, Manchester: Manchester University Press.

Notes

1 Testimony of Eulogia Hernández translated by into English by Sarag Farr, http://sarahefarr.wordpress.com/research/santo-domingo/

2 John O'Hara, Common Wheel, http://www.commonwheel.org.uk/

3 http://soundcheck.wnyc.org/story/134488-mexican-sonidero-parties-its-about-music-and-message/

4 Kester, writing about the authorship of *Faith*, cites letters written by Alÿs to Susan Buck Morss (Kester, 2011: 73).

Chapter 6

FOLi Lab: A museographic urban experiment at the Biennial of Photography in Lima, Peru

Gonzalo Olmos and Valeria Biffi

Introduction

The Museum of Photography Lima, (FOLi)[1] is a new museum dedicated to the promotion of contemporary photography from Peru, and South America more widely. The museum showcases photographic images from a sensory angle, including participatory and experiential activities, as an attempt to promote an understanding of contemporary photography and its practice, implications and cultural significance.

FOLi Lab was a museographic urban experiment at the First Biennial of Photography in Lima, Peru, which aimed to provide an alternative space for contemplation, reflection and appreciation of photographic culture. The project was embedded within the experimental framework of the Biennial and was structured and articulated on three conceptual axes: (1) the creation of an exhibiting display in public space; (2) the installation of a photographic lab for artistic residencies; and (3) the provision of a meeting point for discussion, reflection and research upon the photographic medium.

The museum had a strong interest in promoting research through photography. The FOLi Lab, besides being a photographic intervention in a public space, was a qualitative research experiment that analysed the relationship between contemporary photography and explored the role of a museum in the society. Specifically, the research at FOLi Lab attempted to analyse the views, projections and expectations of the audience, composed mostly of local Peruvian citizens interested in art and photography, concerning a museum of contemporary photography. Qualitative research primarily involved the recollection and analysis of perceptions, meanings and views that the audience gave to a museum of contemporary photography.

FOLi Lab was designed to operate in the agglomeration of the city of Lima. That is, the proposal was to work outside the physical domain of the museum. FOLi Lab became the first and largest architectural and artistic intervention in the city of Lima with the medium of photography located in a public space. The first FOLi Lab experience was a pilot project in the San Martin square in downtown Lima in December, 2011. This event then escalated and developed further in other locations between March and April, 2012: in Parque Kennedy, in the affluent district of Miraflores and in Parque de la Muralla, a poor area in downtown Lima, Peru.

It is important to highlight that precarious spaces are abundant in the capital of Peru, due to the city's unplanned and organic growth. Thus, engaging a broader demographic of the population in Lima – through artistic site-specific interventions – proved to be an educational and pedagogical practice. The museum's main objective was to pilot and promote art-based, socially inclusive strategies for the community. As a result, FOLi Lab made humble efforts and genuine gestures towards public engagement across the wide social spectrum of the population, fostering not only social integration, but increasing shared collaboration and community participation during the Biennial.

FOLi Lab: From the physical containers towards a social and artistic relational platform

The space created for the production of FOLi Lab was realized through the installation of four shipping containers, providing an internal exhibition space of 77.36 m^2. These recycled containers were not only exhibition display spaces, but also a meeting point for the citizens of Lima and photographers through the operation of artistic residencies. The containers also aimed to attract passers-by who took part in the interventions. These individuals eventually became the audience, participating in displays, talking, criticizing and analysing pictures. The architectural language of FOLi Lab was sculptural, expansive and dynamic and reflected the city itself organically.[2] The proposed specificity of the architectural plan was designed to work as a place of contemplation and experimentation for photography. Having a modular design, the containers were naturally interconnected not only in their form, but also in their function.

The audience was composed mostly of Lima's citizens passing by, but also included tourists visiting Peru from different places and walks of life. It is important to highlight that all visitors were recorded systematically through the use of a hand counter by the volunteer network of art school students, registering more than 45,000 visits to FOLi Lab.

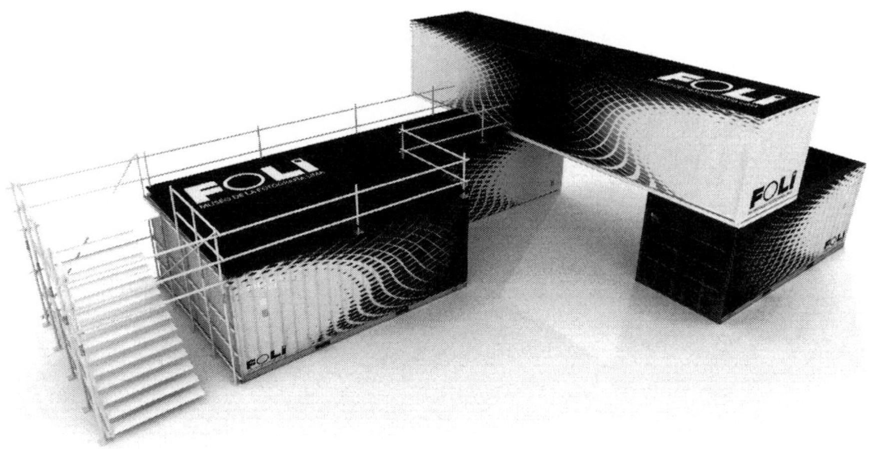

Figure 6.1: 3D render of the FOLi Lab structure. Courtesy of Rafael Contreras.

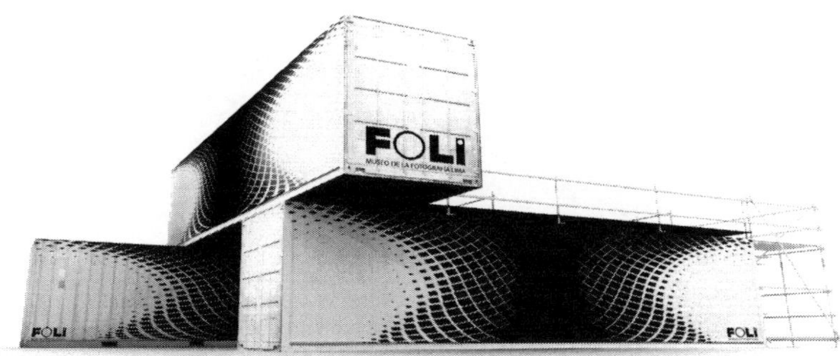

Figure 6.2: FOLi Lab structure built with four shipping containers. Courtesy of Rafael Contreras.

The shipping containers were arranged according to the following functional areas:

Briefing Room FOLi: space created to be a point of contact with the museum, its collection, its members, plans and future projects. Moreover, the visitors had at their disposal an open access and free library with books on visual arts and particularly on photography.

Multimedia Screening Room: space screening the work of 38 photographers from seventeen countries through a 55" LCD display. The artists included the South African photographer Pieter Hugo.

Permanent Exhibition Room: space where the Mexican photographer Alinka Echeverria exhibited her photographic series *The Road to Tepeyac,* winner of the Prix HSBC pour la International Photographie in 2011.

Photographic Laboratory Room: space for experimental photographic residencies where thirteen artists could create their own work across multiple dynamics and photography workshops.

FOLi also developed a program of activities including photo exhibitions and multimedia with the work of 38 established national and international photographers and visual artists, experimental workshops, artists in residence, talks and roundtables, photographic portfolio reviews, night-time projections, photographic laboratory with analogue and digital developing facilities, as well as guided visits to the FOLi Lab.

The FOLi Lab experience was coordinated through the articulation of a set of participants: (1) FOLi team itself; (2) artists in residence; (3) volunteers; (4) people involved in the program of workshops and events; (5) curators; (6) passers-by, who formed the FOLi Lab audience. It could be argued that FOLi Lab was an open platform for experimentation where visual artists and passers-by were integrated into the program of activities in a contingent spontaneous fashion. For instance, one of the activities that drew a lot of public attention was the pinhole workshop, carried out by members of the photographic collective LimaFotoLibre.

Pinhole cameras – small handcrafted cameras – were assembled with simple and affordable materials. With pinhole workshops, passers-by could have learned to make their own cameras, and have taken their photos, developed subsequently in the darkroom in one of the containers. As a result, people in the squares became not solely viewers – an audience – but simultaneously participated in a performative act of making, becoming photographers and models in the photographs. Many admitted they had no prior knowledge in the production of a photograph. In other words, FOLi Lab offered people a platform to transform into manufacturers of cameras and photographs. People learnt in the street, they developed their own photographs, and more importantly, they took their photographs home.

FOLi Lab also offered some outdoor interactive workshops. These workshops included displaying table-top printed reproductions in A4 size of the permanent collection of the museum. However, no information was given about the authors, countries or cultural implications. In these workshops, passers-by were invited to participate and discuss the photographs. These interactive workshops proved to be popular, as sometimes many participants gathered around the table as active observers. The technique was to talk about the evocations that were generated by the photographic representation. Then participants

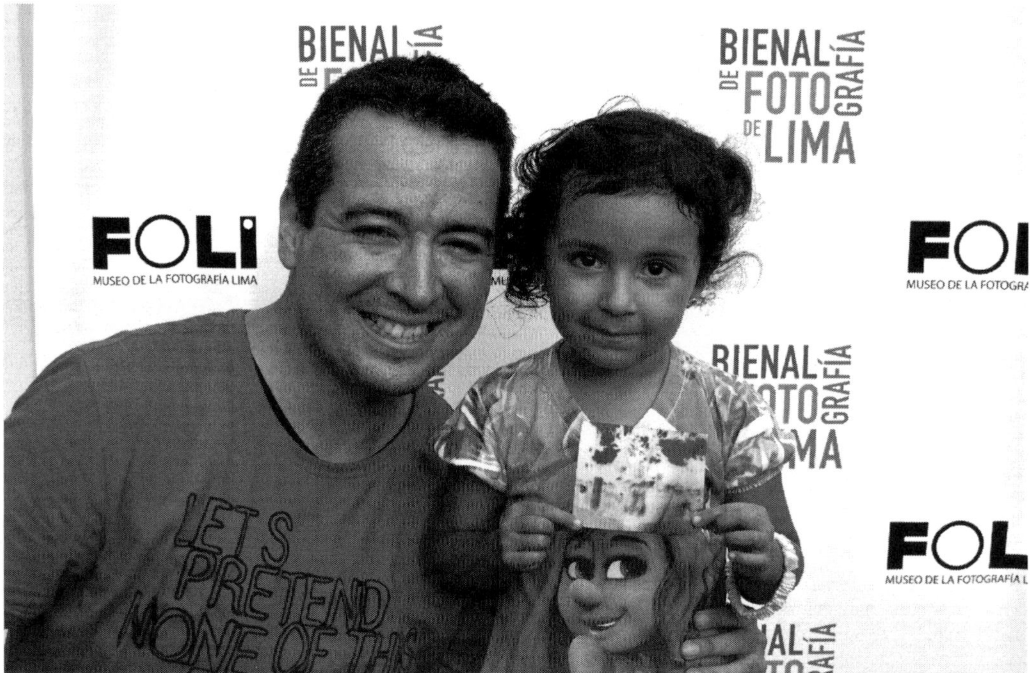

Figure 6.3: Pinhole workshops at FOLi Lab, the First Biennial of Photography of Lima. Courtesy of Gonzalo Olmos.

were asked to associate images with social contexts and situations, as well as cultural and political conditions. Participants distinguished the different perceptions of the same photos, by generation and origin, especially with images that represent sensitive social content, such as the images of *Taller de Fotografía Social* (TAFOS).[3] The discussion generated around the photos led participants to explore how photography serves to reveal a collective imaginary. Also, discussions served to unveil how unfamiliar the audience was in relation to 'more artistic' or abstract work that requires further work of articulation of ideas, evocation and interpretation, as they don't reflect obvious situations as documentary photography. For instance, the specific work of Emma Livingston (*14-5-07 NOA*, 2007) falls into that category. In contrast, a discourse arising around social documentary photos was quickly appropriated and debated.

It could be argued that the FOLi Lab gave importance to both the social dimension and the art-based project in the museographic urban experiment. It placed particular emphasis on the social-interactive aspect of collaboration and the importance of 'the collective' in the shared social experience. This was partly achieved by the training provided to the network of volunteers who were told to be particularly sensitive to the local socio-economic and political conditions. In the field of participatory art, a sense of collective collaboration promotes personal and collective empowerment, as authorship is more egalitarian and democratic (Bishop, 2006). Moreover, the current trend in contemporary art is to involve the public as a way to create active subjects in the creative process by blurring distinctions between opposite binaries of 'performer and audience, professional and amateur, production and reception' (Bishop, 2006: 10).

The curatorship at the FOLi Lab

It is often argued that a photograph's surface is slippery, both literally and metaphorically. It is impossible to study an image that is fixed. It is a personal journey of discovery. A photograph is, as Barthes argued, a powerful and evocative medium that has the power to invite you to daydream in an ideological space – and equally important – to provide you with a fantasy in its representation or associations (Barthes, 1967).

Therefore, the curator's challenge was not to provide a totalizing narrative that is prescriptive, descriptive and discursive. Instead, the curator chose to present various visual fragments, photographic micro-narratives and photographic diversity. This tactical presentation of heterogeneity allowed the audience to develop its own visual micro-narratives and imagine the photographic medium and its representation as a complex maze. This strategy exposed the audience to a dense forest of symbols, suitable for contemplation and experimentation at the urban lab. As a result, the museum's curator, Gonzalo Olmos, opted to give an international dimension[4] to the First Biennial of Photography in Lima. Most of the 38 photographers that were selected included former students of three international schools in visual arts: (1) *Le Fresnoy, Studio national des arts contemporains*, Tourcoing, France; (2) Goldsmiths College of London, UK; and (3) the International Center of

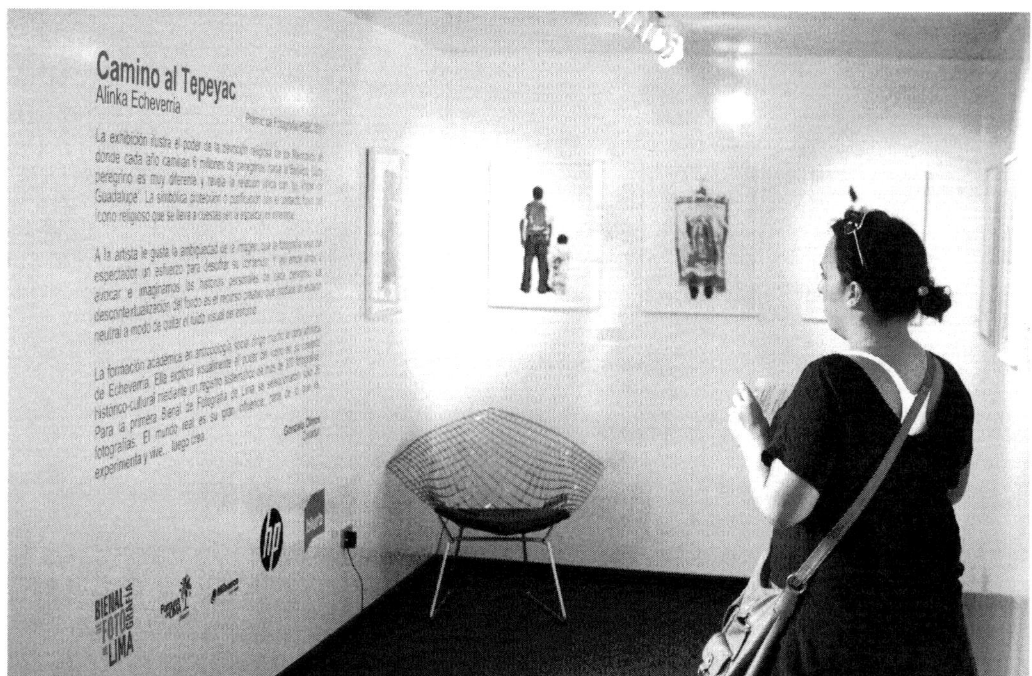

Figure 6.4: The Road to Tepeyac. Permanent exhibition. Alinka Echeverria Photography. Courtesy of Gonzalo Olmos.

Photography of New York, USA. In addition, a parallel program of cultural activities hosted over 40 people, including resident artists, photographic collectives, researchers, educators and street photographers working in squares. To sum up, the program contemplated creative production, knowledge sharing through an educational program articulated with workshops, talks, projections and portfolios reviews, among other activities.

How to build a museum?

The museum used the FOLi Lab as an experimental research platform to explore the interaction of the audience with the photographic image in order to understand the role of photography in contemporary Peruvian society and culture. The purpose of this research was not only to explore the scope of photography from its aesthetic nature, but to understand the potential of possibilities that photography offers to reflect on local social reality.

The appreciation of photographic art in a contemporary museum entails not only looking at pictures, but requires the complex process of observing, discovering, understanding and above all experiencing. One of the main challenges for a new museum was to provide a rich and reflexive cultural space. The museum hoped to make a new proposal for cultural consumption and promote the understanding of photography as a way of reaching out to society.

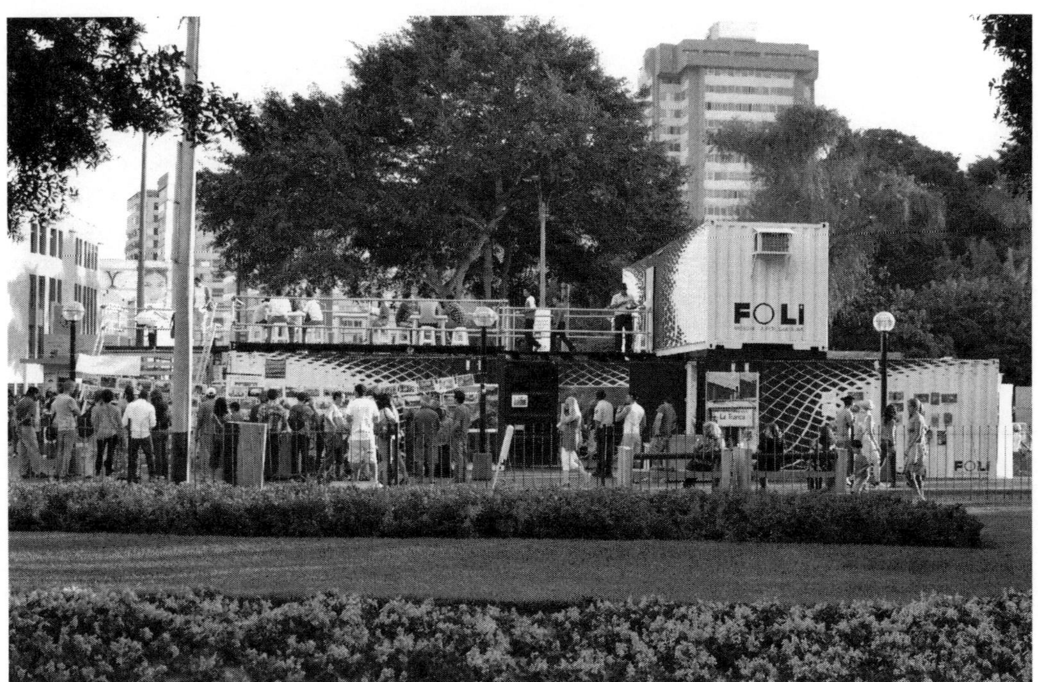

Figure 6.5: FOLi Lab operating in Parque Kennedy in Miraflores district, Lima. Courtesy of Gonzalo Olmos.

Perceptions about the contemporary photography museum were collected through different techniques. In this particular case, photography was the pivotal axis. All the information provided important and insightful data for the researchers. This was later converted into text for easy classification, systematization and final analysis. These techniques were designed not to manipulate or obstruct the flow of information provided by the informants, and it was open to any new information and insights that might emerge. On the other hand, the researchers were participants and observers who, through their own subjectivity, experience and cultural baggage, interpreted the events they saw and information they heard.

The researchers' pivotal axis at FOLi Lab was photography that was approached from four dimensions, including production, contemplation, interpretation and reflections of the audience around these areas based on the experience of the researchers of the museum and views gathered from the informants. The research aimed to experiment, interpret and represent society in terms of photography and generate knowledge about it.

The question that served as the focus of the research was 'what is the role of the contemporary museum'? FOLi's mission – as a contemporary museum – is to reach out and bring culture closer to the people. Museums as cultural institutions are constantly evolving in their mission for new curatorial projects. Nowadays museums are spaces for debate, which questions their own institutional nature (Schubert, 2009). Faced with this new proposal, it was important to recognize what methodologies of display should engage with the public.

We need to go back to the definition of a contemporary museum as a social and cultural construction. Today, orthodox chronologies and historical timelines are no longer the main guiding thread; instead, these have been replaced by exposure to micro-narratives and technological innovation. So little by little, the museum audience becomes familiar with the dematerialization of the artefact. An example in FOLi Lab of this proposition was the invitation of 38 national and international artists into the multimedia projection room, giving a global international dimension to the experimental core of the Biennial.

The action methodology

The research at FOLi Lab was a multidisciplinary effort that combined photography, social psychology and anthropology, using classic techniques of qualitative research. These included participant observation, in-depth interviews, quick surveys and alternative techniques that emphasize participation from the audience in the research process (Flick, 2009; McNiff, 2013; Martin and Hanington, 2012).

Participatory methodologies have been lately widely discussed (e.g. Ramella and Olmos, 2005; Flick, 2009; Pink, 2009). Increasingly, research experiences are committed to fostering the active role of subjects. People who take photos, or people who look at them, have the need to tell a story, or to share something. Photography is not mute, processing a contemplative nature; on the contrary, it serves to reflect, plan, negotiate and criticize. We wanted to utilize the different roles of the audience for photography at FOLi Lab. People acted multiple roles – as consumers of photographs, photographers, respondents and producers of pinhole cameras.

The ethnographical-approach research was undertaken in different contexts, places and events across Lima, such as San Martin square, Parque Kennedy, Miraflores and Parque de la Muralla at Rimac. Data was collected through convenience or opportunity-sampling, namely, the flow of passers-by; people who volunteered to write their views or were approached by a member of the research team. Indeed, one of the techniques used to gather information for the research was to write on post-it notes as a way to quickly gather short testimonies and views about what people would expect from a photography museum in Lima. The idea was to display them on a visible flat surface, easily read by the public, alongside a picture of the person who gave the testimonial. A total of 265 post-it notes were collected and 78 contextual interviews conducted. These were categorized by major themes and then the content was interpreted through affinity diagramming. Affinity diagramming is a process used to analyse clusters of observations and insights from research (Martin and Hanington, 2012). Sticky notes create a constellation or cluster on affinity, which form into research-based themes. The codes (sticky notes) are grouped and categories are formed helping the researchers to easily visualize the insights grounded in the data they analyse.

Another technique used was photo elicitation. This technique aimed to trigger conversation from the contemplation of photographs (Tinkler, 2012; Kuhn, 2007; Harper, 2002). In this case, the photo has value in terms of content and also as a trigger to obtain more information from the evocation, interpretation and memory of those who analyse the photographic images. Photo elicitation narrows the distance between photographer and subject. This technique was successfully used during the interactive workshops. In these workshops, the participants shared their personal experiences, memories and projections about what they expect of a museum, in a fairly open and fluid way.

It was fundamental to include in the research the documentation of the FOLi Lab's experience. Reviewing the audio-visual material allowed us to analyse parts that were not initially considered or felt to be essential in a second revision for analysis. The videos provided details of the subjective world and views of respondents about the FOLi Lab experience. It also had the ability to illustrate not only what happened, but how it happened, allowing recording of interactive processes that unfolded during the experience. The interactive documentary was produced and edited by Freddy Luna.

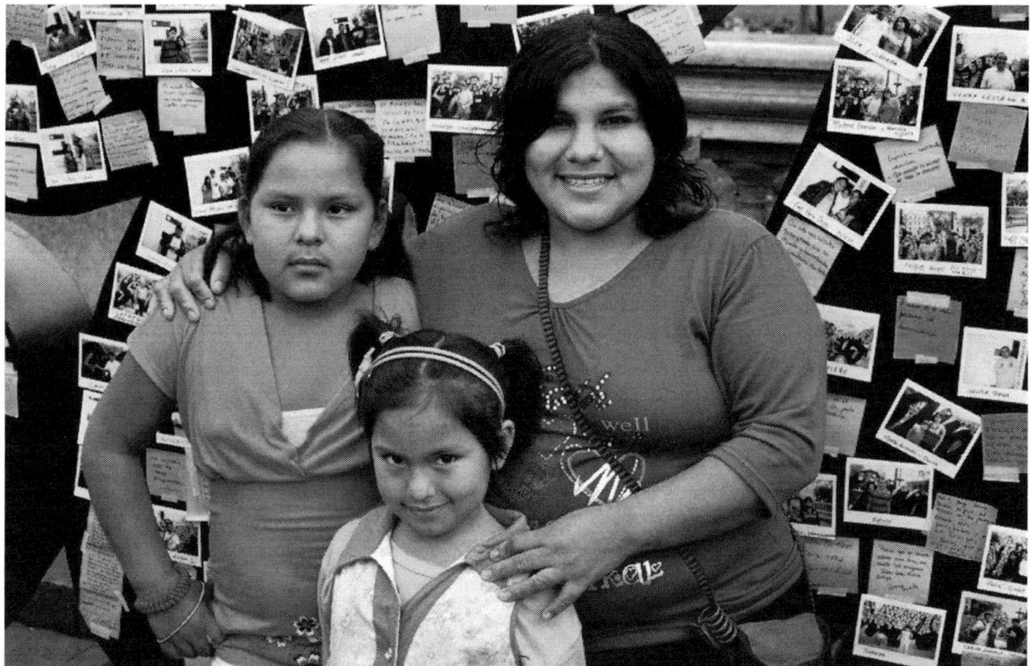

Figure 6.6: Affinity diagramming data-gathering in San Martin square in downtown Lima. Courtesy of Gonzalo Olmos.

Discussion

The research outcomes are directly linked to the main question given to the audience. What do you expect from a contemporary photography museum?

Documentary photo exhibition

Generally, the audience wants a museum that exhibits mainly documentary photography, images that represent the public social environment. The reference to this kind of photography responds to the very common way of thinking about photography: as a reflection of reality. Furthermore, it is the kind of image that society is more exposed to. However, in this particular case, the audience also wants to see images that represent and evoke a familiar reality, a visual reference of common life, their life. This was especially analysed when people used familiar references and meanings to interpret and discuss the pictures shown during the FOLi Labs. Beyond what the pictures themselves seem to represent, people tend to look for shared social and cultural patterns that can be recognized by a larger group. Following what Hall (1959) expressed, the common photographic image, as any other visual method, needs to be consumed over shared cultural patterns in order to be understood, analysed and discussed.

A place to represent culture

The exhibition of photography in a contemporary museum is considered to be an important platform upon which people consume culture and think of their own culture, as some of the responses highlight:

> 'We need more culture diffusion to promote a new and better culture; a museum is a rich source to know our culture.'

Specifically, the museum is projected as a space to represent Peruvian culture and its diversity:

> '[T]he museum (should) show the faces of culture; the museum shows our great culture to the world and also our beautiful culture; to show how wonderful our country and its people are.'

> 'I expect to see Peruvian plurality that shows the theatrical richness of the different communities.'

> 'this project is a great opportunity to get to know each other and to be part of something really great, cheers to Peru!'

Moreover, the notes express allegoric references to a 'civic feeling' which the images that will be hosted in the contemporary photography museum should evoke. From different perspectives, there is a continuous reference to the fact that photography contributes to the generation and acknowledgement of a social identity that is constructed by shared values that unifies people as Peruvians. On the other hand, a photography museum is accepted as a place to represent, recognize and promote the Peruvian qualities: 'we want to spread the values that unify our country'; 'a new place to spread culture, freedom and understanding of our own country.' Here we see a tribute to unity that is constructed from shared values that need to be exposed publicly – in photographic images – to be seen and recognized. Here are the examples of the notes:

> 'We expect to disseminate values that integrate our country… To know the national reality ☺' Post-it response No. 22

> 'Through the images – the museum of photography – should help to know more our society and its people!' Post-it response No. 23

Furthermore, the emergent discourse implies that a museum is mostly useful for local people instead of believing that it is a place that allows representation of their own culture for a foreign audience.

Acknowledgement of the true country

An audience expects to have a museum that 'reveals the truth of local society.' Notes like: 'a place where we can know the reality of the country'; 'the truth about our society, the real face of the country and its people.' It also seems that for the audience there is still something unknown, something hidden about ways society operates and the politics involved. The audience is delegating the educational role to a museum.

When we refer to representation for the true values of society we immediately think of visual and material aspects that can be photographed, in order to be displayed in a museum: material culture, ethnic differences, etc. However, the acknowledgement of the socio-political reality of Peru is also related to less visual aspects of culture that still remain invisible. Here are the examples:

> 'We wish that photography could show the true feelings and essence of the Peruvian man: the struggle; thanks for letting us see our reality and ourselves as a family.'

> 'I would like FOLi to be in other districts, in order to promote the re-integration of social classes and unity among persons' Post-it responses No. 140

The images can serve as a reference point for thinking about ontological questions like how do people want to be recognized as a social group, represented and organized at local and national level. This builds an interest to achieve a visual recognition of an imagined community (Anderson, 1991) that works as a common reference to Peruvians. The aim of this acknowledgement is the search for unity, and deeper understanding of culture.

Common memory

Even when we refer to a contemporary museum, there are competing discourses about the expectation of a museum that include historical pictures that create a visual history and impact on the construction of a collective memory of the common past. This implies an interesting trend about how the audience demands the construction of a visual and public memory. The audience wants a museum that becomes the host of a collection of historical photos that reaffirms a common past, generates individual memory and consequently a collective memory that also becomes a projection of a common future. Some respondents evoked: 'I expect that the museum helps us to see and love our past, doing so, we will be able to love our future'; 'the museum should show our traditions; photography unifies the memory of the past with the present that make us live unforgettable moments'; 'the museum that makes us remember the past with the belief that we will have a prosperous present and future.'

An open museum

The new museum is projected as a place that hosts forms of expressions and evokes feelings, using symbolic and visual language as with photography: 'photography can express emotions that cannot be said.'

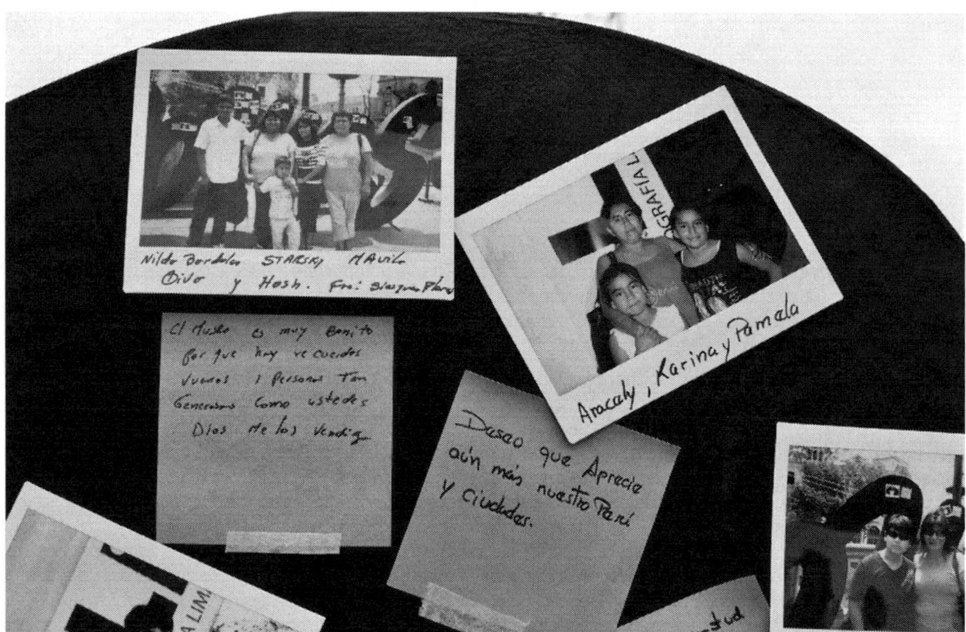

Figure 6.7: Written testimonies of what people expect from a contemporary photography museum. Courtesy of Gonzalo Olmos.

On the other hand, using the public space for a photographic exhibition, FOLi Lab helped the audience to think outside the box and to reconsider that a museum can be very different from the traditional view of a museum as a static place. This new museum is already thought of as a new form of understanding what a museum is in general: interactive, modern, reflexive centre of knowledge sharing with: 'art that reaches people, in a fun way.'

Conclusions

The FOLi Lab team took the conscious decision of working collectively with passers-by in Lima in the flux of daily life. The museum took to the streets and sidewalks of Lima by working 25 consecutive days inside the structure of the urban photographic lab. FOLi Lab as the museographic urban experiment of the Biennial of Photography of Lima was

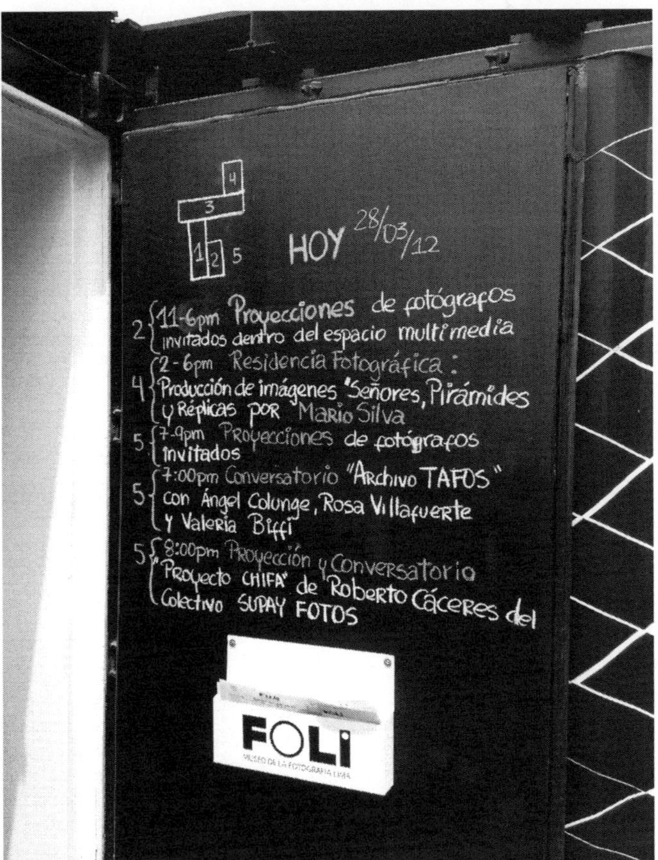

Figure 6.8: Menu of daily programme activities, written on a container door panel, made into a blackboard. Courtesy of Gonzalo Olmos.

a successful experience. In our view, it accomplished the successful integration with the community by fostering photographic culture in a dynamic and participatory platform in the public space. At the end of the event, FOLi Lab had fulfilled the objective of promoting photographic culture by mobilizing more than 45,000 residents and passers-by in the public spaces of the city of Lima.

In our view, it is pivotal to make a distinction and shed light between the physical structure of the space and the notion of social space created at the FOLi Lab. We need to look beyond the notion of space as typology of the physicality and structures of the space, created in the main squares or as mere hardware or 'shipping containers.' But instead, it is necessary to engage in efforts to understand the FOLi Lab in its software, in terms of social interactions, networks and movements created. In short, the visual culture that inhabited the containers was not confined to the physicality of the museum, but lived through the dynamics of relational practice.[5]

FOLi Lab achieved its goal as an experimental laboratory aimed to identify new qualitative methodologies for the promotion and development of a photographic culture. We have mostly highlighted the acknowledgement of photography as a symbolic language that can intensively communicate cultural value and social content for analysis. We could argue that the audience wanted to conceive familiar codes in the pictures they encountered in a museum, that let them analyse and interpret what they have seen. Comparison of their own experiences with the images exposed transformed the experience of seeing photography as a very intimate experience.

It is evident that there is a further need for a reference to common social and cultural codes in order to visually construct a collective identity that can be shown in a museum context. In that sense, the audience wanted the museum to become a 'place where people could find a representation of themselves', and in the collective sense of 'us,' where the social and cultural values could have been shared and represented visually.

References

Anderson, B. 1991. *Imagined Communities: Reflections on the Origin and Spread of Nationalism*, London: Verso.

Barthes, R. 1967. *Elements of Semiology*, London: Jonathan Cape.

Barthes, R. 1984. *Camera Lucida: Reflections of Photography*, London: Vintage Classics.

Bishop, C. 2006. *Participation*, Cambridge, MA: The MIT Press.

Certeau, M. de. 1984. *The Practice of Everyday Life*, Berkeley, CA: University of California Press.

Flick, U. 2009. *An Introduction to Qualitative Research*, London: Sage.

Hall, E. 1959. *The Silent Language*, New York, NY: Anchor Books.

Harper, D. 2002. 'Talking about pictures: A case for photo elicitation', *Visual Studies*, 17 (1), 13–26.

Kuhn, A. 2007. 'Photography and cultural memory: A methodological exploration', *Visual Studies*, 22 (3), 283–292.

Martin, B. and Hanington, B. 2012. *Universal Methods of Design*, Beverly, MA: Rockport Publishers.

McNiff, J. 2013. *Action Research: Principles and Practice*, London: Routledge.

Pink, S. 2009. *Visual Interventions: Applied Visual Anthropology*, London: Berghahn.

Ramella, M. and Olmos, G. 2005. 'Participant authored audiovisual stories (PAAS): Giving the camera away or giving the camera a way?', *Discussion Papers in Qualitative Research*, 10, Methodology Institute: London School of Economics and Political Sciences.

Schubert, K. 2009. *The Curator's Egg. The Evolution of the Museum Concept from the French Revolution to the Present Day*, Manchester: Ridinghouse/Karsten Schubert.

Tinkler, P. 2012. 'Photo-interviews: Listening to talk about photos'. In Tinkler, P. (Ed.), *Using Photographs in Social and Historical Research*, London: Sage.

Notes

1   The acronym in Spanish for Museo de la Fotografía Lima (FOLi).

2   The project was commissioned by the Peruvian architect Rafael Contreras Morales.

3   http://facultad.pucp.edu.pe/comunicaciones/tafos/

4   International visual artists included the following nationalities: Mali, France, Switzerland, Mexico, United States, Argentina, Peru, Italy, Ireland, Chile, Korea, Belgium, Colombia, South Africa, United Kingdom, Holland, Russia, China. The following 38 artists were selected: Afrique In Visu, Alex Franck, Alinka Echeverría, Bakary Diallo, Brendon Stuart, Bruno Stecconi, Carlos Sánchez Giraldo, Sofía Velázquez Núñez, Cesar Delgado Wixan, Cynthia Lawson Jaramillo, Klaus Fruchtnis, Danilo Murru, David Colm Killeen, Eliana Vásquez, Enrique Castro-Mendivil, Enrique Ramírez, Federico Lamas, Gianni Cipriano, Hayoun Kwon, Jeanne Mercier, Jonathan Saruk, Julia Mensch, Laurent Mareschal, Limafotolibre, Manuel Vázquez, Mario Silva, Mónica Heller, Pieter Hugo, Rebecca Locke, Ruben Reyes, Santiago Escobar, Sayed Hasan, Sebastián Norman, Supayfotos, Tessa Joosse, Verso Images, Victoria Sayago, Zhenchen Liu.

5   For instance, Certeau (1984: 117) in *The Practice of Everyday Life* invites us to make a distinction between space (*espace*) and place (*lieux*), concluding that 'space is a practiced place.' Thus, the notion of 'place' needs to be understood in terms of social interactions, networks and movements. Currently, there is a tendency to change the nomenclature from a narrow specificity of 'public space' towards a broader view of the 'public realm.' The latter seems to be a better phrase to suit and describe the notions of the politics of space, physical space and urban design intertwined with ideological, performative and socio-cultural practices.

Chapter 7

OrgansparkZ: Communities of art-space, imagination and resistance

Miguel Imas and Alia Weston

Introduction

Art should comfort the disturbed and disturb the comfortable.

(Banksy, 2005)

Art can imbue and instigate social, political and economic transformation in communities and organizations that operate at the margins of society. Art and creative (activism) can voice and stage actions that can do more than just aestheticize and spectacularize events or experiences lived in these margins (Groys, 2014). For example, in Brazil we find the samba-reggae band Olodum, which has employed music and dance as a vehicle for Afro-Brazilian emancipation. Through the sound of their drums, Olodum has addressed the inequality, marginality and racism that affect most of the Brazilian black population, promoting a cultural resistance towards postcolonial discourses that dominate Brazilian society (Clegg, 1995; Stockland, 2004). Art, as Groys (2014) states, can be influential in directing action towards overcoming the status quo of communities who feel vulnerable and dispossessed. Art, and creative initiatives, then can be a highly effective social vehicle to fight for social transformation or the protection and preservation of grassroots community values.

It is our intention in this chapter to explore art-based creative initiatives that promote well-being, cultures of resistance and social transformation through what we call 'organsparkZ' engagements, i.e., art/creative engagements that can affect and transform communities living in precarity (Neilson and Rossiter, 2006). Precarity, following Butler (2004, 2012), reflects vulnerability, a sense of dispossession, dispensability and substitutability experienced by those who struggle in life and tend to occupy the margins. Jackson (2012) considers that there exists a natural connection between these precarious conditions and creative initiatives that people engage in to promote awareness of their cause. Moreover, she regards creative activities as significant in their attempts to tackle social, health and economic issues, as well as in the promotion of cultural resistance against the main diktats of the society.

Our key conceptual idea is what we come to acknowledge as organsparkZ. Following Mouffe (2007), we consider organsparkZ to be artistic and creative practices embedded in an agonistic approach that foments dissensus from the dominant (political and economic) discourses; aiming to give voice and space for action to those silenced within the framework of existing hegemonic spaces. OrgansparkZ reflects urban sub-cultural activities that occupy and disrupt spaces. They are constituted as fluid and rhizomic (Deleuze and Guattari,

2003); that is they are not fixed practices. They invite fluidity of engagement and dialogical interactions that alter challenging social conditions which emerge from prescribed structures. OrgansparkZers, as we call activists in such contexts, socially, performatively and aesthetically construct an alter-modern narrative of creative resistance that temporarily attempts at defying repression from dominant societal practices.

In the chapter, we expand further our organsparkZ concept. We illustrate our perspective with examples of organsparkZ art and creative engagement from three communities and organizations in Buenos Aires (Argentina), Cape Town (South Africa) and Valparaíso (Chile). We believe these examples illustrate the significance of organsparkZ engagements, challenging hegemonic and prescribed societal practices that repress and sanitize the creative agency of communities and organizations. We conclude with reflections on the importance of organsparkZ art and creative engagements for overcoming social-organizational precarity.

OrgansparkZ: Art-spaces, imagination and resistance

Our exploration of art-based initiatives for social transformation of community life begins with organsparkZ.[1] We build on Mouffe's agonistic approach, placing organsparkZ as forms of co-participative art-activist practices of spontaneous, unrestrained and ante/organized (Boje, 2008) nature that are enacted in primarily (but not exclusively) precarious spaces (Imas and Weston, 2012). These practices evoke creative actions through sub-cultures of subversion that resist and alter challenging social conditions experienced on a daily basis. OrgansparkZ aims to set in flux creative, imaginative acts upon which communities can challenge what has been prescribed on them, or simply use as a vehicle to stimulate engagement with social, political or economic issues that affect them the most. Three key ideas underpin organsparkZ practices: art-spaces, dialogical imaginations and everyday resistance. We articulate each concept separately here but acknowledge that they are highly interconnected.

Art-spaces

Art-spaces indicate two key components in our understanding of organsparkZ. One has to do with our appreciation of art as a force for possible social transformation and the other with the notion of space and how it plays a significant part in the way organsparkZers socially engage in community collaboration.

We see art, and by extension creative acts, as performative actions enacted by individuals, communities or organizations collaboratively in order to resist, contest or disturb social conditions that adversely affect them. For example, Ressler's (2007) video installations about the Bolivarian process in Venezuela enact a process of social transformation that has taken hold among Venezuelan communities. Ressler's work seeks to illustrate the Venezuelan emancipation process from the neo-liberal discourse, providing a global context for engagement and discussion on how precarity can be overcome.

Art represents a social creative engagement that invites co-participation within Kester's (2011) dialogical art and Bishop's (2012) participatory aesthetics. Although differences exist between these two authors' understanding of collaborative art practices, what is pertinent here is the value that they both give to art as a potential for social change. It is a force that can do more than just aestheticize a community or commodify the work of an artist based on that community. Kester, for instance, valorizes art involvement in community life, pointing out the importance of immersion in local conditions from where solutions could be developed on particular socio-political problems (Heartney, 2012). Bishop, on the other hand, places art as a return to a social collective, i.e., less emphasis on the 'artist' as a producer of objects and more as part of a collective that creates situations for co-creation (2012). That is, the emphasis is less on art produced as a commodity, hitherto for profit, but more on the potential it has to create meaningful creative collaborations with or through others.

Art acts in organsparkZ are unrestrained (often non-regulated) and intended to challenge or question the prescribed ways in which society operates (Halsey and Young, 2006). These are practices such as street activities that are written on walls, performed in the streets or symbolized in any other act that questions prescribed societal discourses (e.g. Boal, 2000).[2] They are unexpected and there is more than just an aesthetic or commercial purpose to them (Daskalaki et al., 2008). The recent dispute with the skateboarders, street writers and artists, and BMXers who occupy the Undercroft under the Southbank in London, provides a good example. Attempts were made by the Southbank Centre that owns the space to remove this community to another part of the river (for commercial reasons). The community reacted to this provocation by running a full campaign that invoked art activities to protect and preserve what they have regarded as their legitimate and historical space for running their art. Under the banner of 'Long Live Southbank' they mobilized thousands of people to resist and fight the re-development of the Undercroft Park. The campaign succeeded.[3] The example illustrates how a community can succeed defending their space from gentrification and relocation and, in doing so, preserve their unique creative identities, history and [sub]-cultures (see also Harvey, 2012).

In street art we find communities with a political conscience that seeks to challenge the corporatized city. They enact creative activities that are subversive and on occasions can also be nihilistic (Long, 2104). The fundamental purpose is to express the cry of the community in the way that the community feels and not in the way they are told to feel (John Lennon in Long, 2014).

Space is equally important in our conceptualization of 'art-spaces.' Space, as Gieryn (2000) remarks, is not place. Space represents the abstract, which is detached from material and cultural interpretations. When space is filled with meaning, symbols, practices, discourses, signs, representations and values, it acquires or becomes place (Certeau, 1984). When bodies fill and enact the space with their cultural activities, spaces become of interest and are transformed into meaningful places, landscapes or territories. Meaning, however, does not stay fixed and is constantly in flux (Deleuze and Guattari, 2003) since it is continually questioned from within and outside communities. The example of the Undercroft is useful again here to illustrate this point. The Undercroft space in the Southbank is defined as grey, brutish and unappealing; of no value and certainly meaning. Yet, the communities that use it have been able to socially construct a place that is full of spontaneity, creativity and meaning, defying the fixed notion of what this space is and represents (Richards et al., 2014). This perspective is emphasized by Harrington who states that 'The Undercroft is a free space for people to express themselves on a site of real significance to a global youth culture. It is part of what makes our capital city brilliant' (Catherine Harrington, Director, The National Community Land Trust Network, in Richards et al., 2014). The Undercroft example thus illustrates that meaningful places may therefore be contested. Marginalized communities may be able to reclaim space through art and creative (or other) practices to form narratives of emancipation (e.g. Peteet, 1996). Through their creativity they are able to form, re-transform and re-contest the contested territoriality of a space.

Dialogical imaginations

The second of our ideas underpinning organsparkZ has to do with dialogical imaginations. This is the imaginative capacity to resist precarious circumstances through a collective plurality of creative representations. OrgansparkZ reflects collective imaginations that pursue transformation and emancipation as a fluid network of thoughts that provoke change and oppose centripetal forces of repression (Gardiner, 1992). Imaginations in organsparkZ are constituted as dialogical imaginations (Bakhtin, 1981). Here, imagination reflects a polyphony of possibilities that people have to create potential realities (Bakhtin, 1984a). It is the potential to project and reframe hopes that challenges the present configuration of things (Jovchelovitch and Priego-Hernández, 2013; Scheper-Hughes, 1993). It is the possibility to imagine other 'worlds and realities' that can somehow take shape as a collective effort. The imaginaries here are the centrifugal forces, described by Bakhtin (1981), that challenge dominant prescriptions and construct dialogues that are intertwined, negotiated and contested in spaces created *in-between* (Bakhtin, 1986). That is, the potential imaginaries are products of the intersected meeting of not one but a chain of thoughts and meanings that are ongoing and communicate a polyphony of representations. In dialogical imaginations we see the 'carnivalesque' of everyday creative languages (Bakhtin, 1984b) where everyone embraces one another and is part of a colourful festivity of provoking art/creative space representations that challenge precarious conditions, and do not accept forces of repression.

Grant Kester's (2000) conceptualization of art as well as Saitô's (2006) review of art as collaborative methods provide examples of critical, engaged art practices that reflect organsparkZ's polyphonic and imaginative initiatives. The focus is not on the production of objects by the particular creative 'artist' and their relation with an audience, rather it is on the creative process as a social process that (dialogically) engages communities to challenge and question their status quo. There is connectedness; there is desire to co-create and co-establish links that are based on mutual respect and the realization of the necessity of challenging (political, social or economic) reality as it is pre-conceived and pre-defined by the dominant society. Through dialogical imagination, organsparkZers probe new questions to the social imponderables that they face.

Everyday resistance

The third idea spans from the notion of resistance. This is an everyday resistance that encompasses the everyday practices that people engage in to fight for inclusion and social condition in a mundane and less pronounced way (Vinthagen and Johansson, 2013). It is a resistance that is disguised, or expressed in ways that are not directly confrontational like public protests. This kind of resistance lives within the community as something normal. It forms part of daily routines and culture, expressed in a subtle way, like a creative street stunts. Bayat (2000) calls this form of resistance 'quiet encroachment' by which he means 'the silent, protracted but pervasive advancement of the ordinary people [...] in order to survive and improve their lives' (Bayat, 2000: 545–546). This resisting is not necessarily formally organized or exemplified within a social movement. It is fluid and may appear innocuous to the generally ordered society. It reflects Certeau's (1984) idea of everyday subversive resistance as a practice that is mobile and not fixed. It alters the order of things imposed on a community; it is a creative tactic that emanates from disenfranchised communities to survive the impositions of society. Following Vinthagen and Johansson (2013), everyday resistance as a practice is historically entangled with everyday power, is intersectional as it engages with more than one form of power and is heterogenic and contingent on the performativity of language used by the community to oppose the restrictions of society.

Thus, this triad of conceptual ideas: art-spaces, dialogical imaginations and everyday resistance form the cornerstones for our theorization of organsparkZ engagements. These engagements spark different creative meanings and representations that enable communities to not only resist, but also transform within situations of repression and social precarity.

OrgansparkZ creative engagements

In this section we present three examples of organsparkZ engagements. These examples were collected from fieldwork research conducted in the cities of Buenos Aires (Argentina), Cape Town (South Africa) and Valparaíso (Chile). In Buenos Aires, we participated in an occupied printing factory, Chilavert. In Cape Town, we interviewed people from a youth-development and non-profit organization called Salesian Life Choices (SLC). Finally, in Valparaíso, we explored the hills of the city where some communities have been gentrified and removed. We supported our research in Valparaíso with virtual accounts of art projects conducted by art-based alternative organizations that are active in the city.

The research approach is founded in critical and postcolonial ethnographies (Escobar, 2007), micro-stories (Boje, 2008) and visual traditions that seek to give voice to these communities that exist at the margins. These research traditions underpin a methodology of participation and involvement whereby our descriptions, narratives and interpretations are a critical reflection of who the people in the community are, as well as the kinds of creative activities they engage in. In addition, we also included a methodological stance that invited a more spontaneous and less scripted perspective based on Vincent Moon's *La Blogothèque* take-away shows.[4] Vincent Moon's take-away shows are a series of improvised outdoor video sessions with musicians in unexpected and unusual locations. Moon, an independent filmmaker and sound explorer, employs a 'guerrilla film-making technique,' that is organic and authentic; a mixture of life performances and a finished music video, all done in single-take shots. Moon's approach to music inspired us to explore art and creative initiatives in unusual communities, trying to engage in spontaneous and authentic dialogues that created singular dialogical experiences. It added a sense of spontaneity and originality to our research work and subsequently to the way we positioned ourselves to narrate the stories we collected from these settings. We think that this approach dignifies and accentuates the experiences of the communities and their own capacity to polyphonically construct their potential realities. Below we discuss the three organsparkZ narrative examples from our fieldwork. The examples illustrate different analytical aspects of organsparkZ initiatives, exemplifying the everyday creative resistance practices of the communities, highlighting their occupation of space and application of imaginative practices to overcome a sense of precarity. The narratives are a reflection of the organsparkZers' experiences of living and working in those communities embellished in our own interpretative narratives of those experiences. That is, although our voices reveal our own analytical intentions of these art-initiative experiences, the narratives are a reflection of the spaces we created *in-between* with each of these communities. Our narrative of Valparaíso's hills reflects a visual engagement with what was a *take-away* experience of visual spontaneity. Thus, our analytical voices attempt to visualize what organsparkZers do to overcome in an artistic and creative sense, their position of precarity and dispossession.

Fabrica-sparkZs

In the first of our examples, we engage with *Fábricas Recuperadas* in Argentina. The *Fábricas Recuperadas* (occupied factories) movement emerged as a consequence of the financial crisis suffered by Argentina in 2000 (e.g. Gracia and Cavaliere, 2007; Kosmala and Imas, 2012). Through the crisis, like the recent one in Europe, many businesses were declared bankrupt and thousands of workers lost their jobs. Moreover, as banks were also declared insolvent, workers lost access to their savings. Faced without jobs, a bankrupt state and the impossibility to access their lifetime savings, workers and communities were faced with harsh choices. One of those that was not contemplated and emerged spontaneously was to re-occupy the bankrupt factories and make them work again. This was a risk because it was an illegal action. But it was also a courageous and creative defiance of the unexpected arrangements forced upon them by society.

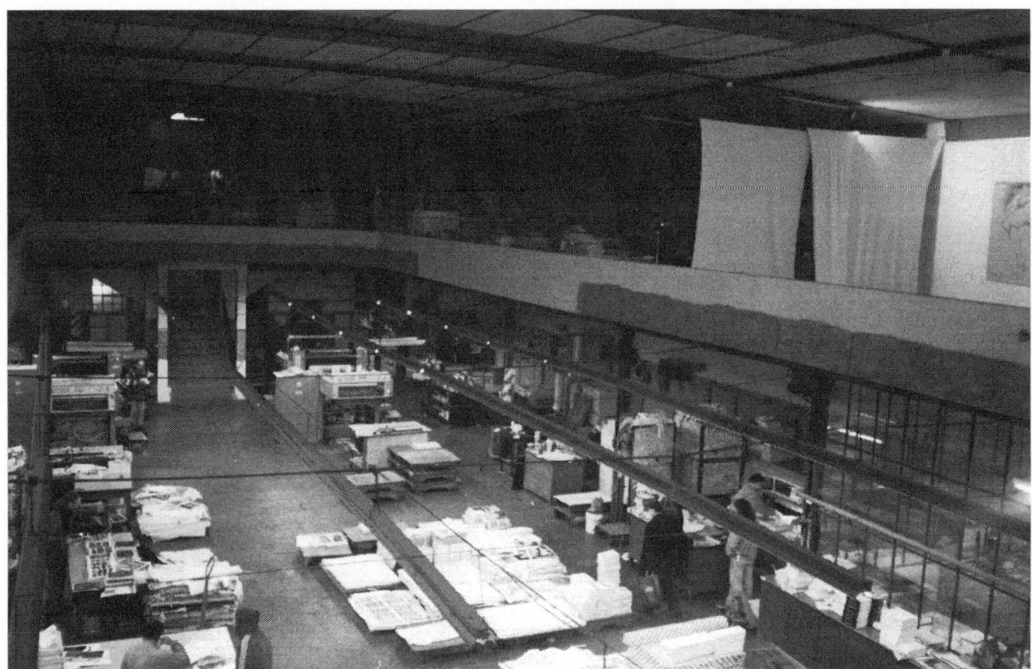

Figure 7.1: *Fábricas Recuperadas* workspace in Buenos Aires, Argentina, 2005. Courtesy of J. M. Imas.

The occupation of the factories by these workers is an illustration of organsparkZ initiatives in social-organizational precarity. Here, organsparkZers applied their collective imaginations to alter and transform their social conditions of unemployment and failure. They contested their circumstances in a way that was creative, resisting the reality that was imposed on them. In this respect they did not subscribe to the narrative that demanded them to surrender their identities, places of work and dignity by becoming casualties of the financial crisis in Argentina (Magnani, 2003). These fábricas-sparkZers (as we acknowledge them), acting upon this forceful removal, re-occupied their places of work, re-invented the associations they had lost and constructed more emancipatory practices of social engagement among themselves and with the communities that surrounded them.

Fábricas-sparkZers were left in a precarious condition as described above. Some of the creative initiatives were to re-construct the meaning of what the factories represented for them and the community. When the factories were run as traditional corporate business, the preoccupation was with the profitability of the companies. There was no major interest but to control the production and the Fábrica workers contributed to the discourse of corporatization. Once they re-occupied the factories, they changed the meaning of the space, re-territorializing it with a plurality of discourses, symbols and practices that reflected a cultural endeavour where solidarity, participation and community building became prioritized (Lavaca, 2004). Building plurality and conceiving different imaginaries from the

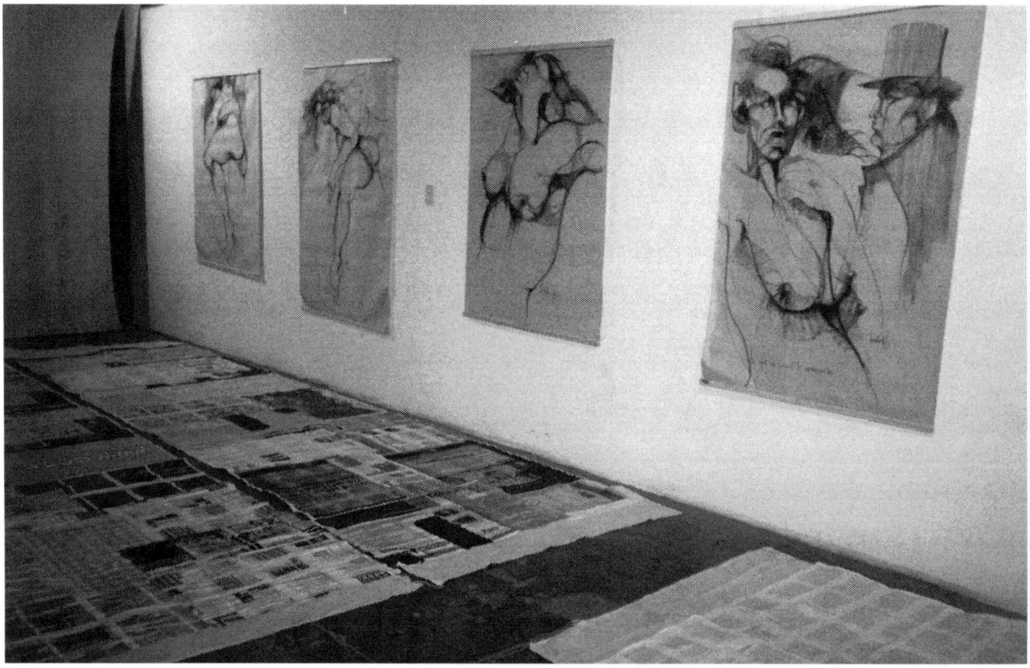

Figure 7.2: *Fábricas Recuperada* used as an art gallery, 2005. Courtesy of J. M. Imas.

one prescribed provided them with an invitation to engage with creative initiatives that stimulated dialogue with the outside community. In this way, the factories became cultural productions that not only produced commercial products but also creative cultural artefacts (of social significance) to sustain life within the communities.

The workers' resistance then was exemplified through creative imagination that defied the fixed representation of a factory. For example, one particular organsparkZ activity was to organize a play within a re-occupied printing factory, inviting the whole community to participate in the production every Saturday. The space of the factory was transformed for these performances. All the fábricas-sparkZers removed the machinery, making room for a stage and accommodating chairs to host the whole community within the factory. This transformed not only the relationship with the space but equally what the space represented in relation to them and the community. It allowed for socialization, participation and creation of mutual understandings of the value of the factory within a community. Through plays, such as the performance of *Les Misérables*, they contested their condition in subtle ways, demonstrating an acute everyday language of resistance.

In addition to the plays, art exhibitions were also conceived inside this factory. Craft and paintings were produced by local community members in order to promote other kinds of creative engagement. The space of the factory was transformed into a gallery open to all. The purpose of the factory was to encourage community engagement and participation rather than commercialization.

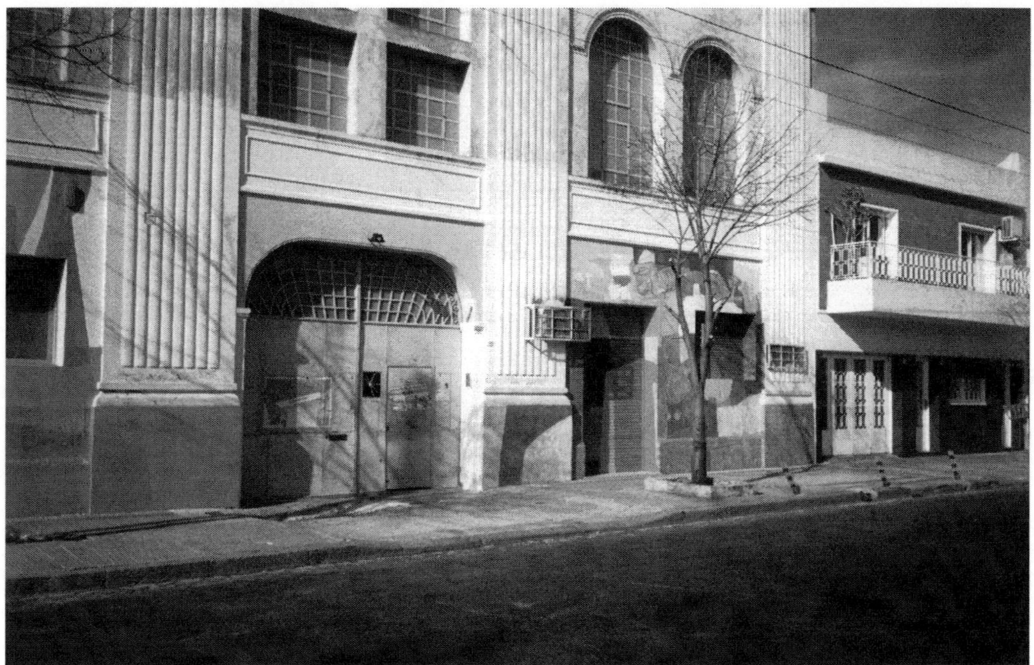

Figure 7.3: *Fábricas Recuperadas'* main entrance in Buenos Aires, Argentina, 2005. Courtesy of J. M. Imas.

Fábricas Recuperadas re-drew the conceptualization of work and organization and by extension opened a dialogue with the community. It allowed for organsparkZ's actions to materialize and contest an otherwise unchallenged narrative that suppressed social and working life. It provided the seeds for dialogical imaginaries that can not only resist through everyday practices, but demonstrated the abundant capacity for creative action when a community is declared as down and out. Overall, this case illustrates the potential of creative tactics that can be employed by organsparkZers to resist social-organizational precarity, and raises expectations for the re-enactment of meaning, work and social life. This example demonstrates that the factory workers were able to overcome the societal repression of economic crisis and remained in the re-appropriated spaces of their factories – transforming some into art galleries and theatres – and creating employment for themselves.

Dance-SparkZs for your life

The following narrative takes us to Cape Town, South Africa and illustrates an example of organsparkZ creative engagement through performance. It conveys a community engaging in spontaneous creativity as a way to overcome a situation of precarity in the form of resource poverty. The organization central to the narrative is Salesian Life Choices (SLC). SLC is a development organization that facilitates social transformation by providing young people in the Cape Flats communities with the skills to initiate change in their communities. The organization runs four main types of projects. These include family stability, youth friendly health services, youth leadership and academic support (as explained by Sofia Neves, Managing Director SLC). The combined aim of their interventions is to generate a social movement that contributes to human 'profit' and instils long-lasting change in communities. The notion of human profit is based on the premise that the organization's wealth is realized from developing human capabilities that overcome societal challenges, rather than wealth from monetary gain. The initiative facilitated the problem-solving capabilities for young people, having positive impact on the wider communities (SLC, 2014a).

Historically, SLC ran on a not-for-profit development model. This meant that it relied heavily on consistent funding sources to sustain their community interventions. It was a tried and tested organizational model that followed a set process and did not encourage alternative thinking or engagement. This formula, however, proved unsustainable. In October 2013, SLC was faced with a situation of precarity when their regular sources of funding were cut. The cuts meant that they would cease to exist as an organization, and this pushed SLC to change.

It was a pivotal moment where all members of the organization were forced to reconsider what it meant to be SLC. Their traditional organizational process had relied on regular income that sustained a standard range of projects. Their dilemma now was how to continue being SLC without the security of a traditional business model and a regular monetary income stream. Their response was to engage reflexively and apply their own philosophy

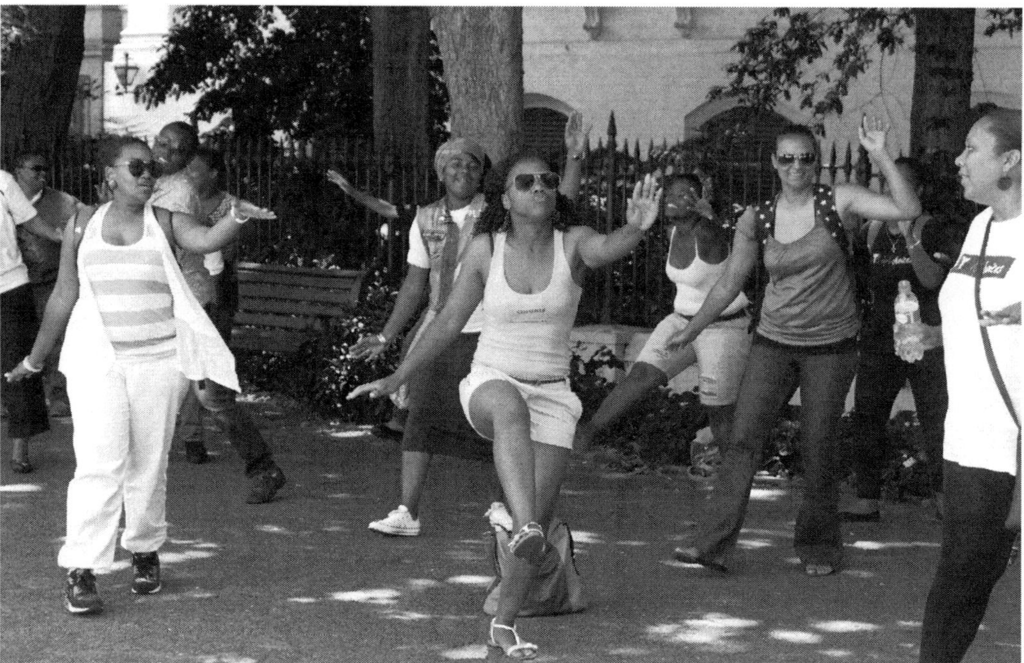

Figure 7.4: Life Choices supporters dancing in the street. Courtesy of Salesian Life Choices.

of promoting optimism. They drew on their wealth of community resources and human profit, rather than relying on financial capital. As a result, rather than focusing on traditional organizational procedure, they began to engage in alternate organizational practices that evoked imagination and resistance.

They evoked dance-SparkZs by launching the 'You Decide Campaign' and inviting the Cape Town community to save the organization with them. Supporters could choose to donate monetary resources or support SLC by joining in with a 'Happy Dance.' The idea was that supporters would learn dance moves and at a given time on the 29th November they would join in the Happy Dance with SLC at Green Point Park and spread joy through the streets. If supporters could not join in with the dance in the streets they could dance at home, at work or at school (SLC, 2013). All of the members of SLC, from the staff to the community members went into the streets together and danced to sustain the survival of the organization. The public rose to the challenge and joined them.

The campaign raised awareness and raised resources, but it also challenged SLC to further engage in organsparkZ and transform their conceptualization and imagination of what it means to engage in organizational activities. The dance practice was so successful for SLC that they became committed to work in a different way. They now focus on their human and community wealth to creatively perform in new organizational ways. A more recent example of this is a campaign '30 Stories in 30 Days' that they initiated to share organsparkZ

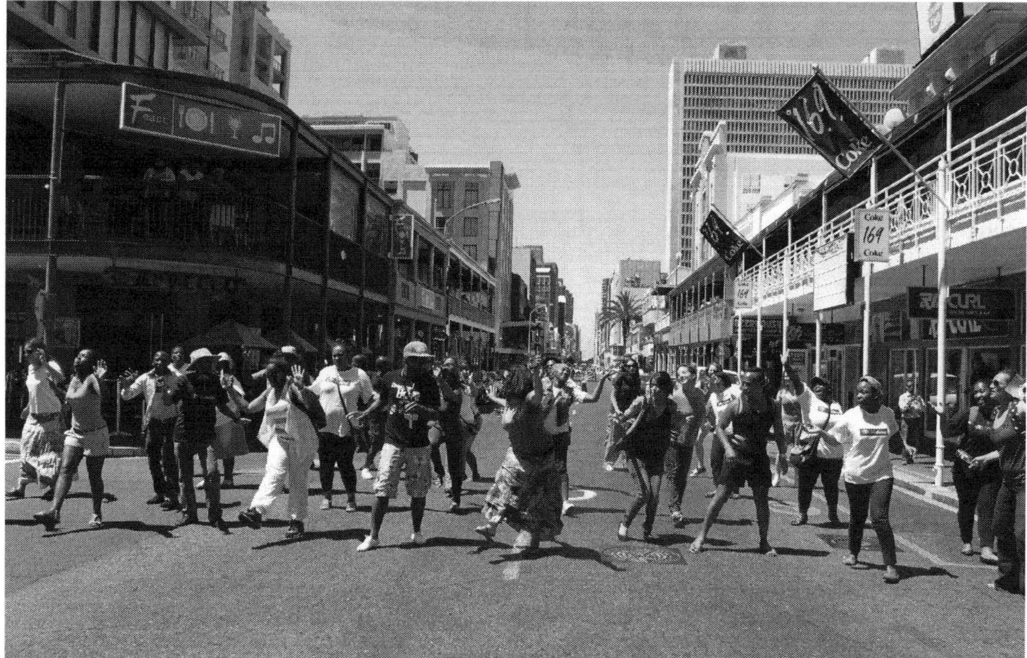

Figure 7.5: Life Choices supporters dancing in central Cape Town. Courtesy of Salesian Life Choices.

stories from and with the community. The campaign embraced storytelling as a form of creative organizational performance (Boje, 2008). They produced an online resource to share personal stories of creativity and resilience in response to human precarity (SLC, 2014b).

These engagements are examples of organsparkZ creative resistance because they embody the essence of spontaneous response to uncertainty of organizational closure. The example illustrates how creative engagement can emerge through organsparkZ of resistance, based on communal need and how this is co-produced as a social movement with and through the community as a form of rhizomic social inspiration. Sofia Neves, the MD of SLC, referred to this process as 'sparks of inspiration' that spread through the community. SLC was faced with closure but they evoked a space of creative resistance and worked with the community to overcome their challenges. In this example, dance was incorporated as an alternative organizational practice that emerged through creative social imagination as opposed to an organized financial plan. Ultimately, this case example shows us how non-traditional organizational practices can initiate social transformation, when organsparkZ engagement is incorporated to promote, protect and defend the community. They achieved this by reimagining organizational practices and creatively organizing through storytelling and dance.

SparkZing imaginations in Valpo's Hills

The third of our organsparkZ creatives takes us to the hills of Valparaíso, Chile. In these hills local communities have been under constant threat from urban 'cleansing' as they do not conform to the new global public gentrified image of the city.

Valparaíso is a port city surrounded by hills. It is the second largest city in Chile and here the main national legislative body is situated. In 2003, it was declared a world heritage centre by UNESCO. This attracted an infusion of capital and private investment in order to develop parts of the city, especially areas that were regarded as highly dilapidated, unsafe, dirty and overlooked, such as the hills. The hills are home to local families and communities. A recent fire that destroyed the environment and killed 15 people exposed the poverty and neglect in which they live. A local writer, Alvaro Bisama, described the tragedy metaphorically (and poetically) as 'when poverty burns down' (2014).

For Bisama, the fire damaged the Valparaíso's image since its inception as a world heritage centre. On the one hand, Valparaíso in the imaginary became an idyllic destination for tourists and a 'chic' place to see and to settle in. For example, Evans (2009) described Valpo[5] as the poetic destination of Chile, where its 264,000 residents cling to the old splendid architecture. Lorenz (2014), writing for the Guardian, describes Valpo as a 'cool' avant-garde art scene, possessing a vibrant colourful and creative atmosphere. In particular, these authors highlight the commercial developments of two hills, Concepción and Alegre, where the multi-coloured spectacle and highly creative narrative of Valpo emerged. Equally, they emphasize a commodified narrative of creative engagements.

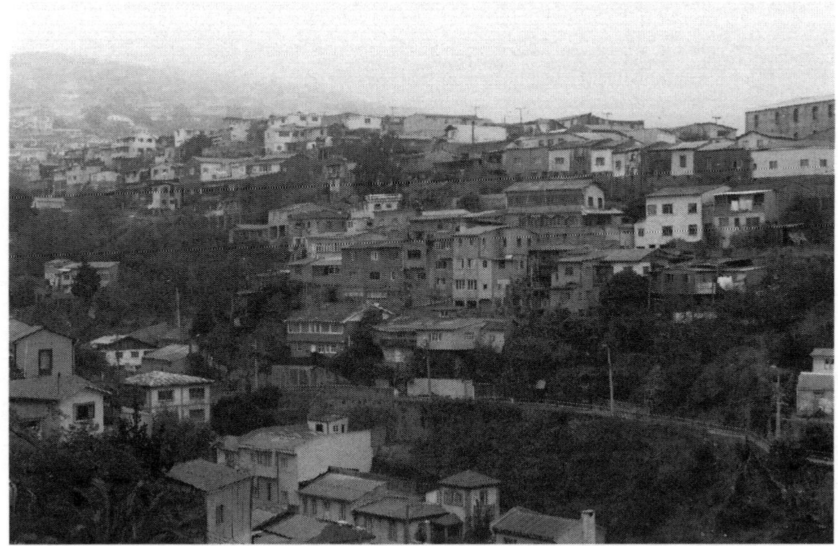

Figure 7.6: Valparaíso Hill Neighbourhood, Valparaíso, Chile, 2011. Courtesy of J. M. Imas.

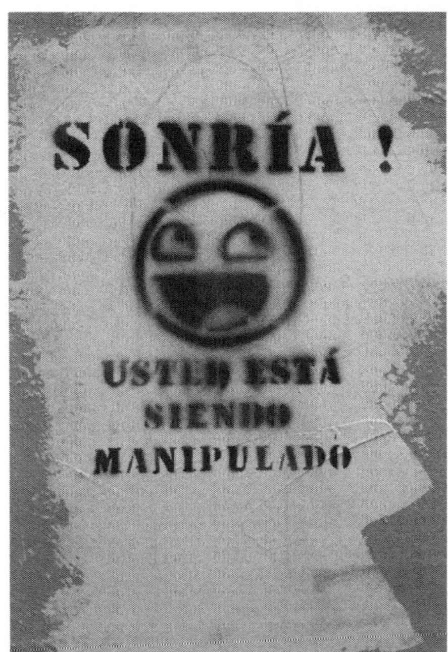

Figure 7.7: 'Smile! You're being manipulated', Graffiti Stencil in Valpo's Concepción Hill, Chile, 2011. Courtesy of J. M. Imas.

On the other hand, the gentrified image of the city hides the less idyllic postcard of the hills where life reflects deprivation, neglect and dispossession. In the 'other' hills, communities have hardly seen any municipal investment or development aid. There is only invisibility, poverty and rejection from authorities and investors, more concerned with the creation of 'tourism' rather than supporting the locals who historically populate these hills. Valparaíso's mayor typified this discourse when he answered one of the victims of the fire: 'who invited you to live here?' This rejection has made local communities more determined to resist the picturesque sanitized discourse of what authorities and private investors want from the city (especially in the hills). As a consequence, valpo-sparkZers have launched collective initiatives that contest the 'embourgeoisement' (Harvey, 2006, 2012) or commodification of Valparaíso's space.

Valpo-sparkZers, working in different art-space workshops, have created a collective map of Valparaíso. This initiative mobilizes different local organizations.[6] The map[7] is a virtual installation that represents the hills' communities under threat. Through these art workshops and the map, locals create awareness and re-educate, in an artistic organsparkZ sense, the population on what is happening in the hills and how the process of gentrification by authorities is destroying their communities. For example, residents started to invite local and international artists to stay in the hills and collaborate in the social construction of discourses that can embody the community existence. Through participation in community life, the communities are able to collaboratively establish dialogical networks with other communities (in Chile and beyond), exporting their collective view of the hills that challenges the gentrified notion supplied by globalized commercial entities.

The map, residencies and workshops expose everyday resistance practices in these communities. They source creative tactics (Certeau, 1984) on how to resist the cleansing and expose their reality in their own terms. For instance, the map, graphically and colourfully, describes areas selected for privatization and creation of new businesses (urban cleansing). It points out the hills where there is structural poverty, i.e., no public transport, collection of rubbish and other basic community services. It brings visibility to the invisible. It invites the community to engage, describing the different resistance actions that can be taken to protect their existence from further displacements. It also points out where workshops and community-based initiatives take place, inviting people to join the valpo-sparkZ movement to act as a collective in order to protect their space and place of living.

Valpo's hill communities and their creative resistance initiatives provide an example of how organsparkZers can act together as collectives to create awareness of perceived precarity and launch subversive and imaginative initiatives that can contribute to socially transformed living. Furthermore, this case illustrates how daily creative resistance tactics can help to launch map campaigns that, instead of defying directly the political authorities, voice resistance that embodies their 'precarious' condition. In this way, by making their precarity visible, organsparkZers challenge the dominant narrative of social development in the city.

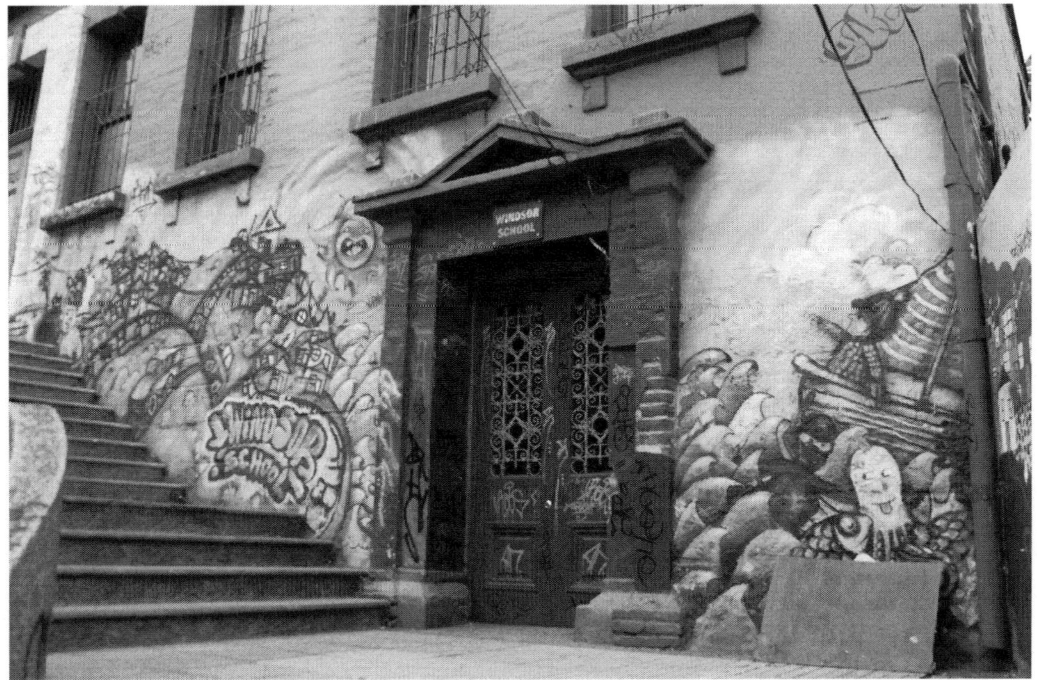

Figure 7.8: Concepción Hill graffiti art, Valparaíso, Chile, 2011. Courtesy of J. M. Imas.

Reflections on organsparkZ interventions

OrgansparkZ conceptually attempts to situate creative endeavours as forms of everyday resistance, dialogical imaginations and art-space initiatives that marginalized communities use in order to improve their living conditions. OrgansparkZ embodies the polyphony of voices that otherwise would not be heard by authorities that often ignore and neglect marginalized groups. Three examples of organsparkZ creative engagement in different parts of the world illustrate our argument. In Argentina we have shown how organsparkZ can initiate social change and transform working lives at the meso-level. Thousands of factory workers lost their livelihoods when businesses went bankrupt. Rather than surrendering to the crisis, workers creatively reimagined what the factories meant for the local communities by staging events and re-use spaces for social gatherings and art exhibitions. In Cape Town, South Africa, we illustrated how a third sector organization, faced with resource poverty and organizational closure, engaged in spontaneous street performance practices. SLC embraced dance as an alternative organizational practice to raise awareness of the organizational future. Here, we see organsparkZ initiatives that invite change through performances to support social causes. In our final example, from Valparaíso's hills in Chile, we show how a marginalized community engaged with art to resist gentrification and urban cleansing by drawing attention to their conditions of structural poverty and how they protect their place of living by resorting to arts-based activities. What these examples have in common is the use of creative strategies to overcome deep and challenging social-organizational uncertainty. These examples show a universal drive to survive and contest situations of resource-centred precarity.

References

Bakhtin, M. M. 1981. *Dialogic Imagination: Four Essays*, Austin, TX: University of Texas Press.

Bakhtin, M. M. 1984a. *Problems of Dostoevsky's Poetics*, Minneapolis, MN: University of Minnesota Press.

Bakhtin, M. M. 1984b. *Rabelais and His World*, Bloomington, IN: Indiana University Press.

Bakhtin, M. M. 1986. *Speech Genres and Other Late Essays*, trans. V. W. McGee, Austin, TX: University of Texas Press.

Banksy 2005. *Wall and Piece*, London: Century.

Bayat, A. 2000. 'From "dangerous classes" to "quiet rebels": Politics of the urban subaltern in the Global South', *International Sociology*, 15 (3), 533–557.

Bisama, A. 2014. 'Ardio Valparaíso', *Revista Anfibia*, http://revistaanfibia.com/cronica/ardio-la-pobreza/. Accessed 4 November 2014.

Bishop, C. 2012. *Artificial Hells: Participatory Art and the Politics of Spectatorship*, London: Verso.

Block, H. 2014. *Sanctioned & Unsanctioned Art in Public Space*, http://www.blockh.net/Block_H_publicspace.pdf. Accessed 5 December 2014.

Boal, A. 2000. *Theatre of the Oppressed*, London: Pluto Press.

Boje, D. 2001. *Narrative Methods For Organizational & Communication Research*, London: Sage.

Boje, D. 2008. *Storytelling Organizations*, London: Sage.

Bradley, W. and Esche, C. 2007. *Art and Social Change: A Critical Reader*, London: Tate Publishing in association with Afterall.

Butler, J. 2004. *Precarious Life: The Powers of Mourning and Violence*, London: Verso.

Butler, J. 2012. 'Precarious life, vulnerability, and the ethics of cohabitation', *Journal of Speculative Philosophy*, 26 (2), 134–151.

Certeau, M. de. 1984. *The Practice of Everyday Life*, trans. S. Rendall, Berkeley, CA: University of California Press.

Clegg, S. 1995. 'The rhythm of the saints', *Electronic Journal of Radical Organization Theory*, 1 (1), http://www.mngt.waikato.ac.nz/ejrot/Vol1_1/clegg.pdf. Accessed 15 October 2014.

Coyle, A. 2012. *Street Art: Berlin Project*, http://www.eftours.com/eLiterature/weShare2012-arianacoyle.pdf. Accessed 26 November 2014.

Daskalaki, M., Stara, A. and Imas, M. 2008. 'The parkour organization: Inhabitation of corporate spaces', *Culture & Organization*, 14 (1), 49–64.

Deleuze, G. and Guattari, F. 2003. *A Thousand Plateaus: Capitalism & Schizophrenia*, London: Continuum.

Escobar, A. 2007. 'Worlds and knowledges otherwise: The Latin American modernity/coloniality research programme', *Cultural Sudies*, 21 (2/3), 179–210.

Evans, A. 2009. 'The poetic streets of Valparaíso', *National Geographic Traveller*, November–December, 46–47.

Gardiner, M. 1992. *The Dialogics of Critique: M. M. Bakhtin and the Theory of Ideology*, London: Routledge.

Gieryn, T. F. 2000. 'A space for place in sociology', *Annual Review of Sociology*, 26, 463–496.

Ginzburg, C. 1993. 'Microhistory: Two or three things that I know about it', *Critical Inquiry*, 20 (1), 10–35.

Gracia, A. and Cavaliere, S. 2007. 'Repertorios en Fábrica. La Experiencia de Recuperación Fabril en Argentina 2000–2006', *Estudios Sociológicos*, 25 (73), 155–186.

Groys, B. 2014. 'On art activism', *E-flux*, 56 (June), 1–14.

Halsey, M. and Young, A. 2006. '"Our desires are ungovernable": Writing graffiti in urban space', *Theoretical Criminology*, 10 (3), 275–306.

Harvey, D. 2006. 'The political economy of public space'. In Low, S. and Smith, N. (Eds), *The Politics of Public Space*, New York, NY: Routledge, pp. 17–34.

Harvey, D. 2008. 'The Right to the City', *New Left Review*, 53 (September–October), 23–40.

Harvey, D. 2012. *Rebel Cities: From the Right to the City to the Urban Revolution*, London: Verso.

Heartney, E. 2012. 'Can art change lives?', *Art in America*, 100 (6), 67.

Imas, J. M. and Weston, A. 2012. 'From Harare to Rio de Janeiro: The Kukiya-favela organization of the excluded', *Organization*, 19 (2), 204–226.

Jackson, M. R. 2012. *Developing Artist-Driven Spaces in Marginalized Communities: Reflections and Implications for the Field*, Washington, DC: LINC, Urban Institute.

Jones, A. 2013. 'A tripartite conceptualisation of urban public space as a site for play: Evidence from South Bank, London', *Urban Geography*, 34 (8), 1144–1170.

Jovchelovitch, S. and Priego-Hernández, J. 2013. *Underground Sociabilities: Identity, Culture and Resistance in Rio de Janeiro's Favelas*, Paris: United Nations Educational, Scientific and Cultural Organization.

Kester, G. 2000. 'Dialogical aesthetics: A critical framework for Littoral Art', *Variant*, 9 (Winter), 1–12.

Kester, G. 2011. *The One and the Many: Contemporary Collaborative Art in a Global Context*, Durham, NC: Duke University Press.

Kosmala, K. and Imas, M. 2012. 'Narrating a story of Buenos Aires' *Fabricas Recuperadas*', *The International Journal of Management and Business*, 3 (1), 103–121.

Lavaca, J. 2004. *Sin Patrón: Fábricas y Empresas Recuperadas por sus Trabajadores: Una Historia, una Guía*, Buenos Aires: La Vaca Editora.

Long, D. 2014. 'Listen to the story: Banksy, Tyler the Creator, and the growing nihilistic mindset', *Journal of Hip-Hop Studies*, 1 (1), 81–121.

Lorenz, T. 2014. 'Chile cool: Art, music and graffiti in laid-back Valparaíso', *The Guardian*, 7 February, http://www.theguardian.com/travel/2014/feb/07/valparaiso-chile-culture-art-city. Accessed 15 March 2014.

Magnani, E. 2003. *El Cambio Silencioso. Empresas y Fábricas Recuperadas por los Trabajadores de la Argentina*, Buenos Aires: Prometeo.

Mouffe, C. 2007. 'Artistic activism and agonistic spaces', *Art & Research*, 1 (2), 1–5.

Neilson, B. and Rossiter, N. 2006. 'From precarity to precariousness and back again: Labour, life and unstable networks', *Variant*, 25 (Spring), 10–13.

Peteet, J. 1996. 'The writing on the walls: The graffiti of the intifada', *Cultural Anthropology*, 11 (2), 139–159.

Ressler, O. 2007. 'An ideal society creates itself: Venezuela and the Bolivarian process', *Art & Research: A Journal of Ideas, Contexts and Methods*, 1 (2), 1–3.

Richards, P., Kitching, B. and Blayney, S. 2014. *Southbank Undercroft: Cultural & Heritage Assessment Report*, London: Long Live Southbank.

Saitô, M. W. 2006. 'Engaging the public: Dialogical art and frameworks to collaborative environments', *Momentarium*, http://www.momentarium.org/research/collaboration.pdf. Accessed 17 March 2014.

Sánchez, A., Bosque, J. and Jiménez, C. 2009. 'Valparaíso: Su Geografía, Su Historia y Su Identidad Como Patrimonio de la Humanidad', *Estudios Geográficos*, LXX (266), 269–293.

Scheper-Hughes, N. 1993. *Death without Weeping: The Violence of Everyday Life in Brazil*, Berkeley, CA: University of California Press.

SLC 2013. *The You Decide Campaign*, http://www.lifechoices.co.za/news/you-decide-campaign-media-release. Accessed 14 December 2014.

SLC 2014a. *About Us*, http://www.lifechoices.co.za/. Accessed 14 December 2014.

SLC 2014b. *The 30 Stories in 30 Days Campaign*, http://www.lifechoices.co.za/media/voices-of-youth. Accessed 14 December 2014.

Stockland, E. 2004. 'Olodum, the revolt of the drums: A case-study of the communication strategies of Olodum from Bahia, Brazil', PhD thesis, Oslo: University of Olso.

Vinthagen, S. and Johansson, A. 2013. '"Everyday resistance": Exploration of a concept and its theories', *Resistance Studies Magazine*, 1 (1), 46.

Notes

1   We have decapitalized 'organsparkZ' in order to emphasize that we see this central concept associated with what Boje (2001) and Ginzburg (1993) describe as 'little people' – those who are deprived of their voice and rights in Capitalist society. Equally, it is not intended to become a grand discourse for the promotion of art (as consumption), but a reflection of how creative initiatives can contribute to giving voice and raising awareness about life in what can be perceived as precarious communities – those ostracized and deprived of a decent existence.

2   We are aware of the commercialization of street art, such as the work of graffiti artist Banksy. However, his – and the work of other street artists – still remains in defiance of the dominant social canons of society.

3   Although the campaign succeeded, we acknowledge that there are still ongoing challenges. In particular, there are tensions over who has the right to the city, as well as how public space in cities can be used. See http://www.llsb.com/ for further details.

4   See http://www.vincentmoon.com/ and http://en.blogotheque.net/ for more information.

5   Valpo is the name given to the city by locals.

6   Local art/creative organizations such as CRAC, Centro Comunitario Espacio Santa Ana (community centre), Radio Placeres, Movimiento de Trabajadores y Trabajadoras Clotario Blest, Revista Escáner Cultural and other individual local participants.
7   The critical map can be downloaded from the following website: http://www.iconoclasistas. net/wp-content/uploads/2014/07/map.jpg

Part III

Resisting: Opening Organizations, Altering Organizing

Chapter 8

Pockets of resistance: A look at the *Mbyá-Guarani* camps in Rio Grande do Sul, Brazil

Cristina Amélia Pereira de Carvalho and Fábio Freitas Schilling Marquesan

We were boundless before. Now, everything is forbidden. We are already unable to work the fields as we used to. We have settled in this small area that we are trying to get recognised by authorities. But if they don't, there will be nothing left for us. We need some guarantees that we can live here, being able to freely express our culture, traditions and pass it on to our children and grandchildren. The fact that we have no land that we can call ours, means that, we cannot fully manifest our culture (*nhandé rekó*).

Excerpt from a letter to government officials from the *Morros dos Cavalos*,
(Identification Report, 2002)

Introduction

Camps of indigenous *Mbyá-Guarani*[1] have emerged in small areas in different cities of Southern Brazil. These camps occupy spaces between fences of private properties and roads, or wastelands on the outskirts of towns. It can be argued that these camps emerged as the result of the Brazilian state's refusal to acknowledge and demarcate indigenous territories (Santana, 2012) and the struggle, suffered by indigenous people, to achieve such demarcation (Oliveira, 1998). Life in the camps came to symbolize local community's struggle to protect their rights.

Centuries ago, when violence and illegal occupation of indigenous land made the *Mbyá-Guarani* people escape to the interior of the American continent, invisibility became essential for their survival. In the 1980s, however, all of that changed with the process of re-democratization in Brazil.[2] Despite the new Federal Constitution's attempt to ensure indigenous peoples' civil and political rights, such as for the *Mbyá-Guarani*, the twentieth century saw a continuous rise in the violation of those rights and a growth of indigenous camps alongside highways at the periphery of cities and society.

The camps' visibility brought some attention to their plight with evidence of their current derelict state, at a time when land reform, as well as diversity, minority concerns and preservation of the environment have been put on the agenda and have begun being widely debated across Brazil (Neves, 2005). The visible excess of the camps presented itself as a social strategy to fight for the community's rights. In this chapter, we argue that these illegal occupations of urban areas of Brazil by the *Mbyá-Guarani* are strategic means for gaining visibility (to recover indigenous culture and lands) and to reclaim the constitutional rights. The *Mbyá-Guarani* camps have been growing, away from

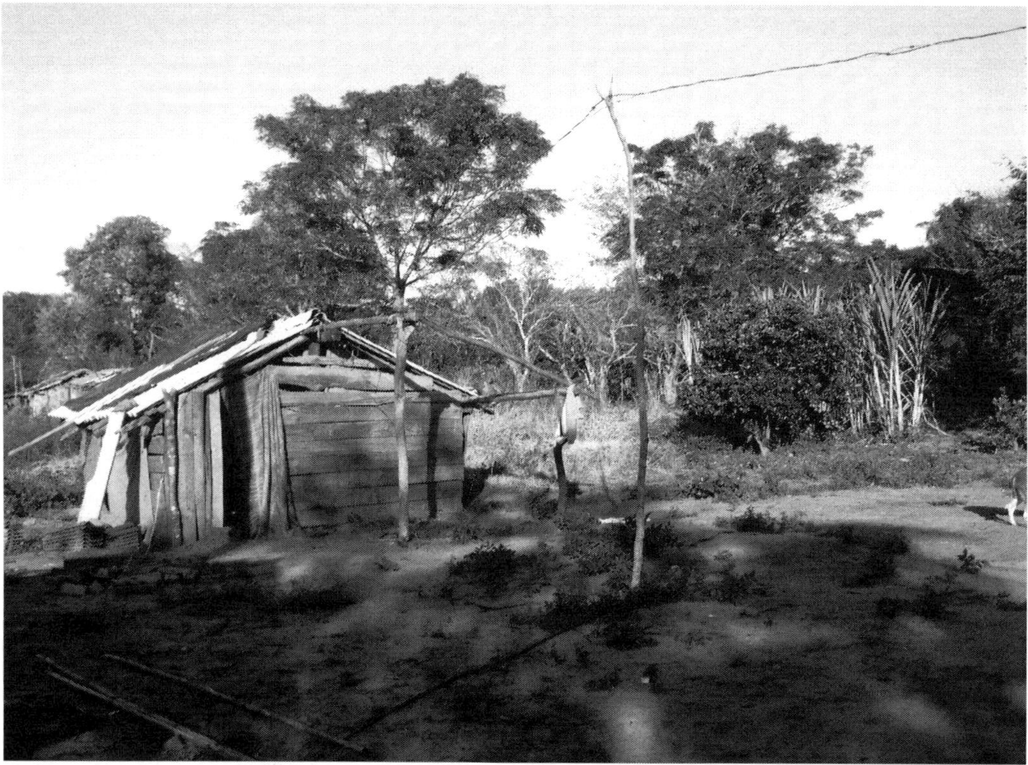

Figure 8.1: Shack in a camp on the roadside. Courtesy of Fábio Marquesan.

their ancestral homes, and surviving from selling traditional handicrafts, and from the support of social programs as well as individual citizens.

We begin the chapter by engaging with the historical foundations of the indigenous issues of Brazil since Colonial times, more than 500 years ago. We discuss the state's ethnocide towards indigenous people. Then, we go to explore the relationship between the concept of territory and the struggle for land and preservation of indigenous identity. Finally, we discuss the *Mbyá-Guarani* occupation, including strategies of resistance in the community's struggle for their constitutional rights.

Historical foundations of the indigenous issue in Brazil

The Brazilian indigenous issue is complex in terms of the temporal, spatial and symbolic scope of the problem. It arose more than 500 years ago in the wake of colonization, which resulted in the expulsion, subordination or annihilation of native peoples. These acts were perpetrated across the vast territory that came to be modern-day Brazil. This significantly impacted the immense cultural and symbolic diversity of the various peoples who inhabited the Southern region of the Americas. The two fundamental elements at the heart of the indigenous issue are the preservation of cultural identity and the struggle for their land.

The form that preservation of cultural identity takes may not be necessarily consensus-based. At the same time, this process represents a struggle for the survival of indigenous people. Brazilian indigenous people can be recognized by their cultural identities. These are preserved by 'maintaining the same organizational format, which prescribes a unified standard of interaction between members and non-members' of a certain indigenous group (Oliveira, 1998: 273). It is in this symbolic perpetuity and homogeneity that an ethnic group identifies itself. However, it is undeniable that 'many of the specificities that characterize indigenous peoples are the result of interaction with Colonizers' (Lima, 1995: 40). The different traditions and social organizations of native peoples emerged out of distinct dynamics throughout history; through interaction with Colonizers and other indigenous groups, as well as adaptation to the natural environments to which they were transferred. Over time, common habits, rituals, practices and values were alterred as a result of continuously changing social practices (Oliveira, 1998).

As such, although indigenous groups do not entirely abandon their identifying traits, their cultures and cultural identities are continuously transforming in a dialectical relationship between stability and change, continuity and alternation. These dialectical dynamics prevent ethnic groups from being perceived as having 'an immutable cultural essence, immune to the changes imposed by different regimes of power over time' (Lima, 1995: 40).

An example of such kind of transformation has also occurred in Rio Grande do Sul, causing significant cultural and genetic miscegenation, the existence of which, according to Catafesto de Souza (2009), is denied by the region's white elite in an attempt to conceal any connection with an indigenous background. This ethnic mixing eventually modified specific cultural elements (Oliveira, 1998) or the cultural essences of indigenous peoples (Lima, 1995).

The idea that this miscegenation made people less indigenous (Catafesto de Souza, 2002) is another facet of the debate over the meaning of 'preserving indigenous cultural identity'. The dispute lies in the possibility of a group identifying itself as different from others and, as a result, being officially recognized by the state as an indigenous group. According to Oliveira (1998: 281), 'any individual descended from a Pre-Columbian people, or any community distinguished from national society by its specific categories and channels of interaction, and claims to be "indigenous"' should be recognized as such'. Despite much disagreement, the government's affirmative action and recent policies included the possibility of citizens and groups declaring that they belong to a certain indigenous community.

The preservation of indigenous identity, and even the very definition of what indigenous identity is and who establishes it, is the subject of ongoing debate at the heart of the indigenous issue. Another central element is the previously mentioned struggle for land. This is a political process by which the state recognizes the right to indigenous communities over part of the national territory. However, as with the defining traits of indigenous identity, matters relating to the ownership and use of land have also changed in light of the fluidity of land borders.

The people of the Plata River basin 'lived under frequent displacements within wide traditional territories, constrained only by the territoriality of their neighbours from other cultural ancestries' (Catafesto de Souza, 2009: 277). This territorial autochthonous lifestyle placed the inhabitants in instant rebellion against the delimitation of spaces imposed by colonizing forces. Archaeological evidence has strengthened anthropological 'indications' that territorial distribution was based on environmental, ecological and cultural factors that were not limited by official, political and administrative boundaries. For the *Mbyá-Guarani* people, villages are an essential part of living according to their laws and habits. They also preserve the privacy of the group and, in the view of the *Mbyá-Guarani*, should contain protected natural resources to ensure their livelihood.

Colonization led to geographic, political and cultural (re)structuring of land. This meant that the remaining indigenous peoples went 'from independence (or interdependence) to units within broader social circuits' (Lima, 1995: 54). This process was governed by 'conversion strategies and the eradication of cultural differences' (Lima, 1995: 59), subjugating native people to successive reorganizations based on social stratification systems they did not understand.

In order to understand the current situation of indigenous communities in Southern Brazil, it is important to consider the territoriality of their original societies. In doing so, it becomes evident that their territorial patterns 'are incompatible with the modern geopolitical criteria established in the Plata River basin from the nineteenth century onwards' (Catafesto de Souza, 2009: 278). Historically, Brazilian indigenous policy has sought to dominate nomadic people (Lima, 1995) and break their resistance, removing them from their native lands and settling them in designated areas defined by a succession of national administrations. This weakened indigenous resistance by eroding key elements of groups' identities and facilitated agricultural expansion by expelling them from their traditional lands, which were rich in natural resources.

For Lima (1995), the height of this movement came with the creation, across the country, of *indigenous reserves*. These were government-allocated tracts of land on which indigenous communities could settle and maintain their livelihoods. However, these areas are also 'territories that have been established with the expenses of an alienation process of internal dynamics of native communities, and are part of a system of land appropriation and control of the State' (Lima, 1995: 76). Therefore, governments imposed further regulation on access to and use of land while mediating its commercialization through registration systems and thus determining its use by the means of property ownership and institutionalized land records. The fragmentation of indigenous villages demonstrates the extent to which this demarcation is determined by agricultural boundaries, roads and even environmental preservation areas.

Indigenism, past and present

Brazil has undergone significant changes since the Revolution of 1930 led by Getulio Vargas. The Provisional Government (until 1934), and then the *Estado Novo* (New State) (until 1945), brought times of political repression but also civil and labour achievements that remain to this day, such as compulsory primary education, women's suffrage, a 48-hour work week as well as entitlement for a paid annual leave.

In 1945, Vargas was overthrown by a *coup d'état*. He returned in 1951, this time through the national election. From this moment on, Vargas initiated the New Republic period, which was marked by a developmental stage illustrated by the creation of the Petrobras corporation and a boost to domestic industry. After Varga's suicide in 1955, Juscelino Kubitschek was elected as president. Known as 'the president who built Brasilia,' he continued the country's developmental stage.

In 1964, a new coup began a long dictatorial period during which individual liberties and the political organization of society were suppressed. It also coincided with a phase of economic growth known as the 'Brazilian miracle.' This dictatorial period ended in 1985. From that year on, Brazil went through a process of political democratization that included the direct election of governors, the neo-liberal economic reform in the 1990s, and the democratic strengthening in the first decade of the twenty-first century.

This brief summary of the country's recent history shows how these complex political, economic and social realities have changed. However, reviewing these details suggests a question: what were the changes regarding indigenous issues during this period?

The statement: 'the Brazilian government's ethnocide attitude towards indigenous peoples has been perfected by applying so-called indigenous policies' (Catafesto de Souza, 2002: 26) indicates that advancements in the rights of indigenous people have not kept pace with the country's political changes. Although the political organization of Brazilian civil society has gained strength in recent decades, the government-centred so-called 'civilizing' initiatives for indigenous people across Brazil appear to continue to harm these native populations.

With their lands administered by white interlopers employing foreign dominant logic, and having been alienated from the connection to nature that is so essential to native communities, the Brazilian indigenous people have been exploited, treated as inferior and stripped of their ancestral roots. This process has happened with the political and managerial support of the National Indian Foundation (FUNAI).[3]

Throughout their history, both the Indian Protection Service (SPI)[4] and FUNAI have implemented income generation and production capacity programs that have exhausted many of the natural resources of the indigenous land they administered. With no regard for the traditional practices or indigenous, ancestral way of life, the government policies implemented by these institutions have failed because they disregarded the specific cultural references and the land rights of these people (Catafesto de Souza, 2009).

Within this framework, the culture and organizational logic of the indigenous communities was disregarded and replaced by models that were alien to the native way of life. This process included the intensive use of the land and all its natural resources to the point of exhaustion, enforced discipline and the subjugation of native people to forms of labour inherent to Western, Capitalist-dominant production. According to Tedesco and Marcon (1994), these political practices, which claim the 'noble purpose' of generating income for native communities but do so by imposing commercial imperatives on indigenous production, were the cornerstone of FUNAI's initiatives in the 1970s. These very initiatives aimed to transform indigenous people into businessmen and their reserves into rural companies, using production models incompatible with their way of life.

Traces of these initiatives are still visible today in the Brazilian government's inadequate policies regarding indigenous people, although it is now 40 years since these initiatives were implemented. Aided by the emergence of so-called cultural economics, the idea of turning Brazilian indigenous communities into entrepreneurial units has gained a new dimension: the production of handicrafts.

Indigenous villages, but particularly camps along highways, have become handicraft production sites, and cities are attractive markets for groups seeking to survive by selling their traditional crafts.

Thus, the *Mbyá-Guarani* families in the precarious camps bordering highways of Rio Grande do Sul survive by selling these handicrafts on the roadside or in the markets and streets of cities like Porto Alegre. Deprived of the land that would allow them to live according to their traditions (*nhandé rekó*),[5] the *Mbyá-Guarani* have lost the ability to determine their own fate. They seek to recover their autonomy by participating in economic projects such as handicraft production in order to generate income.

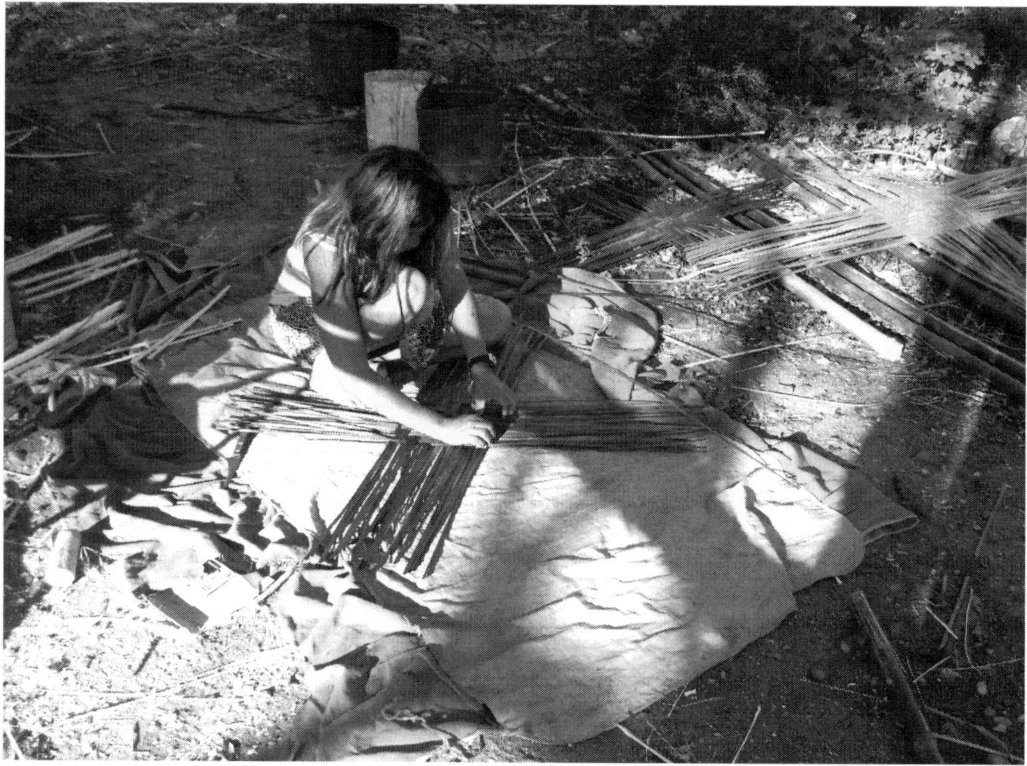

Figure 8.2: *Mbyá-Guarani* child making crafts. Courtesy of Fábio Marquesan.

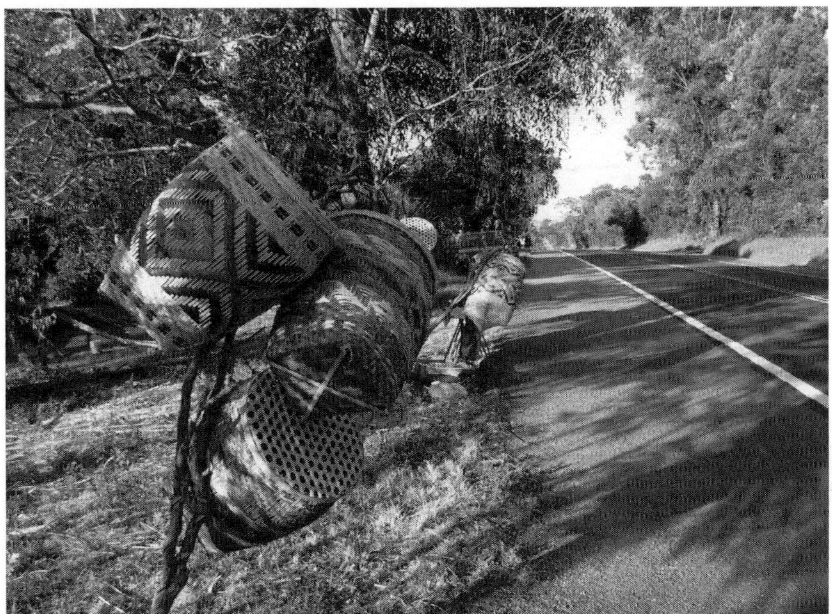

Figure 8.3: *Mbyá-Guarani* crafts exposed on the roadside. Courtesy of Fábio Marquesan.

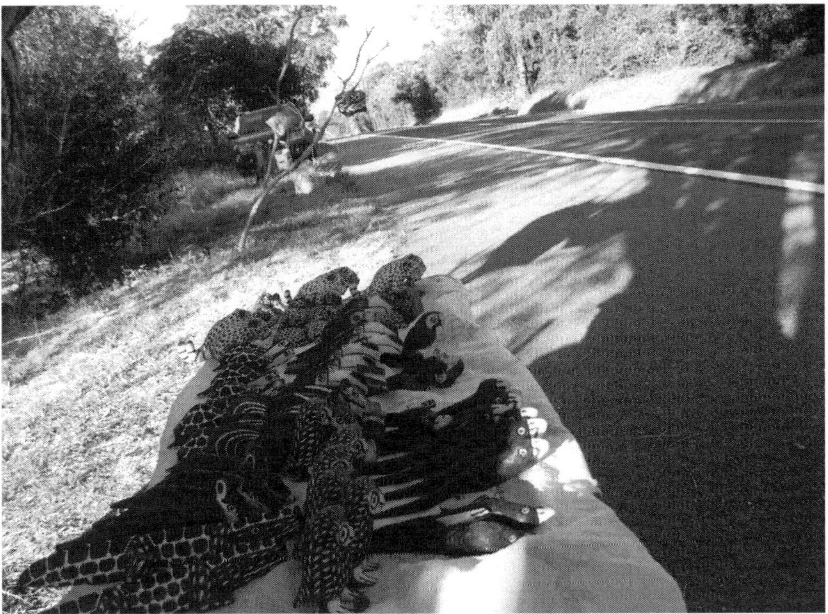

Figure 8.4: *Mbyá-Guarani* crafts exposed on the roadside. Courtesy of Fábio Marquesan.

Territory: The struggle for land and identity preservation

The establishment of a territory involves the appropriation of a particular space by social actors. This is regulated via a political game defined by relationships of power played out in the social arena. Territory is not something static (Saquet, 2009); it involves interaction with power, politics, movement, stability, flow, change, territorialization, de-territorialization, re-territorialization and territoriality. In other words, territory is a political space where power is exercised and cultural and economic interactions are defined. Therefore, in addition to being a physical space, territory is the product and result of temporal, spatial and social interactions that influence the struggle to preserve cultural identity and, specifically, the ownership and use of the land by native peoples.

Thus, the social construction of a territory involves overlapping political, cultural and economic dimensions that form a mixture of interdependent yet inseparable elements. Regardless of the elements within the concept, 'territory' is 'space that is defined and spatially delimited based on relations of power and therefore works as a referential substrate' (Catafesto de Souza, 2009: 59). In other words, territory does not exist without a material basis.

The reality and challenge faced by indigenous people is in 'the desire or need to defend or conquer territories, which requires access to resources by capturing strategic positions and/ or maintaining ways of life and control over the material symbols of an identity' (Catafesto de Souza, 2009: 64). Plein et al. (2009: 52) introduce additional possibilities when stating that 'territorial boundaries are not immutable, but change according to the strategies and resources used to control and delimit the space.' Thus, 'an area can be considered a territory in a certain period and not in another, depending on the interests of those who control it.' Territory can be created and undone in a cycle, 'hardly leaving marks on the landscape'; however, although inseparable from its substrate material, both are not synonymous. In short, 'the results of social relationships are what give territory life and sequence' (Plein et al., 2009: 51). As such, eradicating the nomadism of Amerindian peoples would be 'to utterly divest them of a cultural and political existence separate from the geographic space' (specific territoriality), forcing them to recognize an alien territory imposed on them by outside forces (Lima, 1995: 197).

This illustrates the tactics of attraction and 'pacification' promoted by expeditions under *the great siege of peace*.[6] These tactics always involved freeing up large new areas for agricultural and other predominantly private endeavours. On one hand, the siege confined native ethnic communities to areas controlled by the heads of indigenous posts[7]; and on the other, it gave government authorities access to land that was previously inhabited only by autochthonous populations.

The immobilization of the formerly nomadic *Mbyá-Guarani* people was protected by several legal instruments. The aim was 'circumscribing tracts of land for the establishment of native populations' and to 'add them to the stock of available land under state control' (Lima, 1995: 197); thereby, the remaining land would be made available for private occupation initiatives.

In order to understand the dynamics of the struggle among the *Mbyá-Guarani*, we will consider 'territory' to be a changeable area within a variable geographical region. These areas are demarcated based on relations of power using seemingly contradictory and regressive strategies.

Mbyá-Guarani's territoriality as a resistance strategy

The mobility of *Mbyá-Guarani* is not just a cultural trait of nomadic or semi-nomadic people, but a resistance strategy against institutional violence. *Mbyá-Guarani* groups have fled from Rio Grande do Sul to the interior of the American continent since the Jesuit wars of the eighteenth century. Lugon (1976) cites 1768 as the year in which the last of the *Mbyá-Guarani*'s resistance forces engaged in armed conflict with the combined military contingents of Portugal and Spain – a union that was forged to defeat the indigenous society that dated back to the first Jesuits who settled in the *Missões*, the region of Rio Grande do Sul state, in around 1610.

As the colonization and land occupation process to demarcate the country's borders progressed on land previously occupied by the *Mbyá-Guarani*, 'they retreated to the forests in an attempt to hide from the *encomienderos*[8] and Western civilization' (Madeira, 2009). According to Garlet and Assis (2009), the escapes were an effective strategy that allowed them to evade and resist attempts of assimilation and integration. Garlet and Assis also observed that the current form of spatial mobility among the *Mbyá-Guarani* is not just a migratory predisposition – 'although there is a cultural tendency toward this dynamic, it was exaggerated and intensified by interethnic contact' (2009: 36).

The escape strategy of indigenous people, particularly the *Mbyá-Guarani*, who fled the brutality of Portuguese colonization after the abolition of the Jesuit reductions, contributed to the idea that native people had disappeared from Rio Grande do Sul.[9] This idea, however, masks an unmistakable desire to 'whiten' Southern Brazil and eradicate any trace of indigenous origins and miscegenation.

The slow and gradual colonization process varied between the brutal annihilation of native people and their exploitation for labour by force. In this respect, Catafesto de Souza states:

> In the region of the Plata River basin, many native communities managed to survive in territorial enclaves and natural refuges or wandered, detribalized and *invisible*, through the colonial domain. They survived by establishing asymmetrical social alliances with the agents of European invaders and their heirs.
>
> (2009: 279, emphasis added)

In short, the dispersion of the indigenous *Mbyá-Guarani* and their detribalization did not necessarily result in their physical or cultural extinction, nor did they 'forget their traditional territoriality, despite its highly fractured status' (Catafesto de Souza, 2009: 279).

Nevertheless, this retreat to multiple and dispersed territories made the *Mbyá-Guarani* invisible to the colonizing Western society.

However, although their initial retreat had offered protective invisibility and preserved the existence of the *Mbyá-Guarani* people, their current return to visibility has coincided with the appearance of roadside camps. These spaces are located along highways between the vehicular traffic and property fences. In these small and highly precarious spaces, the *Mbyá-Guarani* people struggle to escape invisibility, surviving by selling their handicrafts. Assis and Garlet report that the *Mbyá-Guarani*'s strategy has changed:

The *Mbyá* realized that by making themselves visible and accessible they would gain a greater advantage in interethnic relations, particularly with respect to accessing geographic spaces suited to their culture. This also resulted in their visibility in censuses conducted by independent researchers as well as official organizations and NGOs.

(2004: 40)

Today, when reclaiming a territory, the *Mbyá-Guarani* primarily assess the area's environmental condition and its layout, instead of relying on anthropological or archaeological records indicating areas inhabited by their ancestors. These methods, as well as the form of land use in neighbouring properties and the extent to which natural resources have been exhausted, can provide indications of the feasibility of surviving according to *nhandé rekó*.

Strategic territorial occupation and indigenous visibility in precarious camps along highways coincided with Brazilian re-democratization in 1985. Assis and Garlet (2004: 40) report that during this period, economic recession in Argentina also led to 'a substantial number of large *Mbyá* families entering Rio Grande do Sul in pursuit of better living conditions.' This migration flow has been intensified since 1988, when the new Brazilian Constitution was enacted, formally expanding the rights of indigenous people. Thus, the *Mbyá-Guarani* population has increased in numbers in Southern Brazil.

Although the slow reversal of the diaspora that has occurred since suggests that re-democratization also brought new possibilities for indigenous people, their camps continue to be repressed by the state. An example of this is the forced eviction, in 2008, of five *Mbyá-Guarani* families from a camp bordering the *Estrada do Conde* (Count Road) between the cities of Guaíba and Eldorado do Sul. Heurich et al. (2010) report that the families were approached by a bailiff, military police officers, the vice-mayor of Eldorado do Sul, the State Prosecutor and several other agents concerned about the families' presence in the area. There were no representatives from FUNAI or the Federal Prosecutor's Office present to defend, protect or support the indigenous families. The group had occupied public land belonging to the National Department of Transport Infrastructure and, although it was not private property, their leader was handcuffed and placed under arrest, and the children were taken to the city shelter.[10]

The example above demonstrates that the occupation of such areas, squeezed between tarred roads and fences without even the most basic sanitary conditions, is a resistance strategy that combines visibility and poverty. Thus, we view the creation of visible derelict spaces as a form of struggle that uses extreme poverty as a tool. It is a form of conscious precariousness, created by a group of individuals who use their vulnerability as a weapon.

Mbyá-Guarani's camps as a struggle strategy

Until the arrival of the Colonizers, the *Mbyá-Guarani* people moved across the South American continent as a nomadic tribe who knew no borders. This enabled them to resist and survive enslavement. The religious conversion of the Guarani people by the Jesuits in the sixteenth century conflicted with the enslavement ideology of the Portuguese empire. However, the *Mbyá-Guarani* in the Jesuit reductions (or missions) were submitted by force to Christianization. The Jesuits taught them the discipline required for work, plant extraction and agriculture, removing them from their nomadic lifestyle.

Territorial disputes between Spain and Portugal, and interference from the Vatican, led to war before the new borders were defined by the Treaty of Madrid[11] (which replaced the Treaty of Tordesillas).[12] As a result, the Jesuits were expelled from Brazil and the *Mbyá-Guarani* were massacred. Survivors were enslaved or absorbed by society (Assis and Garlet, 2004), while others fled to the interior of the continent.

With the borders pacified, an agricultural boom demanded new lands, thus requiring the expansion of the occupied borders (Carini, 2005). This naturally led to conflict with the *Mbyá-Guarani*, who inhabited the fields and forests of Rio Grande do Sul. With the advent of European immigration, the *Mbyá-Guarani* faced a new opponent in the region: the settlers who appropriated land for cultivation. As a result, in order to free up more space for colonial occupation, the state government created the state's first indigenous reserves in the early nineteenth century (Kliemann, 1986; Carini, 2005). Native communities were confined to controlled areas, leaving large territories available to be freely exploited for agriculture, mainly by Italians and Germans who immigrated to Rio Grande do Sul. Confined to small spaces, deprived of the abundant natural resources needed to preserve the *nhandé rekó*, the *Mbyá-Guarani* were now harassed by settlers, who appropriated their land without offering any form of compensation (Carini, 2005).

The situation worsened in the early 1960s, when the state government placed hundreds of settler families onto indigenous land in the north of Rio Grande do Sul confining the native people to an even smaller reserve without natural resources. This reflected the government's strategy regarding the indigenous issue: confining native communities to remote, invisible reserves far from the rest of Brazilian society.

As previously mentioned, re-democratization was followed by the emergence of precarious indigenous camps that remain on the margins of society to this day. These spaces marked the return of indigenous people who had taken refuge in the Brazilian countryside. With the re-democratization of the country, they began to view the strategy of remaining in the camps as a more effective means of gaining visibility and reclaiming their constitutional rights.

The camps are located in risky areas: along busy highways, where individuals are often run over, or on the outskirts of cities, where the communities live in abject poverty. The precarious living conditions include a lack of the minimum necessary infrastructure for maintaining the livelihood of a community unable to live in harmony with nature. In many cases, there is no drinking water, electricity or basic sanitation, and self-sustaining cultivation opportunities are limited by the small space and poor soil quality. For example, at the *Arroio Divisa*, a camp near the city of Porto Alegre, the drinking water of the Mbyá-Guarani inhabitants is the runoff from irrigated rice plantations, sometimes contaminated with waste and toxic substances (Santana, 2012). The shelters, which consist largely of tents made from plastic sheeting and improvised materials, do not offer adequate protection from the elements in a region where temperatures soar during summer and fall to freezing in the winter. In fact, deaths are common among children and the elderly during the harsh winters of Southern Brazil (Balbueno, 2012).

Malnutrition is another visible trademark of indigenous camps. Some communities receive parcels of staple food (*cesta básica*)[13] from FUNAI, but the haphazard nature of these donations does nothing to resolve their poor nutrition. In the small spaces within camps, the *Mbyá-Guarani* try to cultivate cassava, pumpkin and corn, but they cannot always meet the needs of the group. As a result, the main source of income for the *Guarani* natives living in the precarious indigenous camps comes from the sale of handicrafts. This is an important part of preserving their identity as indigenous people, both in their own eyes and on the part of the public that buys these items.

These potential customers are also targeted by the indigenous resistance strategy of exposing the precarious life conditions in the camps. The visible poverty of native communities provokes discomfort and unease in a society that espouses cultural diversity and the inclusion of marginalized social groups.

Final comments on an ongoing struggle

Despite the visibility of the *Mbyá-Guarani*'s camps in Southern Brazil, their struggle is far from over. Many families are still living along highways or at the outskirts of *gaucho*[14] cities in what can be described as a strategy of 'patient and silent resistance' (Santana, 2012: 8). Their aim is to publicly expose their precarious living conditions, including those relating to education and sanitation, and those arrangements that are life-threatening – especially for children, women and the elderly – causing indignation and appealing to individuals' consciences. Thus, they intend to press the political agenda of a government that holds the country up as an example of the eradication of poverty, social inclusion and respect for diversity.

The idea behind the *Mbyá-Guarani*'s resistance is that only human groups subjected to a history of hardships and humiliations could bear to make their own misery an instrument of struggle. That is how the *Mbyá-Guarani* people have been received by the new civil and political democracy in Brazil. For Brazilian indigenous people, democracy is synonymous with the opportunity to make their misery public. The camps were formed as territories of resistance through which native groups reach the consciousness of white society and try to influence governments' agendas. This influence is only made possible through the political embarrassment 'imposed' upon democratic governments regarding the indigenous issue.

We cannot conclude that life in the camps is a choice made by indigenous groups, even if their traditional semi-nomadic strategies were a justification. This way of life is a result of the occupation model of their native land and the imposition of state policies that do not provide reasonable options for native people. According to Liebgott and Bonin 'living on small tracts of land is not suited to communities that consider land as their source of life, their reestablishment of bonds with their ancestors and a celebration of life' (2010: 11).

Yet, in a demonstration of incredible survivability and resistance, indigenous people forced to live in small and precarious camps, dwelling in situations of risk for decades, have made their own precariousness a legitimate strategy of resistance that cannot be underestimated.

References

Assis, V. S. de and Garlet, I. J. 2004. 'Análise Sobre as Populações Guarani Contemporâneas: Demografia, Espacialidade e Questões Fundiárias', *Revista de Indias*, LXIV (230), 35–54.

Azevedo, M., Brand, A., Heck, E., Pereira, L. M., Melià, B. Guarani Retã 2008. *Povos Guarani na fronteira Argentina, Brasil e Paraguai*, São Paulo: CTI – Centro de Trabalho Indigenista, http://pib.socioambiental.org/files/file/PIB_institucional/caderno_guarani_%20portugues.pdf. Accessed 10 April 2013.

Balbueno, R. 2012. 'Inaugurada Aldeia Guarani em Santa Maria', *Notícias Sedufsm*, Seção Sindical dos Docentes da UFSM Universidade Federal de Santa Maria, http://www.sedufsm.org.br/index.php?secao=noticias&id=1035. Accessed 27 March 2013.

Carini, J. J. 2005. *Estado, Indios e Colonos: O Conflito na Reserva Indígena de Serrinha, Norte do Rio Grande do Sul*, Passo Fundo: UPF.

Catafesto de Souza, J. O. 2002. 'A Construção de Políticas Públicas Diferenciadas às Comunidades Indígenas do Rio Grande do Sul: O Caso dos Kaingang'. In Schwingel, L. R. (Ed.), *Povos Indígenas e Políticas Públicas da Assistência Social no Rio Grande do Sul: Subsídios para a Construção de Políticas Públicas Diferenciadas às Comunidades Kaingang e Guarani*, Porto Alegre: Secretaria do Trabalho, Cidadania e Assistência Social.

Catafesto de Souza, J. O. 2009. 'Um Salto do Passado para o Futuro: As Comunidades Indígenas e os Direitos Originários no Rio Grande do Sul'. In da Silva, G. F., Penna, R. and Carneiro, L. C. (Eds), *RS Índio: Cartografias sobre a Produção do Conhecimento*, Porto Alegre: Edipucrs.

Garlet, I. J. and Assis, V. S. de 2009. 'Desterritorialização e Reterritorialização: A Compreensão do Território Mbyá-Guarani Através das Fontes Históricas', *Fronteiras*, 11 (19), 15–46.

Heurich, G. O., Pradella, L. G. S., Fagundes, L. F. C., Huyer, B. N., Volk, M. P. and Marques, R. P. 2010. 'Presenças Impensáveis: Violência Estatal contra Famílias Guarani no Sul do Brasil'. In Assembleia Legislativa do Estado do Rio Grande do Sul, Comissão de Cidadania e Direitos Humanos (Eds), *Coletivos Guarani no Rio Grande do Sul: Territorialidade, Interetnicidade, Sobreposições e Direitos Específicos*, Porto Alegre: ALRS/CCDH.

Identification Report 2002. *Relatório circunstanciado de identificação e delimitação da Terra Indígena Morro dos Cavalos*, http://pib.socioambiental.org/pt/povo/guarani-mbya/1292. Accessed 23 April 2013.

Kliemann, L. H. S. 1986. *RS Terra e Poder: História da Questão Agrária*, Porto Alegre: Mercado Aberto.

Liebgott, R. and Bonin, I. 2010. 'O Contínuo Caminhar Guarani', *Revista do Instituto Humanitas Unisinos (Universidade do Vale do Rio dos Sinos)*, X (331), 9–14.

Lima, A. C. S. 1995. *Um Grande Cerco de Paz: Poder Tutelar, Indianidade e Formação do Estado no Brasil*, Petrópolis: Vozes.

Lugon, C. 1976. *A República Comunista Cristã dos Guaranis: 1610/1768* (2nd ed.), Rio de Janeiro: Paz e Terra.

Madeira, R. M. 2009. 'Ser Guarani, Ser Ambiente'. In da Silva, G. F., Penna, R. and Carneiro, L. C. (Eds), *RS Índio: Cartografias sobre a Produção do Conhecimento*, Porto Alegre: Edipucrs.

Neves, L. M. W. 2005. 'A Sociedade Civil Como Espaço Estratégico de Difusão da Nova Pedagogia da Hegemonia'. In Neves, L. M. W. (Ed.), *A Nova Pedagogia da Hegemonia: Estratégias do Capital para Educar o Consenso*, São Paulo: Xamã.

Oliveira, F. 1998. *Indigenismo e Territorialização: Poderes, Rotinas e Saberes Coloniais no Brasil Contemporâneo*, Rio de Janeiro: Contracapa.

Plein, I., Farias, F. R., Plein, C. and Mondardo, M. L. 2009. 'Território e Territorialidade na Perspectiva de Robert David Sack'. In Saquet, M. A. and Souza, E. B. C. de (Eds), *Leituras do Conceito de Território e de Processos Espaciais*, São Paulo: Expressão Popular.

Santana, R. 2012. 'À Margem: Os Acampamentos Indígenas no Rio Grande do Sul', *Porantim: Em defesa da causa indígena*, XXXV (345), 8–9.

Saquet, M. A. 2009. 'Por uma Abordagem Territorial'. In Saquet, M. A. and Souza, E. B. C. de (Eds), *Leituras do Conceito de Território e de Processos Espaciais*, São Paulo: Expressão Popular.

Souza, M. L. de 2009. 'Território da Divergência (e da Confusão): Em Torno das Imprecisas Fronteiras de um Conceito Fundamental'. In Saquet, M. A. and Sposito, E. S. (Eds), *Territórios e Territorialidades: Teorias, Processos e Conflitos*, São Paulo: Expressão Popular.

Tedesco, J. C. and Marcon, T. 1994. 'As Transformações na Agricultura e as Terras Indígenas'. In Marcon, T. (Ed.), *História e Cultura Kaingang no Sul do Brasil*, Passo Fundo: UPF.

Notes

1   The *Mbyá-Guarani* people are a branch of the Guarani nation, the largest indigenous nation of the South American continent. They live in a vast area including the coast of Brazil, the Chaco region in Paraguay, north-western Argentina, and eastern Bolivia. According to current estimations, a population of about 100,000 individuals is distributed in 500 villages or camps (Azevedo et al., 2008).

2   This period of Brazilian history began in 1985 – which marks the end of the military regime that had ruled the country since 1964 – and extended until 1990. It was characterized by the restoration of elected civilian governments and the adoption of Brazil's current constitution in 1988 that completed the reestablishment of democratic institutions in the country.

3   The National Indian Foundation (FUNAI) is an agency of the Brazilian Ministry of Justice, created in 1967, responsible for establishing and executing indigenous policies.

4   The Indian Protection Service (SPI), FUNAI's predecessor, was created in 1918 to guide the adaptation and integration of indigenous people into the national economy, which included the foundation of agricultural colonies using workforces resulting from official expeditions through Brazilian forests. This was done in order to increase the industrial and agricultural output of indigenous stations by introducing new production methods.

5   *Nhandé [Ñandé] Rekó* is the name given, in Guarani language, to the specific way of life lived by this people. It includes things like the cultural system, the spoken language and the way they interact with other people as well as the way they interact with the natural environment.

6   The expression 'the great siege of peace' is an allusion to the historical survey conducted by the anthropologist Antonio Carlos de Souza Lima, titled *Um grande cerco de paz: poder tutelar, indianidade e formação do Estado no Brasil* (in English, 'A great siege of peace: tutelary power, the indigenous and the formation of the State in Brazil'), in which he discusses the intense and extensive positivist Rondonian harassment, a military technique using pressure and sustained surveillance to restrict freedom of movement, cut off supply and curb independent reproduction (without directly attacking the inhabitants). The main figure in this siege was the positivist Cândido Rondon – a Brazilian military officer famous for his expeditions in the centre of the country and the Amazon Rainforest.

7   Indigenous centralization areas aimed to concentrate large contingents of indigenous people into small areas in order to free up as much land as possible for agriculture.

8   The *encomiendas* were a system of exploiting the land, used primarily for the extraction of yerba mate, in which a 'master' (*encomiendero*) was responsible for indoctrinating the natives, thereby ensuring their exploitation as a workforce.

9   Jesuit reductions (or missions) were settlements organized by Jesuits in South America for indigenous people during the seventeenth and eighteenth centuries. It was a strategy for occupying the territory by Christianizing the indigenous people and then taxing and ruling them according to dictates of the Spanish empire.

10   The National Department of Transport Infrastructure (DNIT) is part of the Brazilian Ministry of Transport and is responsible for building and maintaining the country's roads.

11   In 1750, this treaty established new borders between Spanish and Portuguese empires in South America. Specifically, it settled the exchange of the city of *Colonia del Sacramento* (in what is now Uruguay), which was the property of the Portuguese empire at that time, for the 'region of missions' (in what is now a part of Rio Grande do Sul state, Brazil) that was under Spanish dominion.

12   This is an international treaty signed in 1494 that aimed to divide the newly discovered lands, mainly those in America, between the realms of Portugal and Spain.

13   A *cesta básica* is a parcel of staple foods essential for the survival of a family during the month. It generally contains foodstuffs, personal hygiene items and domestic cleaning products.

14   This is a name given to the inhabitants of the rural pampas' regions of Uruguay, Argentina and Rio Grande do Sul (Brazil).

Chapter 9

Fábricas Recuperadas in Brazil: Contextual experiences

Jacob Carlos Lima, Aline Suelen Pires and Fernando Ramalho Martins

Introduction

This chapter discusses five examples of *Fábricas Recuperadas* and cooperatives in Brazil, focusing on their origins, development, difficulties and dilemmas. The cases presented here represent diverse Brazilian regions and industrial sectors, varying from metallurgy to canvas textile production. The term *Fábricas Recuperadas* started to be used after the Argentine crisis of 2000, in which numerous factories and businesses were occupied by workers who had to self-manage and to claim their collective ownership in order to keep their jobs.[1] In Brazil, a similar process began in the 1980s and was restricted to individual cases, also known as factory-cooperatives (Lima, 2001), or simply cooperatives. In many cases the cooperatives functioned like regular businesses and it was estimated there were around 100 of them by 2007.[2]

At the end of the 1980s, along with economic changes that occurred in Brazil, including the internationalization of policies and the end of industrial protectionism, a great number of factories entered into bankruptcy. In addition, technological and organizational changes contributed to the high level of unemployment that persisted through the following decades.[3] In order to tackle the unemployment problem, a series of factory recovery processes took place, followed by the transformation of those factories into worker's cooperatives. These processes were encouraged by NGOs connected to the trade union movement. At the end of 1990s, the main Brazilian labour confederation, CUT, opened its Solidarity Development Agency in order to facilitate self-management experiences (Lima, 2014; ANTEAG, 2000; Singer and Souza, 2000).

Unlike the Argentinean case of *Fábricas Recuperadas*, however, Brazilian recovery experiences did not manifest as a popular movement and never had back-up support from the trade unions. The Solidarity Economy Movement that originated in the factories during this period occupied a relatively restricted space in comparison to other proposals for social inclusion of workers who were excluded from the labour market. In subsequent years, the economic recovery that took place during Lula's government, i.e. from 2003 onwards, cases of *Fábricas Recuperadas* in Brazil became even more sporadic. Although the factory recovery movement appeared initially as a reaction to unemployment and to precariousness forged by neo-liberal political-economic changes, the self-management cause did not reach a major acceptance among workers, who were more committed to the claim for social rights linked to wage relations.[4] Moreover, even though companies encouraged dismissed workers to organize themselves into cooperatives, they continued to exploit the workers by means of outsourcing and self-management. Therefore, *Fábricas Recuperadas* movement was generally perceived as precarious work experience.

Fábricas Recuperadas: Notes from the Brazilian experience

The discussions of worker cooperatives reappeared in the context of the economic restructuring process and technological and managerial changes that marked the 1980s, accompanied by an increase in unemployment and the crisis of the so-called work or wage society.[5]

As a result of such crisis, new forms of utilization of labour power were created. In this new paradigm where flexibility of products, process and market was central, the wage relation became expensive for organizations, as it incorporated a series of labour rights (such as social security, medical assistance, limited working hours, and unemployment insurance) to the employment contracts. From the 1980s and 1990s onwards, labour market deregulation became the subject of state policies in different countries, turning into a tendency, though with distinct results.

From the beginning of the 1980s, researchers interested in investigating working cooperatives reappeared across Europe, emphasizing new forms of production organization and increase in structural unemployment. Along with the closing of factories, some were recovered as cooperatives and others (re)organized in alternative modes as an answer to the cultural changes in 1970s Europe, the United States and Canada: these included cooperatives of alternative food, care, natural products, schools, bookshops, and so on (Cornforth, 1983; Taylor, 1994; Batistone, 1983; Thornley, 1983).

By the end of the decade, some cooperatives whose aim was to outsource industrial activities appeared in Spain. They were connected to the Catholic Church and to the clothing industry and were moulded according to a new industrial perspective based on the idea of flexibility (Piore and Sabel, 1984). In the beginning of the 1990s, as Guitiérrez (1992) highlighted, clothing cooperatives in some regions of Spain, which were outsourced by big companies, represented between 8 and 10 per cent of the people employed in this sector.

In Brazil, before the 1990s, there were few and very specific experiences related to cooperatives' factories (Claro, 2004) and the discussion about cooperatives was limited to agricultural and credit cooperatives. During the 1980s, some work cooperative experiences were reported by researchers who investigated factories under bankruptcy in different regions including Rio Grande do Sul (Holzmann, 2001), Paraíba and Rio Grande do Norte, as well as experiences supported by the Inter-American Foundation, whose aim was to generate jobs and income for poor people (Lima, 2002, 2004). Only during the 1990s did those experiences spread across Brazil bringing this subject to light, along with the issue of self-management.

In the 1990s, cooperatives were organized in Brazil, on the one hand, as a way to combat unemployment and stimulate income generation and, on the other, as a way to reduce business costs by outsourcing. In the first case, one can include those factories recovered by workers due to financial crises or threats of closure. In general, those processes were supported by trade unions and by NGOs.[6] In the second case, we find the so-called *endowment cooperatives* (Cornforth,

1983), which are the product of an agreement between owners and workers, in which owners transfer part of the factory for employees, who start working as outsourced workers.

Among *endowment cooperatives* includes those created for industrial or service outsourcing or cost reduction. They were organized by (1) companies[7]; (2) the state, through policies aiming to bring industrial investments to regions poorly industrialized; and (3) trade unions (Lima, 2008). In general, these cooperatives have been regarded as false cooperatives, as they do not preserve the self-management principles that were implied by the cooperatives movement. As a result, they are identified as a subterfuge used by companies to evade the formal labour contract and its obligations. At the end of the 1990s, these organizations were closed by the Regional Labour Agencies and Public Prosecutors or had adapted to norms related to cooperativeness.

Finally, it is important to mention that what have been called *popular cooperatives* or *income-generation cooperatives* are those organized either by workers excluded from the labour market (due to age or low qualifications) or by workers in general. The vast majority of these organizations are the result of the recovering and incubation processes promoted by ANTEAG (*Associação Nacional de Trabalhadores em Empresas de Autogestão e Participação Acionária*).[8] This association was created in 1994 with the initiative and support of union leaders and Caritas, an organization linked with the Catholic Church. ANTEAG, Caritas and CUT (Brazilian Labor Confederation or Union Organization) gradually got involved in the so-called Solidarity Economy Movement, whose beginning is linked with the Social World Forum realized in 2001 in Porto Alegre. Cooperatives have a special role in this movement, whose initial proposal was to create a Socialist alternative that would be different from failed experiences of Socialism. This alternative is conceived in terms of a market Socialism, which would represent an alternative to the Capitalist market, in which new solidarity networks would be created by different institutions and social organizations such as solidarity exchange, popular bank and cooperatives. As a consequence, Solidarity Economy cooperatives would be guided by political principles including autonomy, participative democracy in the shopfloor, self-management and collective property of the means of production.[9]

In the 1990s, this movement grew and in 1999, CUT created the *Agência de Desenvolvimento Solidário*[10] (ADS), aiming to support cooperatives and *Fábricas Recuperadas* by advisory services related to their organization and management. Local and state governments, especially those connected to the Brazilian Workers Party (PT), created their Secretariat of Solidarity Economy and during Lula's first government, in 2003, the National Secretariat for Solidarity Economy was created by the Ministry of Labour and Employment. Thus, cooperatives became part of federal public policies.[11]

In the same year, the UNISOL Brasil was created, aiming to organize, represent and join cooperatives, associations and other solidarity economy self-managed enterprises. Along with ANTEAG, UNISOL Brasil became one of the most important Brazilian institutions connected to the processes of support, creation and maintenance of *Fábricas Recuperadas*.

It is worth noting that what happened in Brazil had a more diverse nature than the Argentinean *Fábricas Recuperadas* movement during the 2000s crisis. While in Argentina the movement was more general and started by a great number of workers occupying factories, in Brazil it was limited to a few cases, not becoming a massive movement.

Even among some trade unions there was resistance to the organization of workers in cooperatives, because it was perceived as a form of precarious work. This perception was caused by the fact that cooperatives were not subject to the labour legislation, not having to pay taxes, which brought down labour costs. Besides, it was a way for those who contract cooperative services to avoid responsibilities related to workers management. This fact brings to light some dilemmas related to worker cooperatives, including the distinction between those that are authentic and those that are false cooperatives, and the complex relations and contradictions concerning precariousness, autonomy and possibilities of emancipation by means of self-management.

In July 2012, the Brazilian government promulgated law number 12.690, aiming to restrict fraudulent cooperative cases. The new law established clearer standards concerning the relations with cooperatives, owners and the market. The law established a minimum of seven owners to formalize a cooperative (instead of twenty owners, as determined by the former legislation), and an enhancement of labour rights for associated members. The law also determined the creation of the National Work Cooperative Program (PRONACOOP).

In Brazil, cooperatives and the *Fábricas Recuperadas* movement[12] have been characterized by a great diversity of circumstances, and, as a result, classified according to a continuum that goes from real self-management to a form based on precarious work. It is important to note that self-management cases have not triggered popular claims in favour of self-management cause.

Within the Socialist framing, cooperative movement was discussed by (1) Marx (1977), who considered it as a possibility; (2) Luxemburgo (1974), who pointed to the contradiction derived from the fact that workers play a dual role – as workers and as bosses of themselves, and creates the dilemma of whether to turn the business into a Capitalist enterprise or to be dissolved in the market; and (3) Webb and Webb (1914), who, in the same direction of Luxemburgo (1974), defended the cooperatives' degeneration thesis, in which they claimed that the cooperatives' success leads them to their end as cooperative enterprises, once they become a Capitalist business. This debate marked the end of the nineteenth century and also the beginning of the twentieth century. Further, cooperatives were used in Socialist countries as a state policy while in the occidental countries their growth was connected to periods of economic crises. With the emergence of the welfare state, cooperatives in countries like France, Italy and Spain played a secondary (though significant) role, connected to market economy, comprising another sector that in France became known as the Social Economy.

The *Fábricas Recuperadas* movement lost its power in the 2000s due to economic and employment recovery. Moreover, changes in the insolvency law guaranteed extended payment deadlines for those in the state of bankruptcy, bringing difficulties for the process of factory recovering by workers (Lima, 2012; Leite et al., 2014; Juvenal, 2006).

Concerning factories recovered by workers, a variety of outcomes can be observed after two decades of functioning, varying from success and integration to the market, to experiences including precarious functioning, closure and factory sale. Finally, it is worth noting the experiences of workers from recovered organizations who refused to form cooperatives, because they were in favour of their nationalization.

The examples discussed in this chapter are typical of *Fábricas Recuperadas* in Brazil. All originated in the 1990s and represent different forms of self-management. The first two cases were characterized by a bankruptcy process, which was followed by workers' resistance, leading to the decision of taking control of the factory, making use of self-management. The main difference between these cases is linked with the consequences of the recovering process: whereas one resulted in a successful case of *Fábrica Recuperada* controlled by workers, the other resulted in the sale of the factory to a business group.

The third example was followed by the model bankruptcy-resistance-recovery, but, instead of turning straight into a cooperative, initially it remained in a co-management involving the former owner and workers, and eventually in a factory fully controlled by workers. Three cooperatives were created in the factory space, with each of them specializing in a different product and having a particular management structure (the board of directors and other councils). All of them are under the control of a central committee that is responsible for taking decisions of common interest, being ultimately responsible for this complex formed by three cooperatives. This is the only example in which selected members of a committee have represented workers.

The fourth example was not the result of a recovery process. Whereas in the other cases there was a bankruptcy process, and the recovery appeared as an alternative to guarantee workers' positions, in this case the organization was created as a self-managed company. Since its beginning, founders aimed to build an enterprise in which there was no labour exploitation, and in which everyone could work in a cooperative and, most importantly, egalitarian way.

The final example represents the enterprise recovered, but not turned into a cooperative. Members of the Occupied Factory Movement have questioned viability of this cooperative alternative, as they considered that workers would lose assured labour rights following this path. Thus, they pursued statization of the enterprise instead of turning it into a cooperative, following the Venezuelan model.

Generally there is no self-management model that assures a precise typology. On the one hand, there are those factories that follow the path of cooperative work, in which workers are both owners and managers and, on the other hand, there are those who refuse to follow that path and, instead, try to achieve statization by considering themselves as social movements in which the factory is only a part of the picture.

The Brazilian factories

In this section we present the examples of Brazilian *Fábricas Recuperadas,* pointing out the diversity of experiences related to recovering processes. Data was gathered through visits to enterprises, observation of the work processes and interviews with leaders and workers of the factories and supporting institutions such as ANTEAG, ADS and SENAES between 2011 and 2014.

Case 1: Cooperminas

Cooperminas, which belongs to Criciúma Workers Ltd,[13] is one of the oldest successful cases of *Fábricas Recuperadas* in Brazil. It is located in Criciúma, Santa Catarina State, in the South of Brazil. This enterprise operates in the industry of coal extraction and processing. The coal is sold to energy sector companies and its main client is a thermoelectric company located in Tubarão-SC, a neighbouring city. In 2011, Cooperminas employed 800 workers, from which 400 were associated members and 400 were regular wageworkers. Only five women were members of the cooperative, and another ten were regular employees, all of them occupying white-collar positions.

In the late 1980s, workers organized themselves to claim for their rights and went to Brasilia (Brazil's Capital) to stand up to the statization of the enterprise. Not having achieved success, they decided to collectively deal with production and started the cooperative, with the help of Criciúma Miners' Union. In 1988, this union started to run the organization. The beginning was very difficult and marked by unfulfilled promises from authorities, repossession attempts by the former owners, resistance acts, including workers' camp and clashes with police. Meanwhile, the insolvency case went on for ten years. In 1993, there was an edict that determined the leasing of the company (given that the court understood that the group in control of the organization was not capable of running the business). Workers resisted once more, even by tying dynamite to their bodies and threatening to blow it up if they were not allowed to stay in business. Thankfully, the decision was revised. Only in 1997 did the workers succeed in solving the legal conflict, when an agreement between workers and the former owners was achieved. The company's shares would be sold to the workers, who in return would pay it back over ten years. The workers also had to assume some of the company debts. Although unfair, this enabled them to finish a long and enduring process of legal disputes and take control of the factory. From then on, the cooperative has been growing strong in the market, keeping an increasing production rate, a stable relation with clients and suppliers and also has been investing constantly in modernization of equipment and technologies to minimize environmental degradation, and even investing in the exploration of a new mine (Pires, 2012).

Cooperminas originated from the bankruptcy of Companhia Brasileira Carbonífera de Araranguá (CBCA), which was founded in 1917 and used to be a major company in the Brazilian coal extraction sector. In 1987, after four months of unpaid wages, workers found out that the company was in debt with the government by not paying taxes and also not transferring money for workers' social security funds (Silva, 2005). Besides, according to statements from the cooperative's members, it was found that owners were planning a fraudulent bankruptcy, which would have been harmful for workers, and they could have lost their jobs. As a result, a worker rebellion started, which included strikes and manifestations aiming to pressure government to solve the conflict.

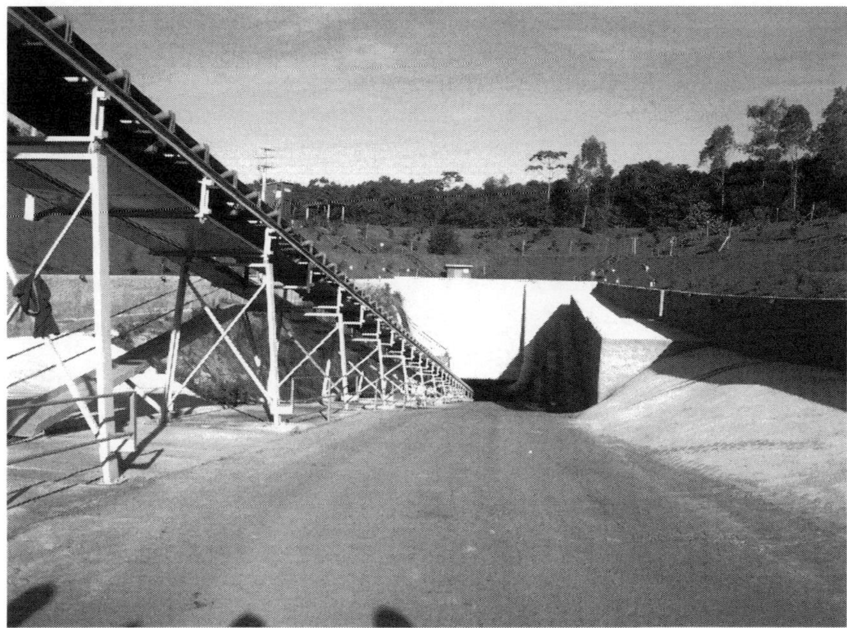

Figure 9.1: New mine, 2014. Photograph by Aline Suelen Pires.

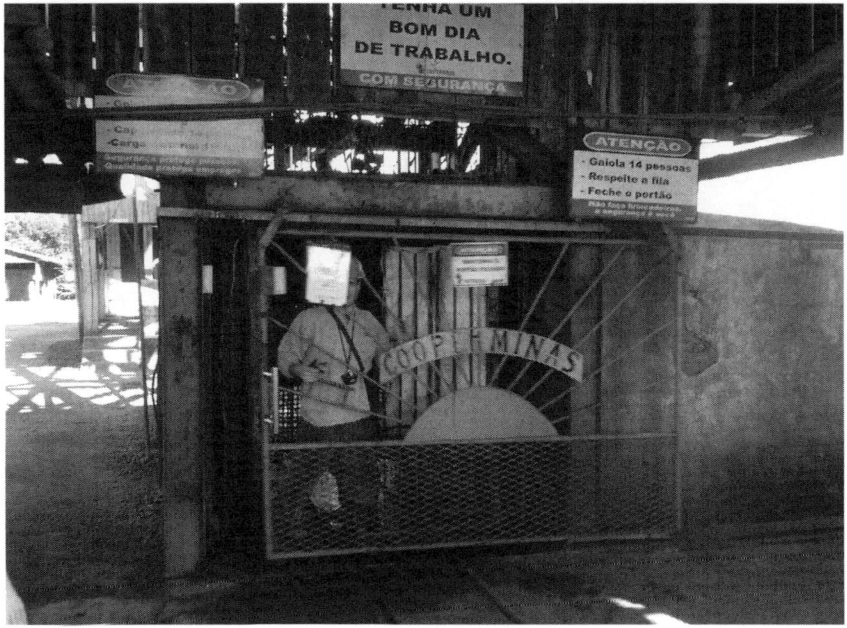

Figure 9.2: Worker in the mine lift, 2014. Photograph by Aline Suelen Pires.

Cooperminas has all the structures and spaces of participation, besides rules linked to job rotation and information access that are expected from a cooperative or self-managing enterprise. However, it is important to note that many workers created difficulties in order for the idea of a consensual or full democracy to become fulfilled. As a consequence, spaces and mechanisms of representation had to be created. In addition, the fact that a great number of employees are not associated members is another controversial issue, because of the subordination and exploitation associated with the maintenance of wage-labour relation. Cooperminas is one of the most successful cases of *Fábricas Recuperadas*. This organization has expanded its market share and has achieved a reasonable level of job satisfaction, according to workers' perception, offering the best wages in the region and reported high levels of satisfaction over time.

Case 2: Uniforja

Uniforja – Central Cooperative from Metallurgical Workers[14] – like Cooperminas, is considered an economic success case of *Fábrica Recuperada* and is also an exemplar and pioneer experience of self-management. In addition, it was the first case in the country where the bankruptcy judge allowed the workers to keep on developing their activities under the condition of equipment and installations leasing, which were part of insolvent estate (Oda, 2001: 18).

The enterprise is located in Diadema, São Paulo's metropolitan region. It is a metallurgical organization, a major Latin American industrial producer of rings, flanges and tube fittings. In 2011, it employed 294 associated members and 290 employees, totalling 584 workers. Among them, only 27 were women. The specificity of Uniforja is that it is a cooperative of the second degree: that is, it is a central organization composed by three others; Coopertratt, Cooperlafe and Cooperfor.[15]

Uniforja began in 1954, in São Paulo city, from Alpaca Produtos Químicos S/A,[16] a factory manufacturing pesticides, paints, cleaning products and chemicals for industrial use. In 1967, it changed its name to Conforja and started producing forged steel connections and piping. After one year, the company was transferred to Diadema-SP. In the 1970s, its production increased considerably due to demand from Petrobrás and other state oil companies. During the 1980s, as a consequence of the economic crisis, the company tried to diversify its production, but by the end of the decade problems began. In the 1990s, the founder of the company fell sick and eventually died. In such a context, it incurred payment delays (including wage payment delay) and debts increased considerably. In 1995, the founder's son opted for co-management, which resulted in an agreement involving the company, the factory commission (formed by workers) and the ABC Metalworkers' Union (Oda, 2001).

In September 1995, the Conforja Workers Association (Assecon) was formed and started receiving support from ANTEAG. However, self-management didn't work very well: collective decisions were not implemented by the company, leaving workers, whose wages were delayed, suspicious. In 1997, Assecon was dissolved, including the self-management agreement (Oda, 2001).

In 1997, workers started considering the possibility of organizing a cooperative, which was realized in December that year with the creation of Coopertratt, which entered into a leasing agreement with Conforja. This experience resulted in the creation of three cooperatives. The leasing agreement was renewed in 1998, including the newly formed cooperatives, and lasted until 1999, when Conforja's bankruptcy was announced. In 2000, the Central Uniforja was created, which was composed of four cooperatives. In 2005, Coopercon (Piping Workers' Industrial Cooperative) was closed due to commercial reasons. Its workers and activities were reallocated to the remaining cooperatives, i.e., Coopertratt, Cooperlafe and Cooperfor (which are still functioning today).

Uniforja used to employ 600 workers, from which 350 were associated members and the other 250 were wageworkers. In 2009, as a consequence of the economic crisis, this number decreased to 500 employees. Apart from specific moments during the crisis, Uniforja has established itself in the market, acquiring quality certifications and even market valuation.

It is important to note that three of the cooperatives presented the following characteristics: spaces for workers to take part in the decision-making process and position rotation mechanisms. Moreover, all of them were successful, legitimate, ... ? in terms of payment of social security taxes. Another important point to highlight is that the huge number of employees brought difficulties in establishing direct relations amongst workers. As a consequence, there has been a constructed hierarchy, and subsequently, a considerable wage differentiation amongst workers.

Interviews[17] with the factory employees revealed that long-serving employees from Uniforja felt a sense of satisfaction linked to the work and also a pride in relation to the history of the organization's recovery. Yet, Uniforja is a big company and workers have related the existence of different levels of commitment with work and also with the collective management. One thing is clear in the workers' statements: considering Uniforja achieved a market position, being a member of this cooperative means stability and brings a sense of safety for workers. However, only those who are associated members can sense stability.

Case 3: Bruscor

Our third case, Bruscor, represents a unique experience in terms of self-management, since its very beginning. However, it is important to note that it cannot officially be called a *Fábrica Recuperada*, as it did not start from a bankruptcy process. Actually, it was created as a self-management organization. It is located in the city of Brusque, in Santa Catarina state. It has been a part of the textile industry, producing strings, ribbon, elastic cords and canvas. These products are sold to the São Paulo clothing industry and also to other small businesses that resell them for the printing industry. For the past three years, the factory has been located in a rented shed.

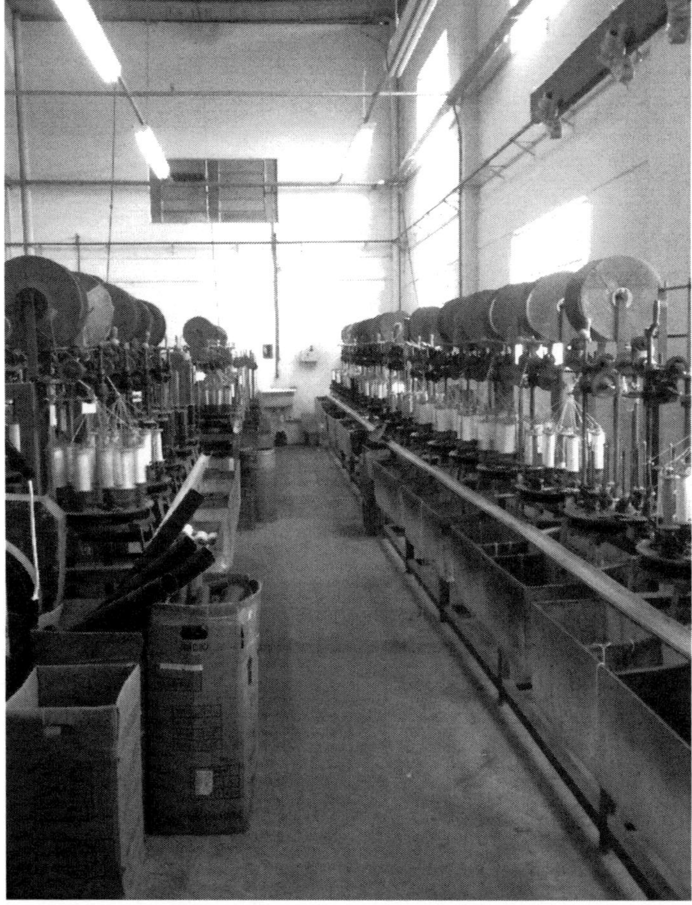

Figure 9.3: Inside Bruscor, 2014. Photograph by Aline Suelen Pires.

There are only eleven members, out of which six currently work there and five are on leave and working for other organizations (companies or government) and, therefore, not earning a wage from Bruscor. Moreover, there are four wageworkers (not associated members) working there. Among the active workers, half are men and half are women.

In 1988, four friends, all of them graduates or graduating students connected to political parties or to the Catholic Church Social Pastoral, joined forces and started up the business (Pieritz, 2008). Each of them invested the money they had (by selling a car, a motorcycle, etc.). The business was started from a former small factory that used to belong to the father of one of them. The initial idea was to develop a business where there would be no labour exploitation and also that would allow them to keep pursuing their political activism. Initially, activities were linked to canvas production, instead of strings and elastic cords. However, due to difficulties in selling their products on the market, the group decided to change production. They bought new machines and started producing shoestrings and ribbons. In 1992, the organization was registered as Bruscor, although among its members it was known as EAPS, which is a short name for the expression: Alternative Company of Socialized Production. A few years later, ANTEAG started to support the company. Along its twenty years of existence, Bruscor has faced many crises that have marked its history. These crises were caused not only by economic factors but also by the obstacles inherent to collective management. In 2009, for instance, some associated members decided to quit the business jointly, because they did not agree with the directions of the organization, including the necessity to adapt to market requirements. It affected the company in terms of not only management and organization but also finance: those who chose to leave had to receive their due share, which brought serious consequences for the business.

The factory has eighteen members and another 22 persons are involved directly or indirectly in the business. It has never been formalized as a cooperative, and currently none of the five founders are working there. The oldest members who have been working at Bruscor became associated around five years after the initial meetings. Nevertheless, at that time they already were connected to former members via the church, especially through a youth church group. Nowadays, some members are still involved with social movements, though less frequently than in the past.

Bruscor is a small business, and hence, there is no division between management and shopfloor workers and, moreover, hierarchy is very simple. There is no general meeting; instead, there are monthly meetings open to all members. Generally, members' participation is not uniform. It is possible to note different levels of participation even among members of the few hierarchical groups that exist there. On the one hand, some of the members are more active, being always ready for solving any kind of problem and, on the other, there are those whose participation is more restricted and formal.

The company has lost some of its biggest clients, and has been trying to recover from this crisis. Although more stable, workers' incomes are still low and the possibility of recovering the market share is limited.

It is possible to affirm that Bruscor's workers face a daily struggle to keep things up. Some workers have parallel activities. They sell products and have small jobs to supplement their incomes and achieve a better standard of living. The great majority of interviewees do not discard the possibility of getting another job in case things get worse. After so many difficulties and disappointments, it is possible to notice that the confidence in the self-management model is no longer the same as the politically engaged people who conceived the idea and built up the organization.

Case 4: Coopermambrini

Coopermambrini is a self-management cooperative that is located in Vespasiano, Minas Gerais, producing different truck bodies and also chassis extension services. The company has clients all around the country and was formed by twelve associated members. Besides

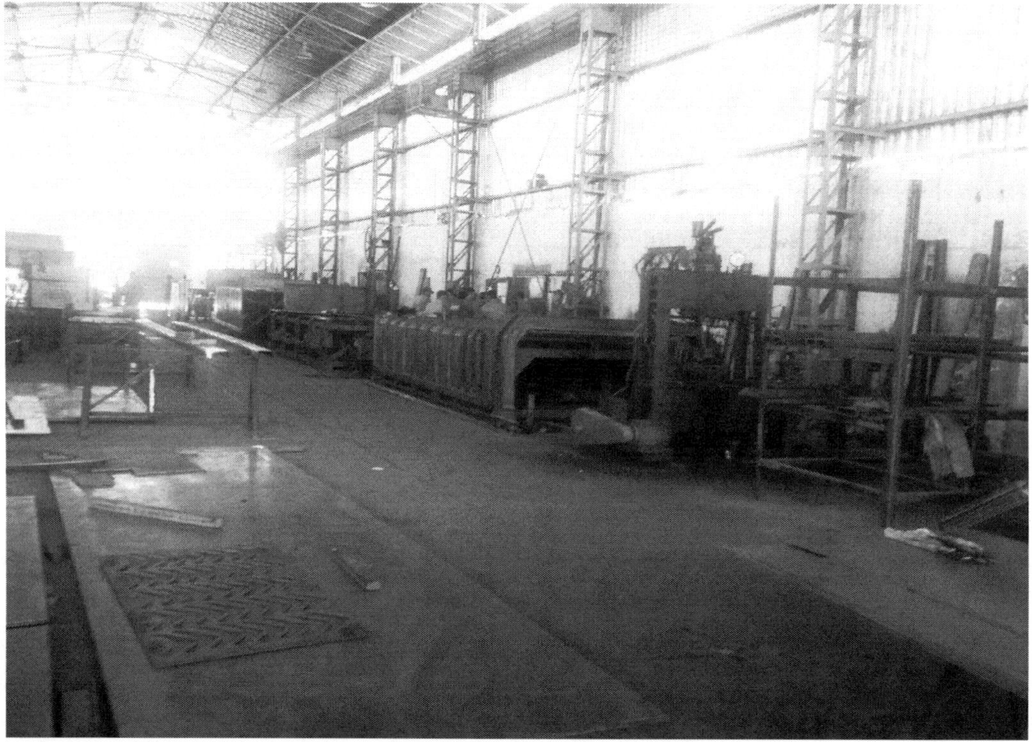

Figure 9.4: Coopermambrini shopfloor, 2014. Photograph by Aline Suelen Pires.

these, there are 36 wageworkers, contracted in accordance with the regular labour regime. All the associated members are men and there are only two women (a secretary and a shopfloor worker) among wageworkers.

What makes this a unique case is that, in 2011, company owners decided to sell to a private group. This cooperative was founded from the bankruptcy of Mambrini Metal-Mecanic Indústry Ltd, which was created in 1946 and was regarded as the biggest body truck producer of Latin America during the 1970s, commercializing its production for clients of different regions. However, during the 1990s the company faced financial problems as a result of economic changes. Taxes and wages were delayed, and personal protective equipment and uniforms were no longer provided by the organization. This situation became even worse, leading Mambrini's owners to transfer factory control to workers in 1997, when the cooperative was formed. At that time, 42 employees worked for Mambrini. Machinery and the industrial plant were accepted in payment of workers' debts (ANTEAG, 2000). Unlike other Brazilian factory recovery experiences, it seems that the present case ran smooth.

Despite this, Coopermambrini faced a series of problems in the beginning. In order to recover the market share, it had to cope with clients' suspicion and the lack of capital. Thus, besides financial problems, cooperators had to work very hard in order to recover clients' trust. As a consequence, workers started leaving the cooperative, reaching the point where only two of them remained. From 2004 onwards this situation started to change, when a group of eight workers decided to take control of the business. After several meetings and, after a reasonable effort, twenty people joined to form the cooperative. Twelve of them still work there.

Coopermambrini has been assisted by ANTEAG (especially during 2004 and 2005 when a group of workers took control of it). It has also been supported by the metallurgical trade union and by local government, which leases the land where it is located. Since then, this cooperative has been able to reorganize itself, regain market confidence and even acquire new costumers and gain some stability.

Given the limited number of associated members, the decision-making structure is rather flexible. Decision-making has been carried out during meetings scheduled according to needs. Associated members earn equivalent incomes, while wageworkers do not. This implies a dubious situation of self-management and the use of wage labour, which is closer to a normal company organization.

In 2011 the company was about to be sold to a three-year partner company. Associated members claimed that Coopermambrini was in good shape and therefore they could retrieve a good price. They reflected that they had overcome a great number of obstacles, challenges and difficulties (some even claimed they had endured starvation). As a result, they felt that they had had enough of the cooperative experience, and considered it a very precarious and stressful experience (Pires, 2012). The organization ceased to be a cooperative.

Case 5: Flaskô

The great majority of Brazilian *Fábricas Recuperadas* have followed the classic model: (1) private enterprise bankruptcy; (2) dissatisfaction and workers' struggle trying to guarantee wages and other rights; (3) support from external organizations that provide advice and support for self-management; (4) cooperative formation; (5) court decision regarding the cooperative formation.

Some groups of workers and left-wing trade unions have regarded this transition from the private enterprise to the cooperative enterprise as a loss in labour rights, instead of a gain. Thus, in their opinion, cooperatives represent workers' subjection to the market economy and are nothing more than a way of exploiting workers by employing them in precarious jobs.

These groups have been defending the nationalization of cooperatives, instead of their formalization. This position implies a particular view concerning the role of the state, one in which the state has to guarantee the right to work (Leite, 1994; Leite et al., 2014). Moreover, it is important to note that these groups share a particular view regarding the issue of autonomy. Whilst cooperatives create collective self-management, which are shared and autonomous, the nationalization of the organizations would maintain subordination of the workers to state or public managers. A public manager, however, is regarded as a collective manager, within the traditional perspective, similar to the dominant perspective in the so-called Socialist states.

This perspective was brought to light by the Occupied Factories Movement that started in 2002, and whose origin is connected to the occupation of three factories that belonged to the same business group. Two of them were occupied in 2002, Cipla and Interfibra, both located in Joinville – SC and one in June, 2003, Flaskô, located in Sumaré – SP. This movement spread and another 35 Brazilian factories were occupied. Only one of these factories remains occupied, Flaskô. In accordance with Raslan (2007) and Araújo (2015), Flaskô's workers did not opt for the cooperative path because they believed that it would mean a loss in terms of labour rights.

Although there have been significant cases of *Fábricas Recuperadas* in which nationalization was defended, including Cipla, Interfibra, Flaskô and Cooperbotões, none of them achieved it. Vieitez and Dal Ri (2007) claim that both forms of workers' responses, i.e. cooperative formation and nationalization of *Fábricas Recuperadas*, are linked with the following goal: guaranteeing workers' jobs.

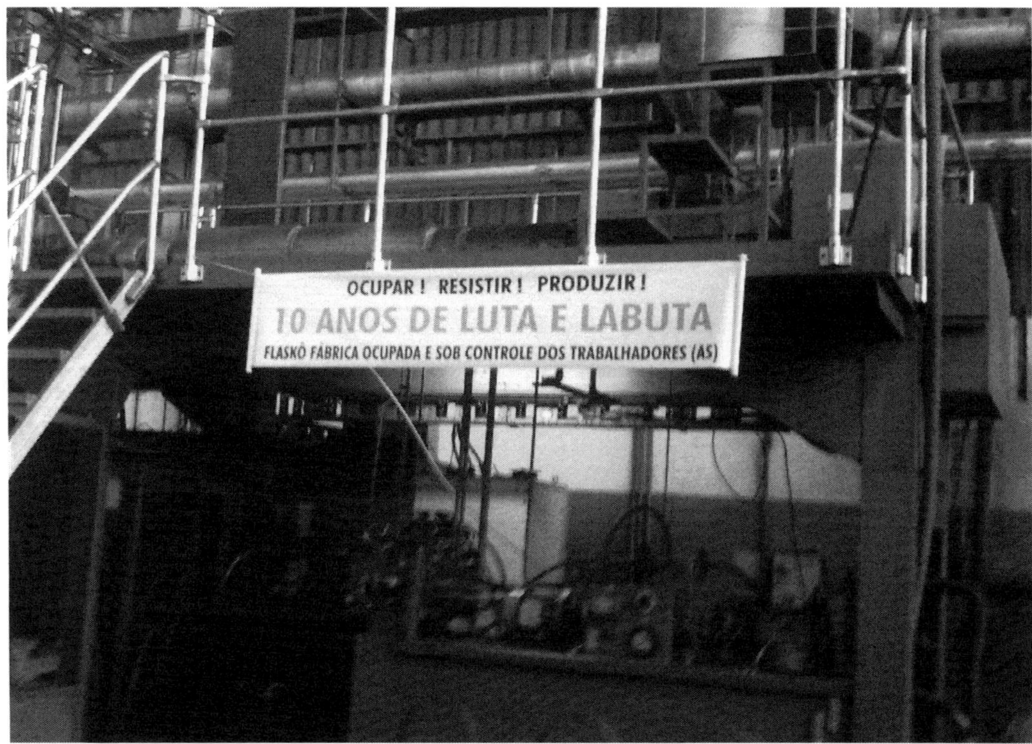

Figure 9.5: Flaskô machine with a logo of Occupied Factories Movement, 2014. Photograph by Aline Suelen Pires.

In 2009, Flaskô employed 78 workers to manufacture industrial containers used to store products including food, cosmetics, crop-protection agents, chemical products and fertilizers. During the mobilization process, Flaskô's workers tried to get support from both within and outside the local community. In that sense, they formed a support network involving homeless and landless workers' movements, local unions, and Argentinean and Venezuelan *Fábricas Recuperadas* movements. Moreover, as a form of getting the community involved, they have been promoting cultural, sporting and educational activities. Finally, it is worth noting that they have reserved part of the factory land for the construction of houses, forming a sort of 'workers village,' providing shelter for workers and local families (Araújo, 2015).

Half of the workforce had actually worked at the factory prior to collective management experience. At the time of the occupation, the company had 71 workers. This number reached the peak of 118 workers, and fell after the 2009 crisis, falling to 70 employees in 2013. Part of the remaining workforce came from other enterprises that made up the Occupied Factories Movement. In terms of age, at least 40 employees are over 40 years old. In terms of gender, twelve women work for the organization, part of them directly in production.

The main decisions have been taken in general assemblies, in which all employees participate. The ordinary assemblies have occurred once a month (but there may be special ones if they need to discuss specific subjects). Every year, a council is elected that makes decisions related to production. In addition to the assemblies, workers participate in other sectorial meetings, having free access to the minutes and other documents. Flaskô's internal communication still occurs through murals and also by means of an internal newspaper that is distributed weekly. The external communication occurs through (1) social networks, (2) organization website and (3) a community radio station on the Internet.

Wages in Flaskô vary in the proportion 3:1; that is, the highest remuneration does not exceed the amount of the lowest multiplied by three. Currently, the enterprise is open from Monday to Friday and workers are distributed in three shifts, from six hours each, with no production between six in the evening and midnight. Thus, the number of working hours is 30 hours per week. The reduction in working hours without loss of payment was one flag defended by the Occupied Factories Movement and is an achievement of which Flaskô is very proud.

So far, Flaskô's legal situation is not well defined. The factory is in the possession of workers, but they do not own the machinery. Workers refused the government's proposal of transforming labour credits into organizations' shares in order to form a cooperative. Factory control belongs to an association, Hermelindo Miquelace Association, founded by workers, who still keep wage-labour status (Araújo, 2015).

Taking Flaskô into account, it was possible to note that, in general, workers have tried to keep themselves politically active in defending the factory and opted for a more egalitarian model of work and society. However, the factory has experienced problems with out-of-date technology and equipment maintenance, resulting in a weakening of its production capacity. Besides, legal issues linked to the factory property seem complicated, generating a climate of instability. Nevertheless, the workers are mobilized to continue fighting, even if the prospects are restricted and the movement shows no sign of expansion.

Conclusions

It could be argued that in Brazil, the vast majority of recovering cases has been motivated by trade unions and other intermediaries that provided support such as ANTEAG. Furthermore, mobilizations in Brazil are by far more restricted.

Workers' perceptions concerning self-management proposals are one of the many obstacles faced by *Fábricas Recuperadas* and cooperative enterprises in Brazil. Workers from these organizations have spent most of their lives under wage-labour logic, in a vertical relation between employer and employee, characterized by hierarchy and subordination. Thus, the adaptation process brings difficulties to management in which collective management presupposes a cultural change.

Returning to the market or recovering the market share is yet another problem faced by these factories. Usually, they achieve a partial success initially, but they are forced to adapt to the market and its costs, which involves the compromise of self-management logic.

It is important to note as well the difficulties of *Fábricas Recuperadas* are often connected to their unsolved legal situations, which involves long disputes between cooperative workers and former owners. In Brazil, a recent change in the bankruptcy law increased the chances of owners to recover the organization, leaving the recovering process even more unlikely to succeed.

It is worth stressing that since Brazilian economic development started in 2000 onwards, there have been a growth in formal jobs and a quantitative reduction in terms of *Fábricas Recuperadas*. Moreover, self-management organizations have never become a trade union banner. Instead, they are only effective when workers' jobs are under threat or when trade unions support them as a form of social inclusion for the unemployed. It has become clear during conflicts between trade unions and *Fábricas Recuperadas* that the union tends to defend the wageworkers and not their associate members. In these cases, associated workers face an ambiguous situation represented by an employer-employee situation.

Currently, the main organization that has supported the *Fábricas Recuperadas* in Brazil is UNISOL, Central of Cooperatives and Solidarity Enterprises. It has been involved with 21 enterprises, distributed in five states, primarily in the metallurgical, textile, chemical and electrical industries. However, it is important to note that the entity itself recognizes that these enterprises tend to deal, in the medium term, with problems related predominantly to the technological gap.

Generally, there have been improvements in working conditions, including better wages, stability and democratization of working relations. However, workers tend to perceive cooperatives with a transitional perspective; that is, they have been working for cooperatives because there have been no available positions in the market, due to their low level of qualification, educational level or age.

It is worth noting the difference between Brazilian and Argentinean experiences concerning factory recoveries. In Argentina, there was an economic crisis during the 1990s and 2000s, resulting in a great number of bankruptcies and popular mobilizations, accompanied by factory occupations aiming to save jobs. These mobilizations started during the 2000 crisis and factories recovered from that moment on were subjected to a particular regulation that brought fiscal advantages for them.

References

Allegrone, V. G., Partenio, F. and Álvarez, M. I. F. 2004. 'Los procesos de recuperación de fábricas: una mirada retrospectiva'. In Battistini, O. R. (Ed.), *El Trabajo Frente Al Espejo: Continuidades Y Rupturas En Los Procesos De Construcción Identitaria De Los Trabajadores*, Buenos Aires: Prometeo, pp. 329–343.

ANTEAG 2000. *Autogestão: Construindo Uma Nova Cultura De Relações De Trabalho*, São Paulo: ANTEAG.

ANTEAG 2009. *Atlas da Economia Solidária no Brasil 2005–2007*, São Paulo: Todos os bichos.

Araújo, A. M. C. 2015. 'O Caso da Flaskô'. In Leite, M., Araújo, A. M. and Lima, J. C. (Eds), *O Trabalho Na Economia Solidária: Entre Precariedade E Emancipação*, São Paulo: Annablume.

Batistone, E. 1983. 'Organization and orientation: A life-cycle model of French cooperatives', *Economic and Industrial Democracy*, 4 (2), 139–161.

Bruno, L. and Saccardo, C. (Eds) 1986. *Organização, Trabalho E Tecnologia*, São Paulo: Atlas.

Claro, M. 2004. *Unilabor: Desenho Industrial, Arte Moderna E Autogestão Operária*, São Paulo: SENAC.

Cornforth, C. 1983. 'Some factors affecting the success or failure of worker cooperatives: a review of empirical research in the United Kingdom', *Economic and Industrial Democracy*, 4 (2), 163–190.

Corteletti, R. F. 2009. 'Trabalhadoras e autogestão: trabalho e vida cotidiana entre operárias de uma fábrica cooperativa em Caxias do Sul', PhD thesis, João Pessoa, Brazil: Universidade Federal da Paraíba.

DIEESE (Ed.) 1994. *Trabalho E Reestruturação Produtiva: 10 Anos De Linha De Produção*, São Paulo: DIEESE.

Dorneles, B. 2003. 'Autogestão e racionalidade substantiva', MA dissertation, Florianópolis: Universidade Federal de Santa Catarina.

Fajn, G. 2004. 'Fábricas Recuperadas: la organización en cuestión', *Labor Again,* Amsterdam: International Institute of Social History, http://www.iisg.nl/labouragain/documents/fajn.pdf. Accessed 20 October 2012.

Faria, J. H. 2009. *Relações De Poder E De Trabalho Nas Organizações*, São Paulo: Atlas.

Gutiérrez, A. C. M. 1992. 'Workers' cooperatives: Are they intrinsically inefficient?', *Economic and Industrial Democracy*, 13 (3), 431–436.

Holzmann, L. 2001. *Operários Sem Patrão: Gestão Cooperativa E Dilemas Da Democracia*, São Carlos: Editora da UFSCar.

IBASE/ANTEAG 2004. *Autogestão Em Avaliação*, São Paulo: ANTEAG.

Juvenal, T. L. 2006. 'Empresas recuperadas por trabalhadores em regime de autogestão: reflexões à luz do caso brasileiro', *Revista do BNDES*, 13 (26), 115–138.

Leite, M. P. 1994. *O Futuro Do Trabalho: Novas Tecnologias E Subjetividade Operária*, São Paulo: Scritta.

Leite, M. P., Pires, A. S., Cherfen, C. O. and Duaibs, R. 2014. 'As fábricas recuperadas no Brasil: um balanço bibliográfico'. In Leite, M. P., Araújo, A. M. and Lima, J. C. (Eds), *O Trabalho Na Economia Solidária: Entre Precariedade E Emancipação*, São Paulo: Annablume.

Lima, J. C. 2001. 'Interiorização industrial e fábricas cooperativas: a experiência nordestina dos anos 90'. In Guimarães, N. A. and Martin, S. (Eds), *Competitividade E Desenvolvimento: Atores E Instituições Locais*, São Paulo: Editora SENAC.

Lima, J. C. 2002. *As Artimanhas Da Flexibilização: O Trabalho Terceirizado Em Cooperativas De Produção*, São Paulo: Terceira Margem.

Lima, J. C. 2004. 'O trabalho autogestionário em cooperativas de produção: o paradigma revisitado', *Revista Brasileira de Ciências Sociais*, 19 (56), 45–62.

Lima, J. C. 2007. 'Workers' cooperatives in Brazil: Autonomy vs precariousness', *Economic and Industrial Democracy*, 28 (4), 589–621.

Lima, J. C. 2008. 'Reestruturação industrial, desemprego e autogestão: as cooperativas do Vale do Sinos', *Sociologias*, 10 (19), 212–249.

Lima, J. C. 2012. 'Cooperativas, trabalho associado, autogestão e economia solidária: A constituição do campo de pesquisa no Brasil'. In Georges, I. P. H. and Leite, M. P. (Eds), *Novas Configurações Do Trabalho E Economia Solidária*, São Paulo: Annablume.

Luxemburgo. R. 1974. *Reforma ou Revolução?*, Lisboa: Estampa.

Marx, K. 1977. 'Manifesto do lançamento da Associação Internacional dos Trabalhadores, 1864'. In Marx, K. and Engels, F. (Eds), *Textos 3*, São Paulo: Edições Sociais.

Menezes, P. C. S. 2008. 'Trabalho e identidade em uma cooperativa de produção na cidade de Nova Friburgo', MA dissertation, Rio de Janeiro: Universidade Federal do Rio de Janeiro.

Oda, N. T. 2001. 'Gestão e trabalho em cooperativas de produção: dilemas e alternativas à participação', MA dissertation, São Paulo: Escola Politécnica da Universidade Estadual de São Paulo.

Pieritz, V. L. H. 2008. 'A gestão participativa e a territorialidade como fatores de fomento a sustentabilidade dos empreendimentos da Rede de Economia Solidária do Vale do Itajaí – RESVI – um estudo multicaso', MA dissertation, Blumenau: Universidade Regional de Blumenau.

Piore, M. J. and Sabel, C. F. 1984. *The Second Industrial Divide: Possibilities for Prosperity*, New York, NY: Basic Books.

Pires, A. S. 2012. 'As fábricas recuperadas: quais são as perspectivas da autogestão?', paper presented at *8th Seminário Do Trabalho: Trabalho, Educação E Políticas Sociais No Século XXI*, UNESP, Marília, http://www.estudosdotrabalho.org/texto/gt3/as_fabricas_recuperadas.pdf. Accessed 20 October 2012.

Pires, A. S. 2014. 'Fábricas recuperadas e os trabalhadores: a autogestão entre a teoria e a prática', PhD thesis, São Carlos, Brazil: Universidade Federal de São Carlos.

Raslan, F. O. 2007. 'Resistindo com classe: o caso da ocupação da Flaskô', MA dissertation, Campinas: Universidade Federal de Campinas.

Rebón, J. 2007. *La Empresa de la Autonomía: Trabajadores Recuperando La Producción*, Buenos Aires: Colectivo Ediciones.

Rebón, J. and Saavedra, I. 2006. *Empresas Recuperadas: La Autogestión De Los Trabajadores*, Buenos Aires: Capital Intelectual.

Silva, E. 2005. 'A atuação do movimento sindical frente ao processo de falência: os casos dos sindicatos dos mineiros/Criciúma e trabalhadores têxteis/Blumenau', MA dissertation, Blumenau: Universidade Regional de Blumenau.

Singer, P. and Souza, A. R. (Eds) 2000. *A Economia Solidária No Brasil: A Autogestão Como Resposta Ao Desemprego*, São Paulo: Contexto.

Taylor, P. L. 1994. 'The rhetorical construction of efficiency: Restructuring and industrial democracy in Mondragón, Spain', *Sociological Forum*, 9 (3), 459–489.

Thornley, J. 1983. 'Workers' co-operatives and trade unions: The Italian experience', *Economic and Industrial Democracy*, 4 (3), 321–344.

Valle, R. (Ed.) 2002. *Autogestão: O Que Fazer Quando As Fabricas Fecham?*, Rio de Janeiro: Relume-Dumará.

Vieitez, C. and Dal Ri, N. M. 2007. 'O controle dos trabalhadores na Cipla – Indústria de Plásticos', *Revista ORG & DEMO*, 8 (1/2), 173–186.

Webb, S. and Webb, B. 1914. 'Co-operative production and profit sharing', *New Statesman*, Special Supplement (2), 45.

Notes

1   For the studies concerning Argentinean *Fábricas Recuperadas*, see for example Allegrone et al. (2004), Fajn (2004), Rebón (2007), Rebón and Saavedra (2006).

2   See ANTEAG (2009), Atlas from Economia Solidária (2005–2007). http://www2.mte.gov.br/ecosolidaria/sies_atlas.asp

3   See Bruno and Saccardo (1986), DIEESE (1994), Leite (1994).

4   Several *Fábricas Recuperadas* did not become cooperatives, experiencing distinct shared management situations. The proposal of self-management was built gradually and with difficulties concerning its understanding by workers. For a discussion of self-management proposal and experiences in Brazil, see Faria (2009), Valle (2002), IBASE/ANTEAG (2004).

5   Worker cooperatives began in the industrial period and during the labour movement of the nineteenth century. Theorists and utopian socialists such as Owen and Fourier considered self-management as a defensive reaction against unemployment and also against living and working conditions of industrial workers. Taking as principle democracy and egalitarianism, they defended workers associations both as a way to make a living within Capitalism and as a way to overcome it.

6   About *Fábricas Recuperadas* organized by ANTEAG (ANTEAG 2000); Valle (2002).

7   Concerning endowment cooperatives in Brazil, see Corteletti (2009) and Menezes (2008).

8   National Association of Workers from self-management organizations.

9   See *Uniforja case*, in which the cooperative tries to adapt to self-management principles and at the same time become competitive in the market (Oda, 2001).

10   Trans: Solidarity Development Agency.

11   The debate on solidarity economy in Brazil begins with Paul Singer, who defended an alternative economy as a way of leading to Socialism. As a movement, the solidarity economy has grouped several social movements and organizations that have dealt with hunger and

social exclusion. Its origins refer back to the 2003 Social Forums realized in Porto Alegre, when the National Secretariat for Solidarity Economy was created.

12 Not all workers' cooperatives are *Fábricas Recuperadas*. Some worker cooperatives are the result of unemployed workers, such as dressmakers, cooks, artisans and street-sweepers, who organize themselves in small production units; *Fábricas Recuperadas* are the result of the recovering of a factory by their workers, taking self-management as a principle.

13 Worker from Criciúma Ltda.

14 Cooperativa Central de Produção Industrial de Trabalhadores em Metalurgia.

15 Coopertratt (Cooperativa Industrial de Trabalhadores em Tratamento Térmico e Transformação de Metais) produces tube fittings made of carbon steel or stainless steel and also provides services connected to thermal treatment for cooperatives that form Uniforja and for the market in general. Cooperlafe (Cooperativa Industrial de Trabalhadores em Laminação de Anéis e Forjados Especiais) produces seamless carbon-steel rings, alloy steel, stainless steel, duplex and special alloys. Cooperfor (Cooperativa Industrial de Trabalhadores em Forjaria) produces automotives – carbon steel and steel forgings. All these cooperatives are located in the same industrial park.

16 Alpaca Chemical Products S/A.

17 Interviews were carried out by Aline Pires.

Chapter 10

New technologies and media activism in Brazil: Reassembling spaces in the context of innovation

Leonardo Vasconcelos Cavalier Darbilly

Introduction

In the Brazilian context, the communication field has traditionally been marked by the dominance of large corporations. For instance, in the past decade, nine families dominated the news production industry across the country, including Marinho (Globo), Abravanel (SBT), Saad (Bandeirantes), Bloch (Manchete), Civita (Abril), Mesquita (Estado), Frias (Folha), Levy (Gazeta) and Nascimento Silva (Jornal do Brasil) (Borges, 2009). Recent advancement of the Internet and the proliferation of new information technologies, generating 'a bombing and the pluralization of information sources' (Alcadipani, 2007: 34), allowed the entry of new social actors in the field, including new independent media organizations, online newspapers, activist bloggers, etc. These new technological changes across the media have facilitated the mushrooming of cyber-activism that attempts to exert pressure on the state in an effort to establish public-friendly policies that can end monopoly practices (Passos, 2011), encourage communitarian radio stations and alternative channels occupied by social movements, non-journalistic websites and networks, as well as promote other forms of exercising free and democratic communication.

This chapter discusses the examples of social practices associated with media activism and explores possibilities of resistance to the traditional organization practices confronting traditional media corporations through the Movement of Progressive Bloggers (BlogProg) and Mídia Ninja.

Resistance and media activism

A perspective of resistance has been increasingly used in the context of organizational studies, which, in turn, is based on a political perspective. Spicer and Bohm pointed out that 'in order for us to understand relations of power and resistance that affect organisations and organisational processes, it is important to look at the struggles of resistance that occur in civil society' (2007: 302). The authors' justification is based on the idea that the orientation from an instrumental to a political approach is vital because it can contribute to the understanding of not only how social movements influence organizations and challenge their hegemonic discourses, but also how these movements develop new forms of organizing. In other words, the political approach of organization dynamics is based on the understanding of the phenomenon of resistance as a collective action that occurs not only in the immediate space of organizations but mainly outside their boundaries. The political perspective of resistance, thus, focuses its analysis primarily on the sphere of civil society as well as how organizations are influenced by civil society actions. It is for this reason that according to Spicer and Bohm resistance can be considered as 'a hegemonic struggle undertaken by social movements […] that seek to disrupt the hegemonic discourse of management' (2007: 1667, 1691).

Discussing the importance of using theories that study social movements as a way of theorizing about the phenomena that occur in the organizational sphere, Misoczky et al. (2008) claim to be interested in 'returning to social movements in order for us to think about theoretical possibilities committed with praxis.' Otto and Bohm (2006), based on Gramsci, highlighted that the hegemonic regime of management is produced not only by means of class relations in the workplace, but that it is also important to analyse the existing political mechanisms of consensus in wider spheres of civil society. The latter, according to the authors, is responsible for the legitimacy or even the cultural and social collapse of this structure.

Within the field of media in Brazil, the changes in organizational sphere are paramount when it comes to discussing the phenomenon of resistance. The use of new communication technologies could be seen as both an open and a hidden tactic of individuals and groups against the dominance of large corporations in the field. In this chapter, we explore the use of new digital technologies by civil society organizations and how technology can be understood as practices of resistance.

Russell discussed a relationship between new forms of activism through the Internet and what she calls digital resistance, i.e., oppositional practices carried out by various groups across the web, having as its main characteristic the fact of acting in the form of a network 'available for copying and adaptation by the vast majority of users located everywhere' (2005: 514). The author explains that many groups that were denied the right to communicate or disseminate their information now exert new forms of resistance to the barriers and filters imposed by mainstream media. This can be made through the promotion of alternative discourse on the Internet and, as a result, their own social networking sites can facilitate political demonstrations online and offline. Russell also points out that resistance to online forms of control continue to develop rapidly, and that 'the technologies that facilitate the political and cultural practices are shaping the collective use of the Internet and integrating it in a more profound way for users around the world – through instant messaging, e-mails "smart" collaborative weblogs, wireless networks, text editors, wiki and social networking' (2005: 513).

Russell (2005) explains that for some groups of tactical media, digital resistance refers to a form of protest that mimics the way in which digital technology, in effect, made itself a new medium. He argues that this type of resistance has emerged through a combination of need and opportunity, and thus several digital 'resistant groups' were denied an access to information and media products or the power to express and control their message. Moraes, in turn, analyses virtual communication and its relation to the scope of citizenship and social justice. Online activist groups seek 'to circumvent the monopoly of dissemination, allowing counter-hegemonic forces to express themselves with ease, as social activists committed to achieving citizenship and social justice' (2000: 142). For Moraes, such organizations, which make use of the virtual space to spread their points of view and communicate their needs, along with numerous individuals and groups that belong to the network, spontaneously form what he defines as an 'online activism' that will broaden the global web of communication (2000: 142).

The concept of alternative communication used by Moraes (2007) in order to analyse online activism is based on the discussions held at the Forum of Alternative Media (Foro de Medios Alternativos), which took place in Argentina in 2004. This forum identified alternative communication as a network that 'builds spaces of affirmation of critical interpretive optics and cooperative journalistic practices with the purpose of defending diversity of information and ethical values.' Thus, alternative communication can be defined as that which acts as a tool for communication in the popular field, without excluding social activism; the implication being that journalists and communicators must be within the conflict, always with a clear tendency to democratize information (Moraes, 2007: 4). Thus, the concept of alternative communication seems to be based on a double ideological insertion of a new communication project, that is, an alignment with processes of social change and a systematic combat against the hegemonic system.

It is worth noting the warnings asserted by Moraes (2007), in which he identifies the illusion that the virtual sphere is free of the contradictions inherent to the Capitalist system. He points out that 'it is a mistake to suppose that online space can overcome the scenario of trans-nationalization of communication, especially in the virtual field where corporate media acts aggressively, controlling the most popular sites and thus increasingly attracting advertisements and sponsorships' (2007: 11).

Also with regard to activism in the virtual sphere, Carroll and Hackett (2006) explain that an important form of activism carried out by militants in the digital realm is one in which communication is seen as being simultaneously a means and end of a struggle, with one of their main goals being the democratization of communication and criticism of corporate control of mass media. In this sense, militants engaged in these practices can be considered as media activists, and the new communication technologies dramatically reduce communication costs and enable new opportunities for the practice of media activism. The authors further explained that the majority of media activist movements attempt to draw on emancipatory practices, with the creation of inclusive dialogues as a way of substituting the mono-logical channels typical of the mass media, defending the universal right of communication, and to work towards a decolonized world. Using Habermas' theory of communicative action, Carroll and Hackett (2006) explain that the struggle that occurs within our society, while attempting to democratize communication, can be classified as a social movement because it is based on networks of activists and dissident cultures. These struggles also employ a repertoire of extra action that requires the mobilization of key resources, such as labour and technology, and reason and justice, which drove many of the social movements in modernity.

Media activism is typically associated with other activist causes, which means that it is constantly breaking political boundaries, ultimately resulting in a lack of collective identity.

However, such a form of activism aims at building a policy of connections more than building its own system of action; the lack of a regularized and clear collective identity between activists 'can somehow indicate success in building inter-sectoral social circles which radical political coalitions require' (Carroll and Hackett, 2006: 100).

Cyber activism and resistance within the media in Brazil: Two examples

This section presents the two examples of resistance organizations created by different civil society groups with the aim of confronting traditional media corporations and promoting social changes to the dominant mainstream media model.

The Brazilian Movement of Progressive Bloggers – BlogProg

The alternative blogosphere in Brazil had its genesis in the mid-2000s, when it emerged in the virtual sphere in the form of political websites and blogs whose main purpose was not only constituting themselves as a space for discussions of a political nature, but also a space for critical reflection about texts produced by dominant media vehicles. Among some of the most well-known political blogs and websites that were the precursors for the Brazilian alternative blogosphere were those run by renowned journalists who worked professionally in the field of traditional media, such as Luis Nassif, Paulo Henrique Amorim, Luiz Carlos Azenha and Rodrigo Vianna. In parallel, there was another blogosphere created by smaller militant leftist groups.

It seems clear that the genesis of the field of alternative political blogosphere in Brazil occurred in the first place because new information and communication technologies and the Internet allowed people to express themselves more democratically online, and enabled different civil society groups to express dissatisfaction to what they considered a dominant model of the conservative traditional media.

The year 2010 was particularly important for promoting significant changes in the alternative political blogosphere in Brazil. As a reaction to what some perceived as a process of increasing manipulation of the mainstream media coverage of the presidential elections with the purpose of benefiting the main right-wing opposition candidate, a group of alternative bloggers decided to organize a movement that could counterpoint the views propagated by the mainstream media at the time. The Movement of Progressive Bloggers (BlogProg) was organized mostly by bloggers from traditional media as well as from other fields related mostly to social movements (Azenha, 2010). They also created an organization called the Centre for the Study of Alternative Media Barão de Itararé, whose main objective was to coordinate the efforts of different bloggers and digital activists that lined the movement, to organize the main events promoted within the field. According to the organization, Barão, as it is known, has helped to strengthen community initiatives and alternative communication channelling, developing projects and researching contemporary

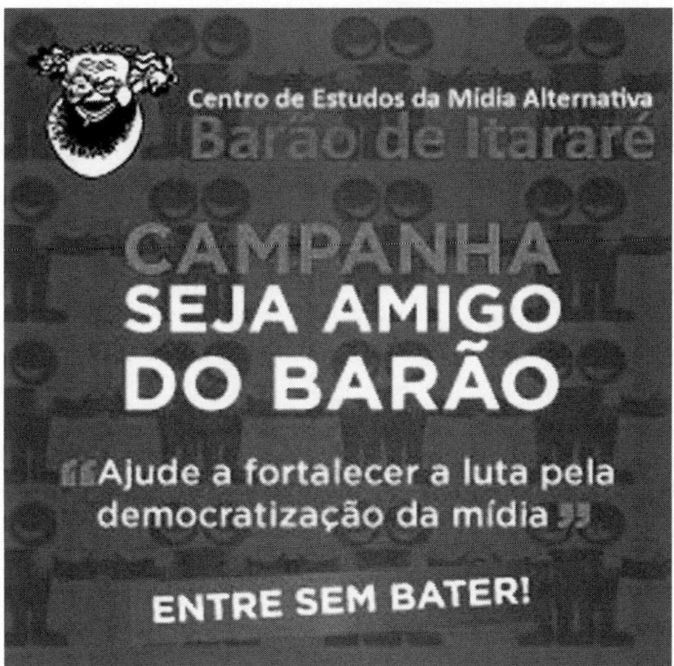

Figure 10.1: Logo for the Centre for Alternative Media Studies Barão de Itararé. Courtesy of the Centre for Alternative Media Studies Barão de Itararé.

media as well as training. The emergence of BlogProg at this time contributed significantly to the strengthening of the field of the alternative political blogosphere in Brazil.

The agents responsible for creating the BlogProg movement also made the important decision to hold regular national and local meetings in order for bloggers and social movement activists to discuss issues of interest to other participants in the movement. Besides this, the meetings became extremely important for them to debate possible strategies for the achievement of its main purpose, namely the implementation of public policies to ensure democratization of the Brazilian media and to prevent the hegemony exercised by the mainstream organizations, allowing other voices to be heard (Vianna, 2010).

According to Darbilly et al. (2013), among many activists that joined the movement since its first national meeting, there are three major groups: journalist bloggers, militant bloggers, and militant organizations. The first group was formed by journalists who came from the traditional media after encountering problems with the companies that they were linked to. They decided to create their own blogs or websites in order to spread an alternative vision of social and political facts. These individuals continue to play a very important role in the movement since they link their names and reputation as important journalists. In this sense, it is possible to say that they act as nodes in the network that helps the movement to gain larger visibility and legitimacy. The second group was also formed by bloggers but, unlike in the previous case, they are characterized by political activism, militancy in favour of democratization of media, digital culture, feminist causes, regional culture and black civil rights, among many others. It consists of a large number of readers and commentators who reproduce the texts published on the blogs and websites of this group, as well as via social networks such as Facebook or Twitter. Finally, the last group consists of different organizations that are also involved in the same issues as the previous group and include various social movements, labour unions, left-wing political parties, foundations, alternative media vehicles and non-governmental organizations that fight for democratization of media.

Among the major achievements of the organization was a news conference granted by former Brazilian president Luis Inácio Lula da Silva to some of its main representatives inside the presidential palace, something that had never happened before (as press conferences were traditionally directed at journalists from the circle of traditional media). The conference was largely described by the movement as a historical event that eventually brought alternative media to the forefront of mainstream media attention (Vianna, 2010). One year after the conference, the ex-president was invited to attend the opening session of the second BlogProg national meeting, which attracted a large

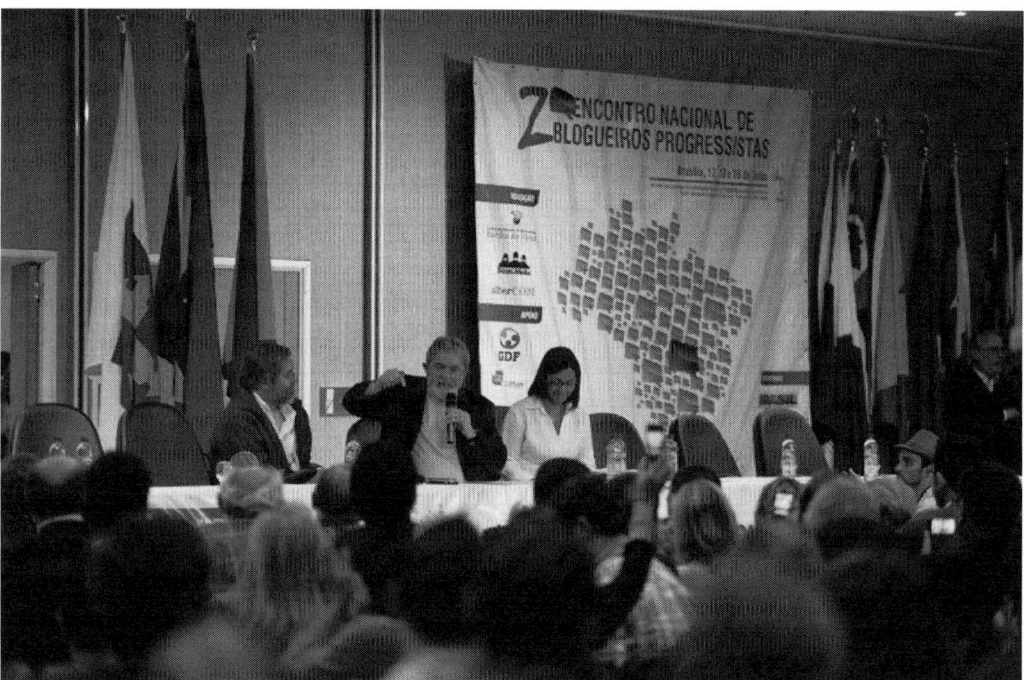

Figure 10.2: National Progressive Bloggers Meeting with ex-president Luis Inácio Lula da Silva. Courtesy of Agência Brasil.

number of people, most of them connected to digital and political activism and social movement representatives. In his speech, Lula da Silva recognized the importance of new technologies in the development of an authentic Brazilian counter-hegemonic media that can privilege a diversity of voices and point of views, especially those who represent Brazil's periphery (Borges, 2011).

I have pointed out elsewhere that the movement clearly adopts organizational practices that emphasize horizontality, decentralization and participation in the process of decision making (Darbilly, 2014). Although there is a national committee composed of representatives from many regions, this commission is responsible only for the process of organizing the annual national meetings and tries not to interfere with local decision-making processes. That is why participants argue that the movement can be considered as an inorganic organization since it does not have any formal role and does not represent anyone. Also, the movement rejects the idea of any formal leadership, since the blogosphere is characterized as a space where everyone can express their points of view and ultimately exert influence. Influence, in this sense, is related to the capacity of someone to argue and convince other people about their own ideas. Also, financial resources obtained by the movement come from donations from many civil society organizations like social movements, unions, alternative media vehicles and especially from other bloggers. It could be argued that an important strategy implemented by movement participants was the decision to create a financial fund and legal aid to be made available to bloggers who could be the target of the lawsuits by the mainstream media organizations. The fund constitutes an example of planned action aimed at not only strengthening online activism and freedom of speech, but also clearly reinforcing the willingness of alternative groups to continue challenging dominant organizations without the fear of being penalized (Darbilly, 2014).

The Mídia Ninja

According to Soares (2013), the Mídia Ninja group (Independent Journalism, Narratives and Action) is a group formed mainly by young people who have used information and communication technologies such as smartphones and social networks to disseminate socio-political events such as protests and manifestations. It can be described as a decentralized organization that has as its main representative journalist Bruno Torturra, former managing editor of a well-known traditional media magazine called *Trip*, where he worked for eleven years.

The Mídia Ninja has its origin in another group called Fora-do-Eixo (FDE), a collective network created in 2005 that organized music festivals and other cultural events independently (Costa, 2013). According to Watts (2013), this largely student-run movement, which started in the Brazilian cities of Rio Branco, Cuiabá and Londrina in 2005, has spread to more than 200 areas and encompassed representation of universities, political parties and financial organizations. The movement's initial role was to promote

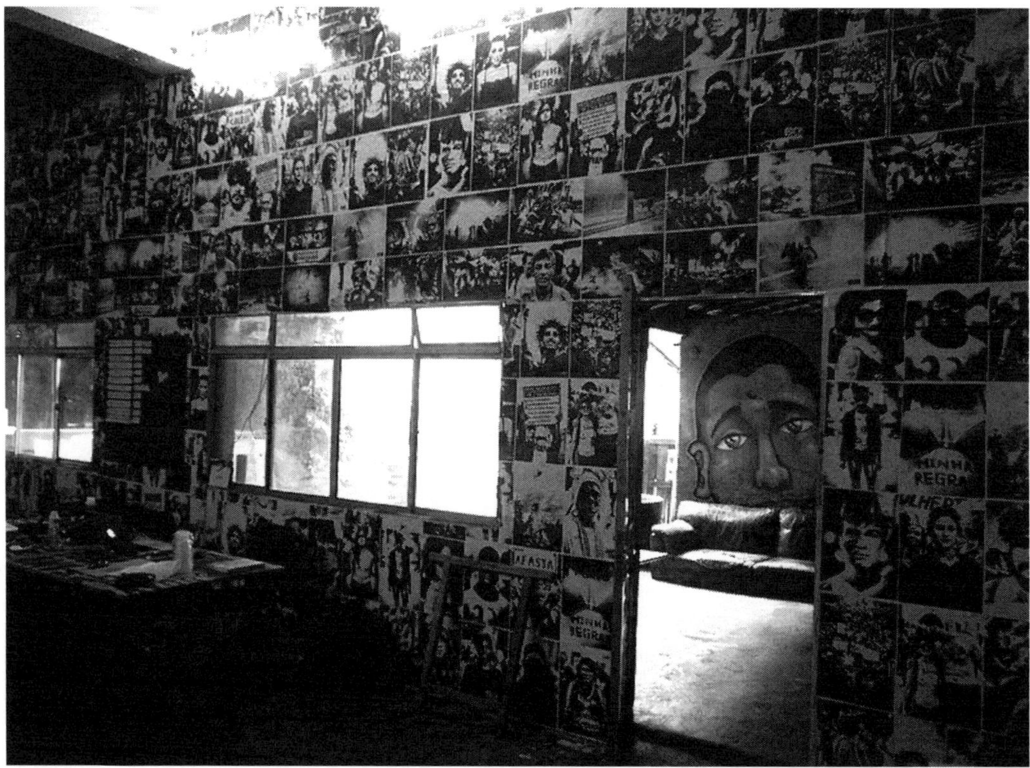

Figure 10.3: Midia Ninja's headquarters in São Paulo, Brazil. Wikimedia Commons.

gigs and live broadcasts of concerts and conferences, but it quickly found an extra mission covering events across the favelas and streets reporting on smaller protests that nobody else reported on. Although there is no specified budget for the Mídia Ninja, Costa (2013) explains that between 3 per cent and 7 per cent of the FDE budget is available for Mídia Ninja in order for development.

The visibility of the group grew especially due to the public protests that took place in Brazil in June 2013. The main objective of these protests was to force local governments to reduce rates of the increased bus fares. Moreover, the protests began targeting the poor quality of public services such as health and education, while criticizing large spending on events like the World Cup 2013 and the Olympic Games, perceived by protesters as abusive. As the protests grew to more than a million people in 52 cities during the Confederation Cup football tournament, the Ninjas saw a surge in support because people at that moment were extremely dissatisfied with the coverage of the events by the mainstream media. Rede Globo, in particular, was perceived by many as a media organization that traditionally tends to criminalize social movements, and its opinions about the protests were considered biased right from the beginning. After one journalist linked to Globo called the protests a 'waste of

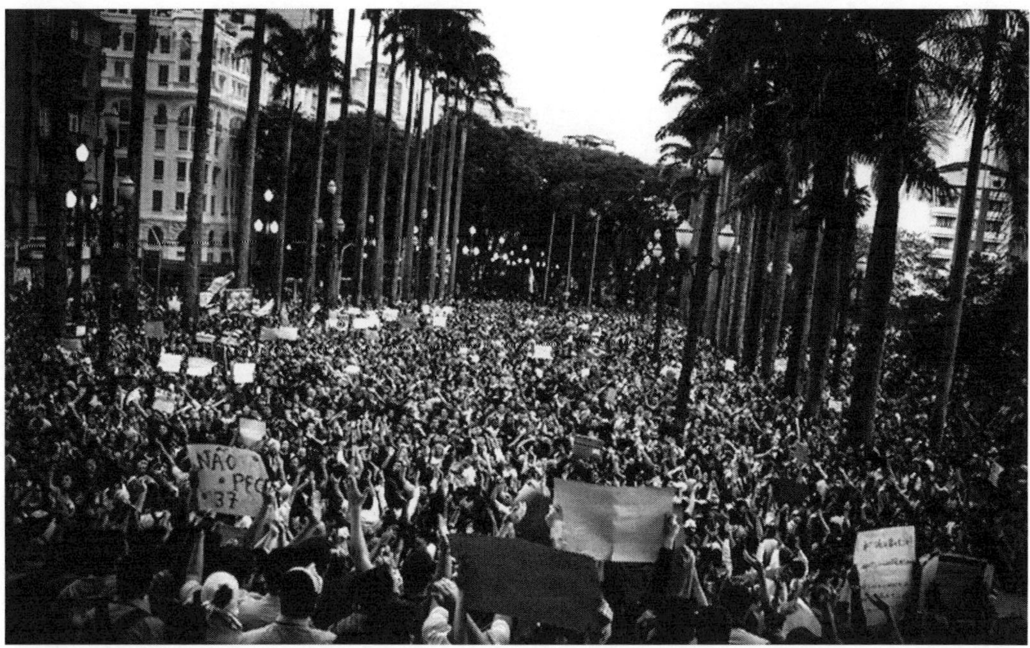

Figure 10.4: Protest against the rise in public transportation fares, 2013. Courtesy of Mídia Ninja.

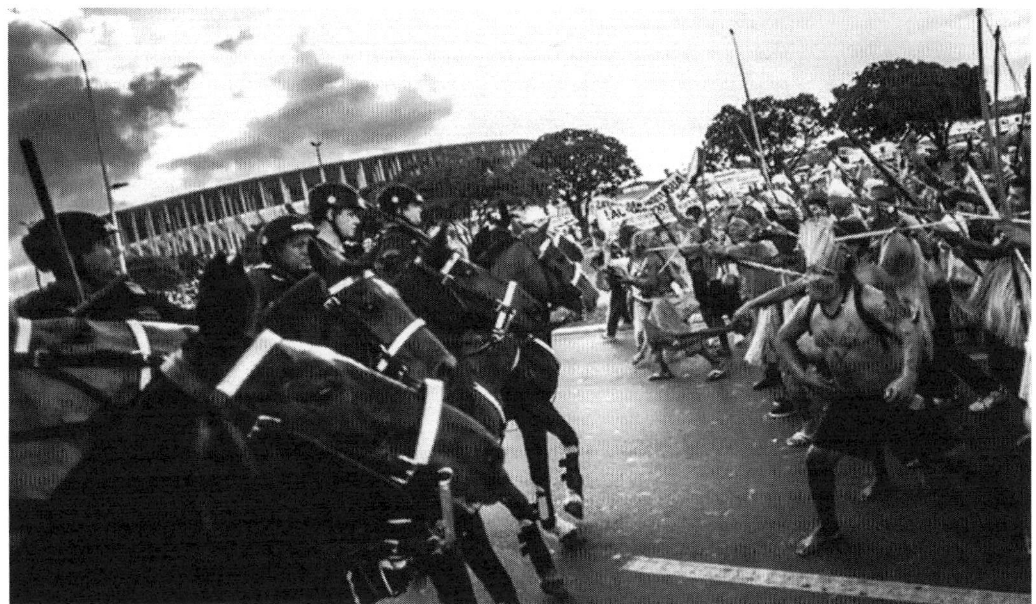

Figure 10.5: Protest against the World Cup in Brazil, 2014. Courtesy of Midia Ninja.

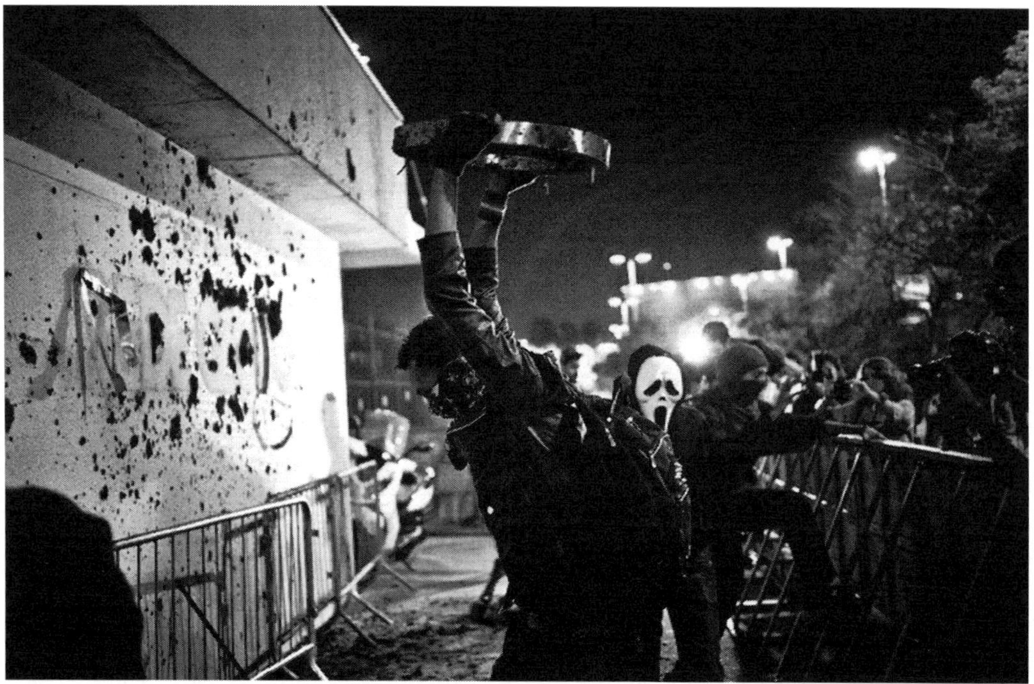

Figure 10.6: Protest against TV Globo and in favour of democratization of media, 2013. Courtesy of Mídia Ninja.

time,' traditional media itself became a target and it was almost impossible for mainstream journalists to cover the protests live without suffering some kind of inconvenience.

On the other hand, the Ninjas were among the first to collect and broadcast images of police violence against the protesters. Much of the reportage was filmed and broadcast live from mobile phones. The coverage was also gathered from images posted online or sent to the groups through social media. Besides having gained more support from the protesters, the traditional media began to mention the group in several of its stories, and represent some of the images already transmitted by Ninjas.

The group's goal is to bring Mídia Ninja information to a larger portion of the Brazilian population. The group fights for the democratization of content creation, the right to inform people and thus modify the role of the media that is concentrated in the hands of few (Mazotte, 2013). This is the main idea of the socio-political activists, who want to offer a counterpoint to traditional media, to show other points of view of the same event, so that citizens do not rely solely on the information transmitted by large corporations. Another goal of this group is to mobilize protests, helping to create a network that helps not only the public with more reliable information, but also the journalists who cannot find room in the market.

In relation to its current structure, Mídia Ninja is formed by a cultural production and communication net that covers the whole country. Costa (2013) argues that currently the

Mídia Ninja group has about twenty people working in the production of content, divided into teams. They are located in the cities of São Paulo, Rio de Janeiro, Belo Horizonte, Fortaleza, Porto Alegre and Salvador. The Mídia Ninja also has hundreds of employees who send in their work in the form of videos, photos and texts. Their publications are mostly made in their Facebook profile, and the information published is mainly about events within the south-east region, with occasional international information.

According to its members, Mídia Ninja is not funded by any institution and their hope is to enlist the help of the public. Through collective financing campaigns, such as crowdfunding on the Internet, they raised funds for equipment. Mídia Ninja's future plan is to make available on their website monthly subscription content that will enable readers to make donations, and thus, remunerate some of their members for expenses such as accommodation or equipment use. The longer-term challenge is how to maintain the financial integrity of a group that wants to become a more powerful force for social change but does not want to compromise its non-commercial values.

Conclusions

The perspective of resistance may allow for the analysis of the media field in Brazil as a space marked by disputes between traditional organizations and newcomers, where different kinds of strategies are developed and implemented in order for these groups to achieve their goals. Thus, social protagonists located in it – like journalists, mainstream media corporations, bloggers, social movements, among others – adopt different strategies in order to achieve their objectives.

The two examples of social movement organizations analysed in this chapter have contributed significantly to changes in the structure of the Brazilian communication field. The emergence of new information and communication technologies allowed different participants that did not traditionally belong to the media industry to express and disseminate their opinions without having to pass through the filters of large organizations that own the biggest communication vehicles. If until recently mainstream media organizations, as shown by Borges (2009), held the most powerful position and had the power resources needed to keep their position, technological changes enabled the entry of new social voices challenging the mainstream media domination.

Different groups that now have the opportunity to express themselves through the use of new digital tools also use them as a form of refusal to the hegemonic model practiced by the large media organizations based on an established power for decades. Such digital resistance practices are not only intentionally recognized by those who propose changes in order to produce content and practice a different kind of journalism, but are also recognized as such by those who still exercise a dominant position in the industry.

Therefore, it seems possible to affirm that the expressions of resistance analysed in the examples of the Movement of Progressive Bloggers (BlogProg) and Mídia Ninja and put into practice by many social factions (parties, bloggers, unions, non-governmental organizations, guerrilla groups, among others) can be characterized as more open form of resistance. This is because they clearly aim to combat mainstream media monopoly in the communication field. In the case of the BlogProg movement, it is clear that its primary aim is to fight for the implementation of some kind of public policy in the Brazilian context that can allow democratization of a media that for many decades has been monopolized by a few large media corporations that used to control all stages of the process of production and distribution of information. In this sense, the creation of the movement can be described as a strategy that consisted of an alliance or a net of different civil society groups who understood that the use of new technologies could provide them an opportunity not only to express their point of views, but to openly resist the dominant discourse and practices implemented by mainstream organizations. The different national and regional meetings organized by the movement, as well as the many counter-hegemonic actions it has implemented, show that their performances are not restricted to the virtual space but, on the contrary, find its main course of action in the real world.

Media activism as a form of activism practiced by militants in the virtual sphere has as one of its main goals the democratization of media and the mass media monopoly of criticism. In the second example, it seems correct to describe Mídia Ninja as a militant alternative journalism. Combining new technologies with their commitment to transparency, the Ninjas do not care about formal quality, do not select or edit, but show live, in real time, what their cameras are capturing. In this case, virtual and real spaces are not distinguished and people are able to watch live many contradictions, violence and conflicts. In this regard, Mídia Ninja can also be characterized as a counter-hegemonic movement of resistance to the traditional media corporation practices. The mass protests that occurred in Brazil in 2013 were one of the main events that made them become well-known across the country. It seems appropriate to consider digital resistance as a form of media activism, since, as pointed out by authors such as Moraes, such groups and organizations have well-defined strategies of action that seek to 'assume transformative visions in the relationship with readers and society in general, in management methods, forms of financing, and especially the interpretation of social facts' (2007: 4).

The two examples of media activist organizations described in this chapter show different experiences or new forms of organizing that are capable of resisting and contesting the traditional model of news production and dissemination. In other words, these experiences can be seen as alternative practices implemented by different civil society groups that not only reject the notion of neutrality that is central to traditional organizations, but that explicitly assume its ideology. This ideology, according to their participants, is based on the fight for social transformation and social justice in a country still marked by heavy social exclusion and poverty, despite all the improvements achieved over the past decade. Compared to the corporations in the communication field, these experiences can be considered as informal, incipient, fragmented, sometimes irrational forms of organizations that are guided by an alternative logic of action. Based on the ways BlogProg and Mídia

Ninja organize their activities and develop strategies for resistance, they can be categorized as morphing organizational spaces promoting transformational change in a society.

The precariousness that marks these organizations is directly related to their logic, different from that of the market-based system (Ramos, 1981). While the latter is characterized by a set of language, methods, tools and techniques oriented towards the imperative of efficiency and profit (Solé, 2003), these alternative organizations adopt forms that can support social causes in which they are engaged. Thus, the main characteristics implemented by these organizations, such as a non-hierarchical structure, a participative decision-making process, the lack of formal leadership and alternative forms of financing, as well as their informal and fragmented way of acting, are elements that point at their precarious nature.

References

Alcadipani, R. 2007. 'O declínio dos jornais', *Revista De Administração De Empresas*, 6 (2), 31–35.

Azenha, L. C. 2010. 'O encontro nacional de blogueiros progressistas', *Viomundo*, http://www.viomundo.com.br/opiniao-do-blog/o-encontro-nacional-de-blogueiros-progressistas.html. Accessed 17 March 2013.

Bocchini, L. 2013. 'O Barão de Itararé está te chamando. Blog do Lino', *Carta Capital Online*, http://www.cartacapital.com.br/blogs/blog-do-lino/o-barao-de-itarare-esta-te-chamando-1849.html. Accessed 2 September 2013.

Borges, A. 2009. *A Ditadura Da Mídia*, São Paulo: Anita Garibaldi.

Borges, A. 2011. 'As críticas de Lula no II BlogProg', *Blog do Miro*, http://altamiroborges.blogspot.com.br/2011/06/as-criticas-de-lula-no-ii-blogprog.html. Accessed 20 August 2013.

Carroll, W. K. and Hackett, R. A. 2006. 'Democratic media activism through the lens of social movement theory', *Media Culture Society*, 28 (1), 83–104.

Centro de Estudos de Mídia Alternativa Barão de Itararé 2013. 'Objectivos', http://www.baraodeitarare.org.br/index.php/2012-09-08-21-55-06/objetivos. Accessed 25 August 2013.

Costa, L. M. 2013. 'O linchamento da Mídia Ninja', *Observatório da Imprensa*, http://www.observatoriodaimprensa.com.br/news/view/o_linchamento_da_midia_ninja. Accessed 31 October 2013.

Darbilly, L. V. C. 2014. 'Blogosfera, estratégias de subversão e o campo da comunicação no Brasil: uma análise do Movimento dos Blogueiros Progressistas sob uma perspectiva de estudos organizacionais', Doctoral dissertation, Rio de Janeiro: Getulio Vargas Foundation.

Darbilly, L. V. C., Simões, J. M. and Vasconcelos, F. C. 2013. 'Práticas de Ciberativismo e o Campo da Mídia Política Alternativa no Brasil: uma análise do Movimento dos Blogueiros Progressistas a partir da perspectiva de Pierre Bourdieu', paper presented at *XVI SemeAd: Seminário em Administração*, Universidade de São Paulo, 24 October.

Furtado, C. 1978. *Criatividade E Dependência Na Civilização Industrial*, Rio de Janeiro: Paz e Terra.

Mazotte, N. 2013. 'Mídia Ninja: um fenômeno de jornalismo alternativo que emergiu dos protestos no Brasil', *Knight Center*, https://knightcenter.utexas.edu/pt-br/blog/00-14113-

midia-ninja-um-fenomeno-de-jornalismo-alternativo-que-emergiu-dos-protestos-no-rio-de. Accessed 31 October 2013.

Mielli, R. 2009. 'Pela criação de políticas e espaços públicos de comunicação'. In Mielli, R. (Ed.), *Comunicação Pública No Brasil: Uma Exigência S Democrática*, São Paulo: Anita Garibaldi, 9–12.

Misoczky, M. C., Flores, R. K. and Bohm, S. 2008. 'A práxis da resistência e a hegemonia da organização', *Organizações E Sociedade*, 15 (45), 181–193.

Misoczky, M. C., Flores, R. K. and Silva, S. M. G. 2008. 'Estudos organizacionais e movimentos sociais: o que sabemos? Para onde vamos?', *Cadernos EBAPE.BR*, 6 (3), 1–14.

Moraes, D. 2000. 'Comunicação virtual e cidadania: movimentos sociais e políticos na Internet', *Revista Brasileira de Ciências da Comunicação*, XXIII (2), 142–155.

Moraes, D. 2007. 'Comunicação alternativa, redes virtuais e ativismo: avanços e dilemas', *Revista de Economía Política de las Tecnologías de la Información y Comunicación*, 9 (2), http://www.seer.ufs.br/index.php/eptic/article/view/226/224. Accessed 15 March 2016.

Nassif, L. 2009. 'A mídia em debate', *Conteúdo*, 4, 10–15, http://www.contee.org.br/noticias/contee/pdf/revistaconteudo_n4.pdf. Accessed 1 February 2013.

Otto, B. and Bohm, S. 2006. '"The people" and resistance against international business: The case of the Bolivian "water war"', *Critical Perspective on International Business*, 2 (4), 299–320.

Ramonet, I. 2010. *A Tirania Da Comunicação*, Petrópolis: Vozes.

Ramos, A. G. 1981. *A Nova Ciência Das Organizações: Uma Reconceituação Da Riqueza Das Nações*, Rio de Janeiro: Editora FGV.

Russell, A. 2005. 'Editorial: exploring digital resistance', *New Media Society*, 7 (4), 513–515.

Sá, N. de 2013. 'Grupo Mídia Ninja se projeta ao cobrir protestos ao vivo', *Folha de S. Paulo*, http://www1.folha.uol.com.br/poder/2013/07/1317943-grupo-midia-ninja-se-projeta-ao-cobrir-protestos-ao-vivo.shtml. Accessed 31 August 2013.

Soares, L. 2013. 'Por que a mídia tradicional tem medo da Mídia Ninja', *Pragmatismo Político Online*, http://www.pragmatismopolitico.com.br/2013/08/por-que-a-midia-tradicional-tem-medo-da-midia-ninja.html. Accessed 31 August 2013.

Solé, A. 2003. 'L'entrepise: une invention latine?'. In *Colóquio Internacional Sobre Poder Local, 7, Salvador. Anais*, Salvador: Nepol.

Spicer, A. and Bohm, S. 2007. 'Moving management: theorizing struggles against the hegemony of management', *Organization Studies*, 28 (11), 1667–1698.

Vianna, R. 2010. '2010: ano dos blogs sujos e do Sujinho', http://www.rodrigovianna.com.br/palavra-minha/2010-ano-dos-blogs-sujos-e-do-sujinho-ano-da-bolinha-da-dilma-e-da-nova-direita.html. Accessed 30 September 2013.

Watts, J. 2013. 'Brazil's ninja reporters spread stories from the streets', *The Guardian*, http://www.theguardian.com/world/2013/aug/29/brazil-ninja-reporters-stories-streets. Accessed 25 August 2013.

Chapter 11

Organizing culture in favela *Fluminense* in Rio de Janeiro: The dynamics of precarity

Alketa Peci, Daniel S. Lacerda and Vanessa Brulon

The law is ruthless only for us favela people
and protects the scammer
he should be the first in your list,
heads up, officer!
Se Liga Doutor/Heads Up Officer

(Bezerra da Silva, 1999)

Introduction

According to the official census, 6 per cent of the Brazilian population live in favelas, and this number can rise to 40 per cent of the population in some urban centres (Cavallieri and Vial, 2012). More than just a social problem, today the concept of a slum is widely referred to as a feature of urban settings shaped by modern development, whose effects are resisted through the organization of the excluded (Imas and Weston, 2012). Poverty and the perceived precarious nature of these areas make them the most common targets of social change programs, including culturally led interventions. These interventions are designed to serve as anchors for regeneration and social projects, a current trend in many cities around the world (Santos et al., 2004).

Although favelas contain a large number of organizations of different types and a life of their own, they continue to be viewed through a prism of absence: historically defined by what they lack or what they do not represent (Souza e Silva, 2009). Cavalcanti (2007) highlights the terms of poverty and illegality as most associated with definitions of a favela, and as explained by Zaluar and Alvito (2006), favelas are usually associated with shortage, absence and emptiness. This prejudicial discourse on favelas is consumed also by political society, perpetuating the discrimination (Lacerda, 2014). Observatorio de Favelas, a social research organization dedicated to research on favelas and the urban phenomena, produced a report based on a seminar 'What are favelas, anyway?' (Souza e Silva, 2009), in which the authors argue that stigmatized perceptions of favelas set negative parameters as references to the social representation of this phenomenon. Instead, favelas should be defined in what they are, and 'recognized according to their socio-territorial specificity' (Souza e Silva, 2009: 3) as explored for example in the investigation of their 'underground sociabilities' (Jovchelovitch and Priego-Hernandez, 2013).

In many countries in South America and elsewhere, areas considered as economically underdeveloped are often the focus of social projects and involvement of cultural organizations, indicating certain assumptions about the potential of such projects in changing the dynamics of inequalities. The introduction of a new cultural attraction and cultural interventions are aimed at the transformation of *space*, which is formed by 'an indivisible, integral and contradictory set of systems of objects and systems of actions, not taken in isolation but as a unique scenario in which history unfolds' (Santos, 2006: 39). Santos' definition unfolds from the geographic conceptualisation of produced space, in which any social setting carries with its historical happenings and present relations. Any spatial change is committed, thus, to the entwined processes and social relations. In that sense, external or internal interventions can produce space, changing the systems of objects and systems of actions that compose this space, and redefining its own practices.

This chapter is particularly interested in comprehending how cultural organizing practices produce space, transforming it in terms of its symbolic, political and technical dimensions. Instead of focusing on organizations as structured social entities, the theoretical and empirical argument is based on the notion of organizing practices, which requires that 'several different collective actions be connected according to a pattern that is institutionalized at a given time and in a given place' (Lindberg and Czarniawska, 2006: 293). According to Lefebvre (1991), practices form social space as much as its representations. Hence, organizing practices are situated in a particular social context, which may allow the agents to appropriate their social space, leading to various spatial transformations. In Brazilian cities, where the formation of favelas is a common phenomenon, the progress of Capitalism silences the voices of others who inhabit favelas. The installation of cultural organizing practices may be an attempt to give dwellers their voices back.

This chapter looks particularly at how organizing practices encompassing a variety of cultural initiatives in an exemplary favela of Rio de Janeiro, which henceforth will be called favela *Fluminense*, mediate the effects in the transformation of space. This favela is a good example of a space with flourishing cultural initiatives promoted by various governmental agencies and artistic workshops sponsored by the Human Rights Secretary, NGOs, as well as events organized by local groups. The insights that emerge from this investigation contribute to the understanding of cultural organizing processes applied in favelas, and the increasing depth and range of actions performed by both the Brazilian government and civil society, which enact multiple transformations within the confines of the so-called favela territory.

Favelas, cultural organizing practices and transformation of space

Lefebvre (1991) explains that every 'space' is socially produced. Spaces are continuously transformed by human action, and contain in themselves social relations that occupy and transform the space. Every spatial setting contains much more than its material artefacts, as it is the outcome of a set of operations undertaken over time, whereby each operation changes the space previously transformed. In Lefebvre's accounts, the growth of productive forces is the reason for the growing transformation of urban landscapes. Accordingly, Milton Santos understands space as social fact (Santos, 2008a) and, similarly to Lefebvre, emphasizes the dual function performed by space: 'it defines itself by the set [of systems of objects and systems of actions], but is also determined by it; space is simultaneously producer and product, determinant and determined' (Santos, 2008a: 163).

Thus, space encompasses power relationships, means of production, physical settings, social relations, and so on. Drawing on this foundation, we argue that space may be an important category that substitutes previous traditional categories of organizational analysis, such as system or environment, which could lead to a reductionism of the social phenomena (see also Vieira et al., 2010; Vergara and Vieira, 2005). This assumption applies especially to the analysis of precarious spaces, which due to their nature are constantly changing spaces, and require the use of categories that reflect the mutual determination between subjects and objects of a social materiality (Lefebvre, 1991; Santos, 2006, 2008a, 2008b). This is particularly important for the analysis of urban spaces, which often produce favelas as a product of their development.

An important feature of Brazilian cities is the presence of favelas. The population living in favelas is growing three times faster than the urban population (Coelho, 2004). In Rio de Janeiro, where the biggest favelas are located, 1.4 million people (22 per cent) were accounted as living in favelas in the last census. The first urban settlement that received the name of favela in Brazil (*Morro da Providência*) emerged during the late nineteenth century, also in Rio. In the early twentieth century, favelas began to expand, and Pino (1998) argues that problems such as inflation, unemployment and high rental prices were the main causes of this social framework. Aggravated by the migratory trend towards urban centres, the growth of favelas accelerated and by 1950, 7 per cent of the total population of the city of Rio de Janeiro was already living in favelas (Oliveira, 1985).

According to Valladares (2000), in the early twentieth century the issue of favelas left academia and started to be discussed by society in general, showing concern for the future of this population and triggering a major debate around what should be done about it. Recently, this debate has taken on even greater significance, inasmuch as the favela has become the symbol of another social issue: the lack of public security (Ramos and Paiva, 2007). Today, many public policies and private initiatives pursue agendas aimed at changing the spaces of favelas to provide better quality of life for the dwellers and encourage integration with the rest of the city.

Organizations today are believed to be the protagonists of social relations, and individuals are drawn to organizations in order to satisfy a great range of social and personal needs. Traditionally, organizations were defined as groups of individuals who pursue shared objectives. However, Marsden and Townley (2001) caution us against the common mistake of reducing an organization to its intrinsic strategic objectives, extracting the social relations from its operation. Aiming at an understanding of organizations beyond their formal boundaries, we share the view of Dale and Burrell who see organizations within the social processes that construct and are constructed by space, and suggest organization is 'a social form or institution that facilitates collective action' (2008: 33).

A processual perspective of organization especially suits the domain of civil society organizations. The values driving voluntary organizations are much more substantive and less associated with strategic or instrumental goals (Lacerda and Vieira, 2011), and as such organizational actions should not be subordinated to a given aim. Organizing practices can result in different structures including projects, networks or formal institutions. We focus here on the social relations produced by the collective coordinated actions, related to cultural activities in particular.

As a social phenomena, organizing practices should be seen in the light of social practices. As proposed by Schatzki et al., the study of social practices can solve the issue of relying only on individual or invisible entities to identify what distinguishes a collective group from outsiders: 'to insist that the bedrock of all order and agreement is agreement in practice is to cite something public and visible, something that is manifested in what members do' (2001: 1). Focusing on the public and visible features, the analytical identification of organizing practices may be embedded in the nature of such practices, for instance in the cultural activities.

To define cultural organizing practices, we will consider here the different ways of understanding culture. We adopt here the categorization presented by Williams for the three dimensions of cultural analysis: ideal, whereby culture is an aesthetic process for achieving the absolute values of human perfection; documentary, consisting of the registered body of intellectual and artistic work; and social, which anthropologically describes as a certain way of living with shared meanings and values (2001: 41).

Culture can also be organized as a way of resistance. Said (1993) defends that culture can mitigate damage from an urban existence that can be potentially aggressive, and the perception of culture as a way of living is emphasized by Saraiva and Carrieri (2012), as a characteristic of the organization-city, wherein it is necessary to understand culture as a metaphor in which the dynamic of the population defines their place.

This chapter attempts to evaluate how favela dwellers can resist the discourses of Capitalist expansion through cultural organizing, illustrating the contradictory existence of favelas, and explaining how the actions of groups can be the mediators for the production of space (Lefebvre, 1991: 77). Cultural organizing practices account, here, for the social role of culture. Cultural organizations are expanding, making 'the space of culture an important factor in the quality of life of society' (Goulart et al., 2003: 124). Our focus on cultural organizing practices broadens the range of cultural activities that, particularly in the case of favelas, may not always be manifested as a formal organization.

Each cultural organizing practice is also a potential force for changing the territory. This is the conclusion produced in the project Solos Culturais (Cultural Lands) that mapped out the existing cultural activities across different favelas (Rocinha, Alemão, Manguinhos, Cidade de Deus and Penha) across Rio (Barbosa and Dias, 2013). Challenging the common sense that regards favelas as devoid of culture, the project found more than 800 recurrent cultural activities across these five favelas (including music, performing arts, and visual arts). On average, for every 640 favela dwellers, there is one organization promoting local cultural manifestations. The report revealed that creativity is their tool for overcoming the lack of proper cultural equipment for their art. In Cidade de Deus, for example, one of the sites previously used by drug traffickers to kill, was the place chosen to promote a storytelling activity called 'London Tea,' where people would sit at a table decorated with British adornments and tell their stories about the favela (Barbosa and Dias, 2013: 104).

In the same direction, geographers were proficient in demonstrating that space is closely related to culture (see Santos, 2006), which is even pointed as one of its dimensions (Saquet, 2007). Culture reinforces local identity, and is such an important component of the territory itself that Santos stated that the territory, composed of land and population, can itself be thought of as 'an identity, the fact and the feeling of belonging to what we belong' (2008a: 96). This is expressed in our case especially by the word favela itself, usually evocated by dwellers to reinforce their identity as bound to their territory.

Cultural Studies contribute to the debates on development by rejecting the alienated production of space. In effect, the relationship between culture and development is a key topic in contemporary discussions about development, both within academic and practical experiences (Loiola and Miguez, 2007). Brazil has been largely influenced by the ideas about development of the academic, ex-minister Celso Furtado, who argues that development policy should be used to enhance the process of cultural enrichment (Furtado, 1984: 32). This is precisely what will be shown in the studied case: examples of how cultural organizing favours development.

However, Santos (2008b) also warns that, as a result of the process of imposing elements of mass culture, the development model of hegemonic countries has been followed by other countries, with no consideration for the cultural aspects of each country, which would have led to an appropriation of the local model as the key for development. Again, in the studied case, we believe there are striking examples of how cultural practices, which strengthen the shared meanings and values of a given people, may prevent functional implementation of a hegemonic development project.

For Santos (2007), cultural enrichment could be achieved also through the social appropriation of technical and technological means, ultimately aimed at the socialization of natural spaces. In this sense, through the appropriation of technical means, we could produce space from our values and our culture, with no imposition from the outside. On the other hand, when exchange value supersedes use value as the driving force of productive organization, organic solidarity becomes impossible, and the external influence emerges as the determining force of regulation – this is the origin of deterritorialization (Santos, 2007: 82). People in favelas are constantly exposed to such constraints. Outsiders determine their productive and social life, and the appropriation of technical means is one of the ways to resist the alienation of territory.

Thus, for the appropriation of technical means to work as a resistance against the alienation of territory, it should be driven by local cultural values, and not have mass culture as its end. As Swidler (1986) explained, in opposition to the idea of cultural values guiding actions as ends, the strategies of action themselves could be cultural products. Culture provides people with a repertoire of capacities with which the world is faced, and the capacities produced within the favela are the less constraining ones for their own subjects. The case of *Morro do Fluminense* presents the description of strategies of actions developed within the favelas in order to appropriate space in its social and technical dimensions.

The organization of *Morro do Fluminense*

Morro do Fluminense is located in the South Zone of Rio de Janeiro. The whole complex houses around 10,000 residents squeezed into an area of only 128,000 m^2 (IPPRio, 2011). There are many infrastructural issues such as lack of basic sanitation, waste disposal and leisure spaces. *Fluminense* is, currently, one of the favelas with the largest number of cultural projects in the city of Rio de Janeiro, thanks to its location in one of the city's richest neighbourhoods. This makes it the target of high-profile projects, such as the Corporate Social Responsibility project by the most influential media group in the country.

From this community emerged one of the most celebrated samba musicians in Brazil, who denounced many of the social oppressions occurring in favelas. The reality that inspired much of the work of the famous samba singer also stimulated the creation of various organizations founded by the dwellers themselves or by external movements, aiming to provoke a social change in living conditions of the *Fluminense* area, such as the reduction of youth crime or the or the development of skills for young people to enhance their employability. We could argue *Fluminense* has become one of the most thriving favelas in Rio de Janeiro in terms of cultural interventions.

The data collection for this study coincided with a time of great transformation for the community in the years 2011 and 2012. In 2010, the recent public security program for favelas' 'pacification' was implemented at *Fluminense*. Even though the program is publicized as liberation for the local residents, Lacerda and Brulon (2013) showed that the logic behind this is the control of resources by non-residents. In effect, trafficking was still very active in the favela, although residents have been liberated from arbitrary criminal commandments. Amidst the atmosphere of revolt against a government that publicizes what has not yet been delivered, and the constant renegotiation with the as yet not well-established Pacifying Police Unit (UPP), cultural organizing had a lot to say. We were there to listen.

We targeted practitioners of various cultural manifestations and local inhabitants. The collected data were interpreted according to two key theoretical categories. The first category was organizing practices encompassing cultural initiatives, here defined as the social production of coordinated and collective modes of cooperation organized around specific cultural manifestations (Dale and Burrell, 2008; Williams, 2001). In order to operationalize this category, we worked with the following indicators: collective actions aimed at developing values of human perfection; collective actions for producing/promoting registered intellectual and artistic works; and collective actions that reinforce shared meanings and values. Another key category was relation between culture and transformation of space, which was defined as cultural initiatives that lead to the material transformation of territory (Eagleton, 2000; Furtado, 1984; Goulart et al., 2003; Santos, 2006). In order to operationalize this category, the following indicators were used: reinforcement of a local identity; promotion of political citizenship; and appropriation of technical means.

No social territory can be homogeneous, and neither is the analysed favela. Some places are more evidently precarious than others, as reported by one of the dwellers: 'There are two

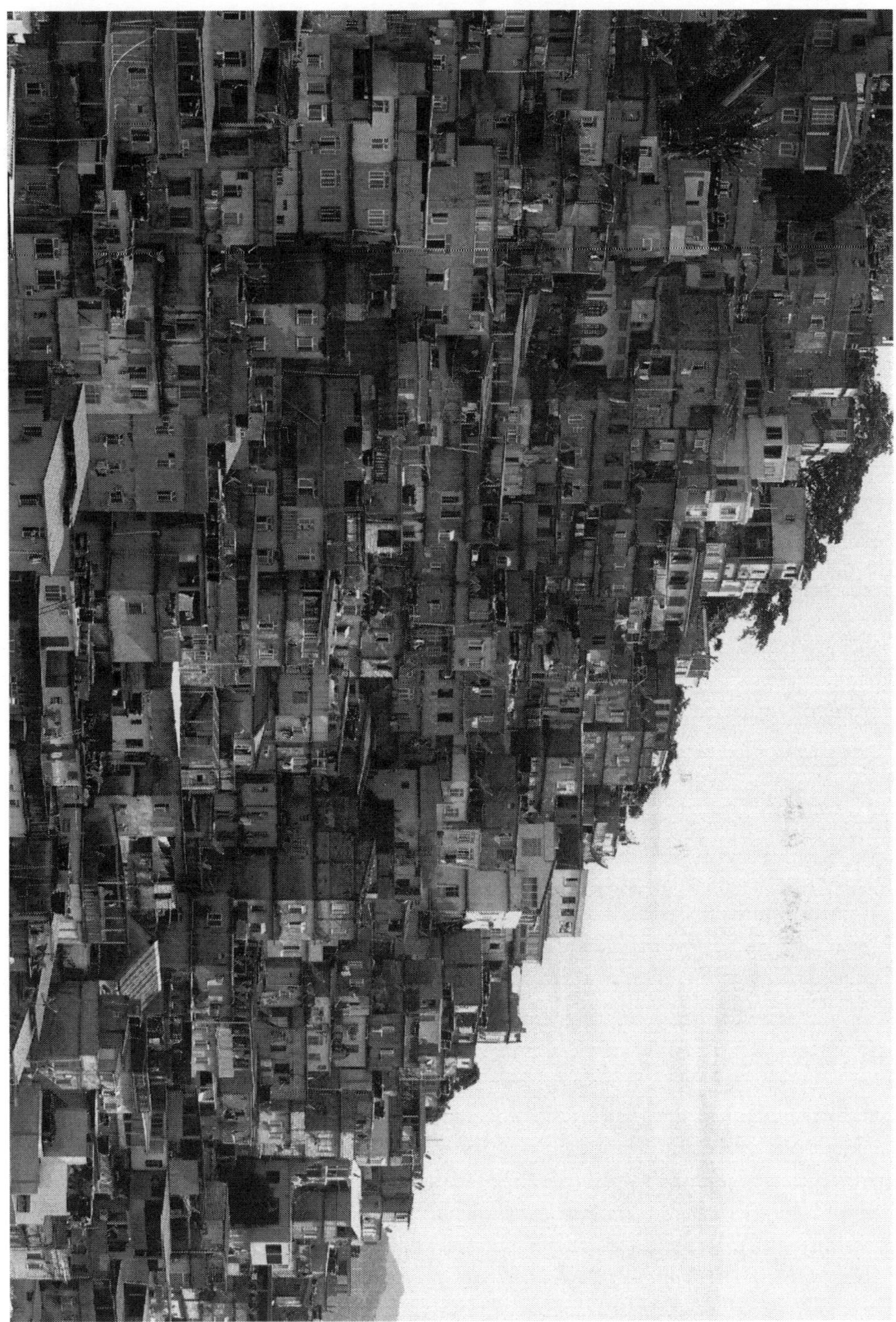

Figure 11.1: Landscape view of one of the communities, 2014. Photograph by Rodolfo Abreu.

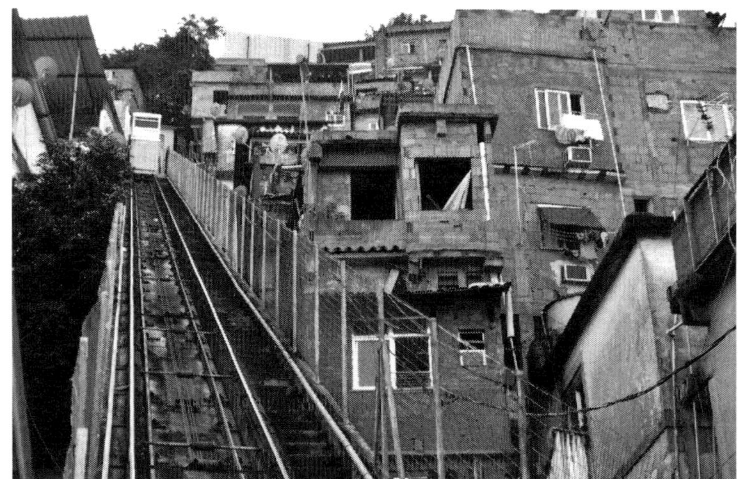

Figure 11.2: Funicular railway up the hillside, 2013. Photograph by Rodolfo Abreu.

realities in here. One is the reality of good houses, where there is sanitation … and the other is the hidden one, where people have nothing' (Sandra, inhabitant). The abundance of cultural organizations in the territory is probably associated with its location in an affluent zone, with easy access to public transportation, which led one of the interviewees to characterize it as 'a super privileged space … I mean, in terms of location, right, and … and even in cultural terms' (Andrea). Previous surveys by local organizations (Residents Association and Local Museum) found about 50 to 60 organizations operating in the favela, most of them promoting cultural activities.

Given the diversity of cultural manifestations concentrated in *Fluminense*, there are a variety of cultural organizing practices going beyond the formal limits of particular organizations. These practices are networked across formal organizations' boundaries, resulting in shared facilities, actions and programs. We describe below examples of cultural activities including music, dance, painting, design, photography and literature; and what was supposed to be emerging from these activities: the autonomy provided by the association between art and technique; cultural manifestations as political actions; and the identity formation from collective gatherings and re-signification of space.

The community seems to be bonded to musical manifestations, and this is not surprising considering that some genres, such as samba and funk music, were born in the favelas, indicating the historical effervescence of musical manifestations in these settlements. During the period of data collection, one of these groups was a grassroots organization struggling to become formal through legal registers and external sponsors. By means of local pressure, they managed to get a concession to use a public space inside the favela. Nearly every day, the practitioners got together to clean and prepare the space for formal classes and performances. However, while they were renovating the space, the children

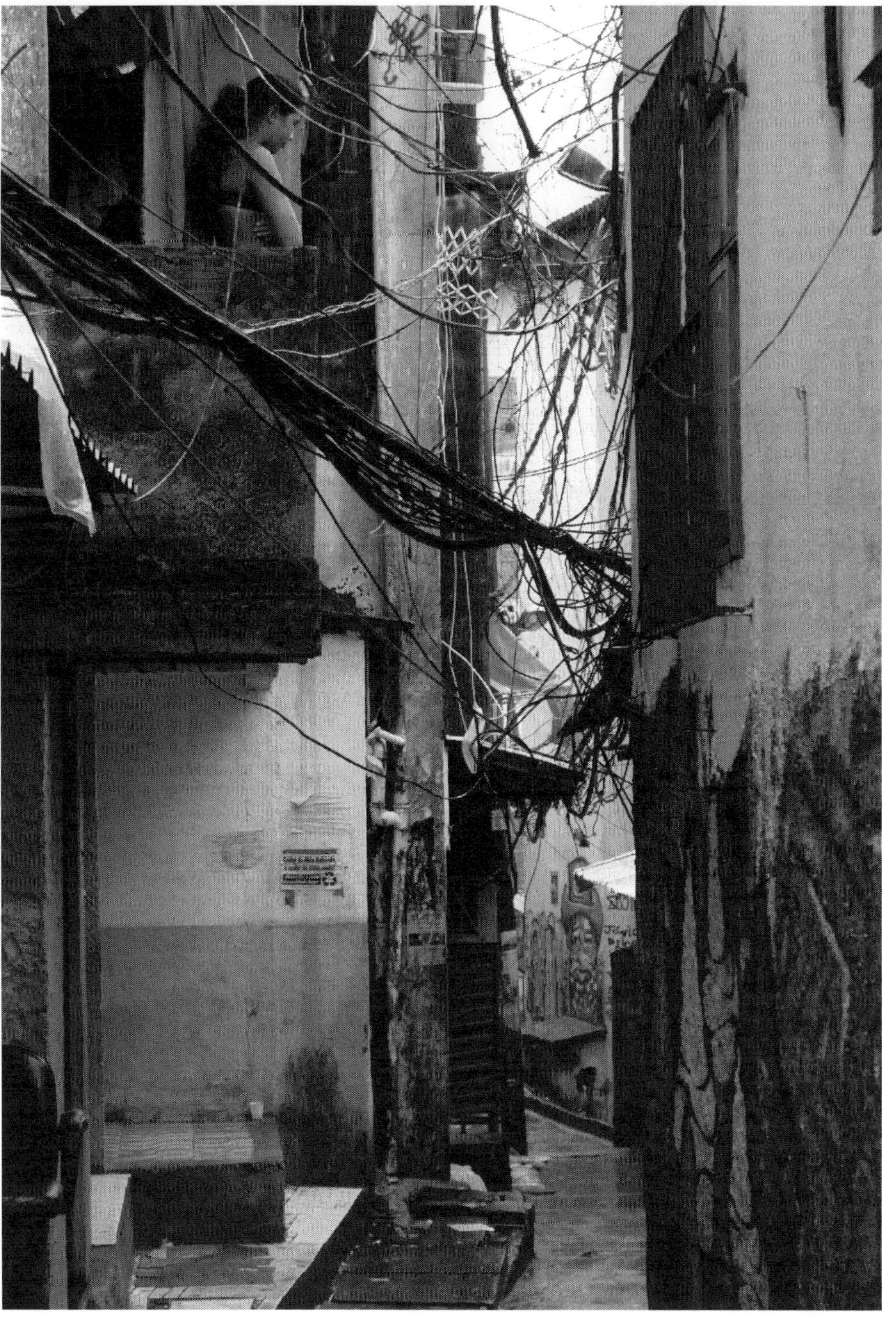

Figure 11.3: Alleyway in the favela with energy-tapping wires and graffiti on the walls, 2013. Photograph by Rodolfo Abreu.

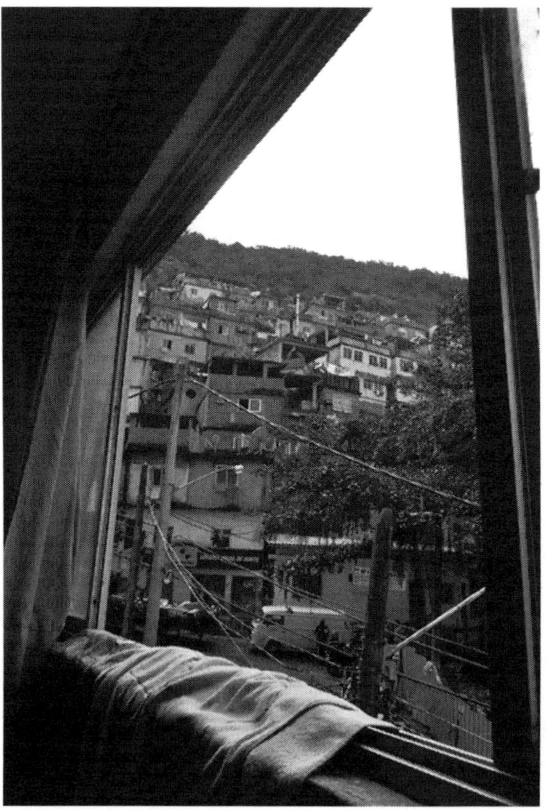

Figure 11.4: Main road seen from a resident's window, 2013.
Photograph by Rodolfo Abreu.

played, sung, practiced their instruments, studied for school and did all sort of activities (always supervised by adults). While the organization was formally inoperative and had no results to present, the organizing practices were intense and the benefits to the children were visible: strengthening their link to the local space, improving their musical abilities and exploring creativity. The question of what is *good* music is relative to taste. In an overall complex network of practices, funk and rap shared the slum space with genres that are traditionally unfamiliar to favela dwellers, such as hall, jazz, tap-dancing, ballet.

How would it be possible to focus on the individual as a whole, accepting their autonomy and at the same time working on their cultural development? In a sense, the answer came from cultural practitioners who demonstrated a strong link to the territory, such as in the photography project: 'these curators are concerned with understanding the context in which they are embedded, you see?' (Ana, practitioner). In these cases, the observable effect was the strengthening of the local identity. Following the explanation of several cultural practices in the community, a practitioner of the project Photosun evaluated the changes:

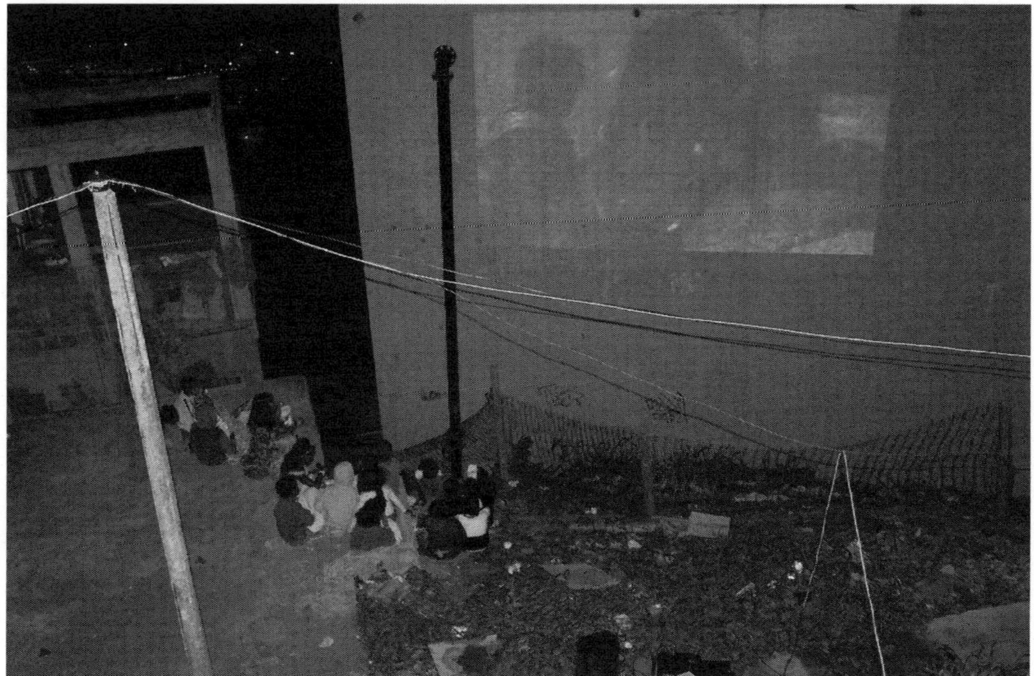

Figure 11.5: Film projected on the community water tank wall, 2012. Photograph by Rodolfo Abreu.

in two years I've seen almost everyone I've worked with changing from one year to the next in their attitude toward the community and in relation to their colleagues and the desire to promote activities or not. […] Nowadays they have a much stronger relationship with the community as a whole.

(Leticia, practitioner)

In Singsoft, some children that took part in the project, now teenagers, work as musicians and teach other children instruments. But one of the strongest examples is Cutting Art, a cooperative of seamstresses that produce T-shirts and purses with designs that represent the community in some way:

Seamstresses who had worked in manufacturing and did not want to work with bosses anymore, because they had small children, organized it here, together, each one had their machine at home, brought them over here, and began making repairs.

(Gil, practitioner)

The group became bigger and more organized. They then produced clothes, purses and bath clothes, stamped with designs that emulate the community. The dwellers themselves created most of the drawings, representing shacks or clusters of people. The seamstresses were proud of how they discovered how to reinforce shared meanings and have an income at the same time. Although they also do some small work of repairs, they insist in using their work to represent the community and for that they dedicate the biggest part of their work time.

The option to sell clothes with images that represent the community, with drawings created by the dwellers, is just possible because they have no bosses; they are the owners of their technical means. They are aware that this choice also bears undesired setbacks, such as the absence of a fixed salary and the fluctuation of their profit from month to month. But the autonomy to choose what to produce and the recognition from the community – that refers to them as real artists – according to them pays for the sacrifices.

The autonomy and recognition is also a political project. This concern was evident in activities that gave them a voice, and the ability to manifest themselves and fight for their own rights. This was the case with the engaged activities of Photosun and the everyday message of Singsoft, to generate an awareness of what it means to be a citizen. In effect, the rise of a political conscience seemed strongly associated with education and information, and when this education comes through cultural practice and identity awareness, it seemed easier to point at the direction of emancipation.

One of the biggest collective practices promoting artistic work in the community is the project Canvas Houses, organized by the Local Museum. The project aims to represent and narrate the history of the favela through paintings on the walls of houses. On the main pathways up *Fluminense* hill, murals can be seen on the walls of houses portraying the story of the favela, and explaining how the community has developed over the years. The twenty painted walls, funded by partnerships with public agencies, are explored through a local tour guided by locally trained residents, explaining the history of the favela from the dwellers' point of view.

The representatives of the program reinforce the importance of transmitting local culture through the Canvas Houses. Other than documenting artwork by local artists, it reinforces the shared meanings and symbols of the favela. The full circuit is depicted in a book that is distributed for free to the favela inhabitants. One of its members, who is also a resident, depicts the central idea of the project:

Because all this tells a story. You see here? It is telling the story of the Copacabana Fortress. Yeah, when there was that Sergeants' Revolt, the soldiers were all here, [...] so it tells about the time that they were not allowed to build brick houses, people in favelas could only build wooden or zinc houses [...] here is the story of water because it was a little water tap, and they had to refill cans to bring water home. And while people stood there waiting to fill the can, they sang, it was the appearance of *samba*, get it?

(Celia, practitioner)

This project was appreciated: 'that's where we praise our memory, our history, our way of living, walking, talking, communicating [...] and [we praise] all this together, congregating with all the other institutions' (Celia, practitioner). Praising their history, the local residents learn to be proud of their 'way of living'. It contrasts the shame they are constantly taught to assume for being from the favela. While the society reprehends them for being poor, they learn that they have something to be proud of.

By painting the walls, the group is also re-signifying the space (building a new place). A good example is depicted by the aforementioned project Solos Culturais, in which spaces formerly used by the traffickers were re-signified by new practices such as storytelling. This could also be seen in *Fluminense*: a graffiti artist paints over the red 'X' signs that were made by government officials to mark the houses allocated for demolition after expropriation, showing cultural practices manifested as practices of resistance.

There is evidence that cultural organizing practices are contributing to the transformation of the local territory through reinforcement of a local identity, promotion of political citizenship and appropriation of technical means.

Conclusions

It seems evident that cultural organizations and their input in the community as well as organizing practices have a strong effect in the transformation of space, understood in the totality of objects and actions (Santos, 2008a). And while all practices generated transformations in space, some of them generated stronger effects than others.

Sometimes the effect realized by a set of practices may seem controversial, as in the events of micro-emancipations that pushed the members towards the pursuit of an outsider world, even leading to an outflow of resources from the community. This is the case, for example, when Singsoft tends to valorize erudite music, or the ballerinas go to Europe in order to improve themselves in ballet techniques. But, even in those cases, the overall benefit of improved education within the community and the development of the skills can have an indirect impact, such as economic growth provided by more options of jobs as musicians or music teachers, or as ballerinas and ballet teachers. This shows also that the effects of organizing practices are interrelated.

All the cultural practices, then, contribute to transformation of space. In case of *Fluminese*, the most visible transformation was indeed the reinforcement of local identity, which is produced by organizing practices of cultural heritage and the sharing of meanings and values. For instance, the mural-document of the history of the community on the walls made young people learn their own history, which for many years had been forgotten. It could be argued that cultural practices can indeed strengthen local identity, even in case of generated resistance to a hierarchized view of culture and its values.

It is interesting to note the cultural exchange that favelas are establishing with the *asfalto*, which might be an indicator of a strong local identity being able to produce its own cultural products. Some of the cultural organizing practices promoted by favela dwellers receive attention from people outside favelas, and spread all over the city. Funk music, for example, a type of music produced inside favelas, is a resounding success among young people from the upper classes. And this cultural exchange is also promoted by the pacification policy, which makes people who want to go into the favelas feel safer. In this sense, people can go inside favelas and, for example, consume the products of Cutting Art, watch a presentation from Singsoft or visit the project Canvas House, getting in touch with local culture and with the history of the community.

The benefits of organizing practices for the recognition of otherness and reinforcement of local identity have also been reported in other studies. Raposo, for example, analysed a group of break dancers in *Favela da Maré*, revealing that participation in an urban tribe relieves the feeling of subordination through solidarity, and restores their pride in a recognized and valued existence: 'a way of building alternate identities and performing collective actions that overcome the stigma with which they are associated' (2012: 336). This network with similar social practices outside the favela (break dancers in other communities) reinforced their feeling of belonging, enlarging their spatial references, in the same way as the cultural manifestations at *Fluminense* did.

Above all, organizing practices encompassing cultural initiatives in favelas, regardless of their primary purpose, show that these territories have their own identity, values, history and culture. The organizing practices analysed here challenge stigmatized perceptions of favelas, which reinforce the idea of favelas as territories of emptiness. Despite the gaps in the provision of welfare and poor living conditions, favelas also have strong presence, highlighted even more by cultural initiatives.

References

Banco Mundial 2012. *O Retorno Do Estado Às Favelas Do Rio De Janeiro: Uma Análise Da Transformação Do Dia A Dia Das Comunidades Após O Processo De Pacificação Das UPPs/ Bringing the State Back into the Favelas of Rio de Janeiro: Understanding Changes in Community Life after the UPP Pacification Process*, Washington, DC: The Worldbank, http://documents. worldbank.org/curated/en/2012/10/17431100/bringing-state-back-favelas-rio-de-janeiro-understanding-changes-community-life-after-upp-pacification-process-o-retorno-estado-favelas-rio-de-janeiro-uma-analise-da-transformacao-dia-dia-das-comunidades-apos-o-processo-de-pacificacao-das-upps. Accessed 15 March 2016.

Barbosa, A. 2012. 'Considerações introdutórias sobre territorialidade e mercado na conformação das Unidades de Polícia Pacificadora no Rio de Janeiro', *Revista Brasileira de Segurança Publica*, 6 (3), 256–265.

Barbosa, J. L. and Dias, C. G. (Eds) 2013. *Solos Culturais*, Rio de Janeiro: Observatório de Favelas do Rio de Janeiro, http://observatoriodefavelas.org.br/wp-content/uploads/2013/05/SolosCulturais_ISSUU-2.pdf. Accessed 23 June 2014.

Bezerra da Silva, J. 1999. 'Se Liga Doutor', CD, *On Bezerra da Silva – Ao vivo*, Rio de Janeiro.

Cavalcanti, M. 2007. 'Of shacks, houses, and fortresses: An ethnography of favela consolidation in Rio de Janeiro', PhD thesis, Chicago, IL: University of Chicago.

Cavallieri, F. and Vial, A. 2012. *Favelas Na Cidade Do Rio De Janeiro: O Quadro Populacional Com Base No Censo 2010*, Rio de Janeiro: Instituto Pereira Passos.

Coelho, S. 2004. 'Pesquisadores quantificam crescimento espacial e populacional de favelas cariocas', *Fiocruz*, http://www.fiocruz.br/~ccs/arquivosite/novidades/out04/favela_sarp.htm. Accessed 12 January 2013.

Dale, K. and Burrell, G. 2008. *The Spaces of Organization and the Organization of Space: Power, Identity and Materiality at Work*, London: Palgrave Macmillan.

Delicato, C. T. 2007. 'Cidades e favelas, pelos olhos de quem?', *Revista de Discentes do Programa de Pós-graduação em Ciências Sociais da Unesp Marília*, 1 (1), 39–51.

Fleury, S. 2012. 'Militarização do social como estratégia de integração: o caso da UPP do Santa Marta', *Sociologias*, 14 (30), 194–222.

Furtado, C. 1984. *Cultura E Desenvolvimento Em Época De Crise*, Rio de Janeiro: Paz e Terra.

Goulart, S., Menezes, M. F. and Gonçalves, J. C. 2003. 'Composição e características do campo organizacional dos museus e teatros da região metropolitana do Recife'. In Carvalho, C. A. and Vieira, M. M. F. (Eds), *Organizações, Cultura E Desenvolvimento Local: A Agenda De Pesquisa Do Observatório Da Realidade Organizacional*, Recife: EDUFEPE.

Imas, J. M. and Weston, A. 2012. 'From Harare to Rio de Janeiro: Kukiya-favela organization of the excluded', *Organization*, 19 (2), 205–227.

Instituto Pereira Passos Rio (IPPRio) 2011. 'Estatisticas municipais – assentamentos precários', Instituto Pereira Passos, http://portalgeo.rio.rj.gov.br/amdpgint_ms.asp?gtema=5&gcod=100&gcod_sub=319>ipo_topo=Tem%E1ticos>ipo_sub=1. Accessed 6 January 2013.

Jovchelovitch, S. and Priego-Hernandez, J. 2013. *Underground Sociabilities: Identity, Culture and Resistance in Rio's Favelas*, Brasilia: UNESCO.

Lacerda, D. S. 2014. 'Rio de Janeiro and the divided state: Analysing the political discourse on favelas', *Discourse & Society*, 26 (1), 1–21.

Lacerda, D. S. and Brulon, V. 2013. 'Politica das UPPs e espaços organizacionais precários: Uma análise de discurso', *RAE*, 53 (2), 130–141.

Lacerda, D. S. and Vieira, M. M. F. 2011. 'Market rationality inside voluntary sector: An analysis of five organizations in Rio de Janeiro, Brazil', *Voluntas*, 22 (3), 875–893.

Lefebvre, H. 1991. *The Production of Space*, Oxford: Blackwell.

Leite, M. 2012. 'Da "metáfora da guerra" ao projeto de "pacificação": favelas e políticas de segurança pública no Rio de Janeiro', *Revista Brasileira de Segurança Pública*, 6 (2), 374–388.

Lindberg, K. and Czarniawska, B. 2006. 'Knotting the action net, or organizing between organizations', *Scandinavian Journal of Management*, 22 (4), 292–306.

Loiola, E. and Miguez, P. 2007. 'Sobre Cultura e desenvolvimento'. In *Proceedings III ENECULT – Encontro de Estudos Multidisciplinares em Cultura*, 23–25 May, Salvador: Faculdade de Comunicação/UFBA.

Marsden, R. and Townley, B. 2001. 'A coruja de Minerva: reflexões sobre a teoria na prática'. In Clegg, S. R. (Ed.), *Handbook de Estudos Organizacionais*, São Paulo: Atlas, pp. 31–56.

Oliveira, J. S. 1985. 'Repensando a questão das favelas', *Revista Brasileira de Estudo de População, Campinas*, 2 (1), 9–30.

Pino, J. C. 1998. 'Labor in the favelas of Rio de Janeiro', *Latin American Perspectives*, 25 (2), 18–40.

Ramos, S. and Paiva, A. 2007. *Mídia E Violência: Novas Tendências Na Cobertura De Criminalidade E Segurança No Brasil*, Rio de Janeiro: IUPERJ.

Raposo, O. 2012. 'Coreografias de evasão: segregação e sociabilidade entre os jovens do break dance das favelas da Maré', *Etnográfica Online*, 16 (2), 315–338.

Rio+Social 2012. *Territorios – Upp Social*, http://www.uppsocial.org/territorios. Accessed 12 February 2013.

Said, E. W. 1993. *Culture and Imperialism*, New York, NY: Vintage.

Santos, A. C. M. S., Kessel, C. and Guimarães, C. (Eds) 2004. *Museus E Cidades*, Rio de Janeiro: Symposium.

Santos, M. 2006. *A Natureza Do Espaço*, São Paulo: Hucitec.

Santos, M. 2007. *O Espaço Do Cidadão*, São Paulo: Universidade de São Paulo.

Santos, M. 2008a. *Por Uma Geografia Nova: Da Crítica Da Geografia A Uma Geografia Crítica*, São Paulo: Universidade de São Paulo.

Santos, M. 2008b. *Por Uma Outra Globalização: Do Pensamento Único À Consciência Universal*, São Paulo: Record.

Saquet, M. A. 2007. *Abordagens E Concepções De Território*. São Paulo: Expressão Popular.

Saraiva, L. A. S. and Carrieri, A. P. 2012. 'Organização-cidade: proposta de avanço conceitual a partir da análise de um caso', *Revista de Administração Pública, Rio de Janeiro*, 46 (2), 547–576.

Schatzki, T. R., Cetina, K. K. and Savigny, E. V. 2001. 'Practice as collective action'. In Schatzki, T. (Ed.), *The Practice Turn in Contemporary Theory*, London: Psychology Press, pp. 1–26.

Souza e Silva, J. (Ed.) 2009. *O que é a Favela Afinal?*, Rio de Janeiro: Observatório de Favelas do Rio de Janeiro, http://www.observatoriodefavelas.org.br/observatoriodefavelas/includes/publ icacoes/164308ca4eebfdf4fd62ab414e0ad4fb.pdf. Accessed 5 January 2013.

Swidler, A. 1986. 'Culture in action: Symbols and strategies', *American Sociological Review*, 51, 273–286.

Valladares, L. 2000. 'A gênese da favela carioca: a produção anterior às ciências sociais', *Revista Brasileira de Ciências Sociais*, 15 (44), 5–34.

Velloso, J. P. R., Pastuk, M. and Pereira Jr., V. 2012. *Favela Como Oportunidade: Plano De Desenvolvimento De Favelas Para Sua Inclusão Social E Econômica*, Rio de Janeiro: INAE.

Vergara, S. C. and Vieira, M. M. F. 2005. 'Sobre a dimensão tempo-espaço na análise organizacional', *RAC – Revista de Administração Contemporânea (Impresso)*, 9 (2), 103–120.

Vieira, M. M. F. 2004. 'Por uma boa pesquisa (qualitativa) em administração'. In Vieira, M. and Zouain, D. (Eds), *Pesquisa Qualitativa Em Administração*, Editora FGV: Rio de Janeiro, pp. 13–28.

Vieira, M. M. F., Vieira, E. F. and Knopp, G. C. 2010. 'Espaço global: território, cultura e identidade', *Revista Administração em Diálogo*, 12 (2), 1–19.

Williams, R. 2001. *The Long Revolution*, London: Bencore Editions.

Zaluar, A. and Alvito, M. 2006. *Um Século De Favela*, Rio de Janeiro: Editora FGV.

Chapter 12

A much mended thing: Notes from the North

Cristina Molina and Dean (Rocky) Rockwell

Amy Clampitt, 'A Hermit Thrush' (1999)

Precarious spaces raise concern. It is the direct confrontation with crisis or instability that prompts the urgency for change. We begin from a post-crisis viewpoint. Through an exchange of a two-year correspondence, we detail our experience of contributing to spaces that are actively being restored.

One defined space is the American city of New Orleans. The city's below-sea-level construction, history of racial tension, and role as catalyst for the birth of jazz music have earned it an infamous reputation. The other spaces are affordable housing units throughout the United States. Both spaces have been activated in positive ways after an initial collapse. For New Orleans, the devastation caused after hurricane Katrina has begun an initiative among cultural producers to question the initial problems of the city, and propose solutions for maintaining physical and cultural infrastructure throughout. While biking across the United States, Dean witnessed how the American housing crisis has prompted nationwide initiatives to rebuild and restore housing for those on a low-income.

Dear Dean,

Which is better for creative production? Feeling safe? Or feeling unstable? We project these questions onto the architecture of our cities, onto the natural world, onto our objects and onto our varying states of consciousness. We agree that a combination of both precarity and stability proves to be fruitful.

I propose that as long as one has inward structural stability, then one can deal with most external precarious situations, perhaps even thrive in them. While reading *A Paradise Built in Hell* by Rebecca Solnit, I was struck by the main thesis of the book – contrary to media distortion, when confronted with disaster communities typically tend to band together in forms of altruism.

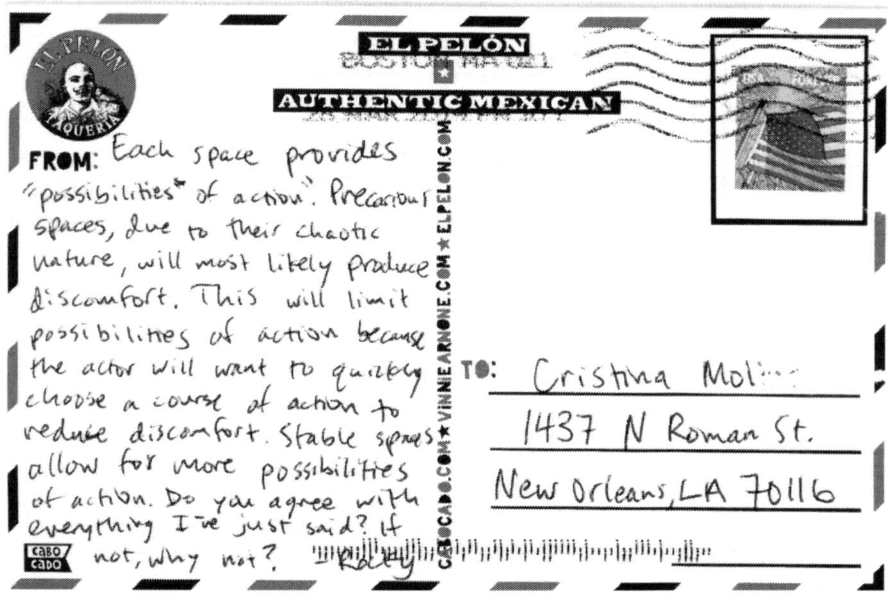

Figures 12.1–12.2: *A Much Mended Thing*, 2014. Courtesy of Cristina Molina and Dean Rockwell.

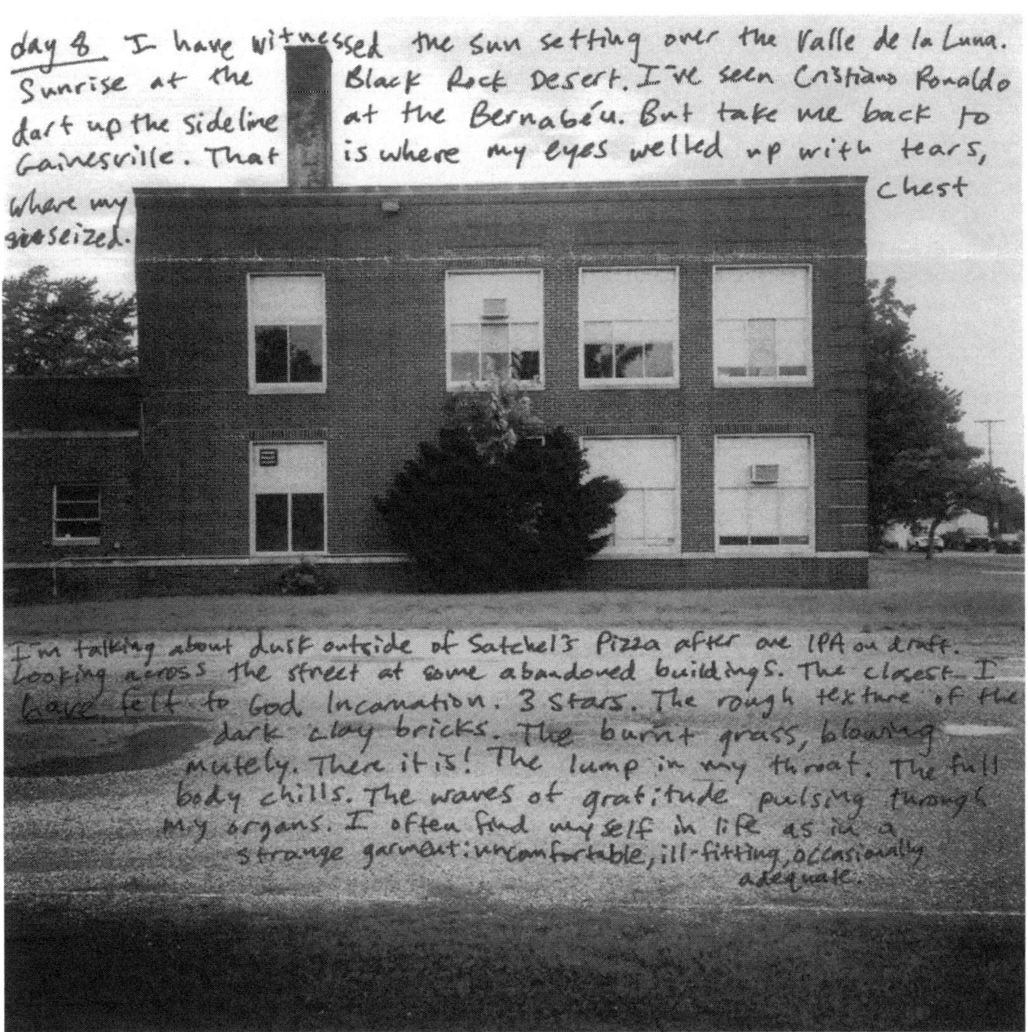

Figure 12.6: *A Much Mended Thing*, 2014. Courtesy of Cristina Molina and Dean Rockwell.

No one claims that New Orleans is a safe place to live. The general sentiment is "I'd rather die in New Orleans than live anywhere else." That's a quote that I often hear, but can't credit to any one author. It's a firm position that grips the people who decide that any risks are worth it. So many people I've met say they come here on vacation and then never leave. The city has gripped me. It's an uncanny magnetism; NOLA is like a siren that intoxicates, welcomes, and seduces you into settling in. Then you see all the dark undertones; an obvious racial divide between neighborhoods, poverty, corruption, over indulgence... and you still decide that it is your home and you will be loyal to her. For me, it's an honest way of revealing what we all are. we all have darkness, we are deeply flawed, and contain a certain amount of evil desires with in us. My position is that I feel more comfortable if that darkness is blatant rather than obscured. I have always been suspicious if the sunny and highly—overly efficient cities of California for instance. where is the ID in that scene?

Maybe that contrast is what is so attractive. like a lover that you constantly quarrel with, but when you make love it is the most passionate, and when things are right they are so right, but when things are blue it casts over your whole vision and everything turns a shade of violet and celeste. I don't think that deep inside, any one in this city feels completely secure, and I'm not sure that any one wants to be. That's part of the appeal, that one day you can lose it all.

what I do know is that when the city was completely devastated, a third of the people who live here now rushed here because they could embrace some darkness in order to build something for others and themselves. It feels good to be part of the wild west of the south. More thoughts on the next letter.

with warmth,
Cristina.

P.S. just booked my ticket to Tokyo! I leave May 1st

PPS: your letter just arrived in the mail — I don't agree with you. I will explain.

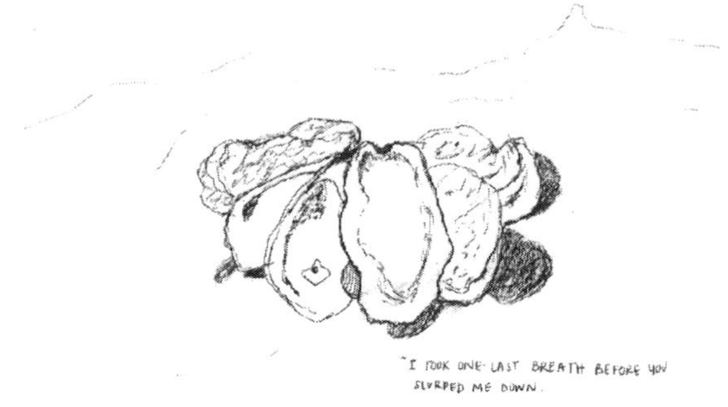

Figures 12.7–12.8: *A Much Mended Thing*, 2014. Courtesy of Cristina Molina and Dean Rockwell.

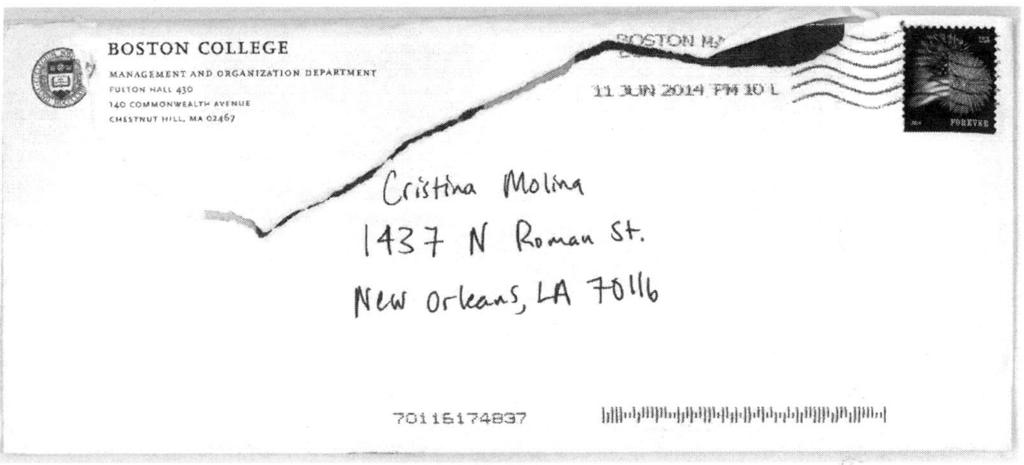

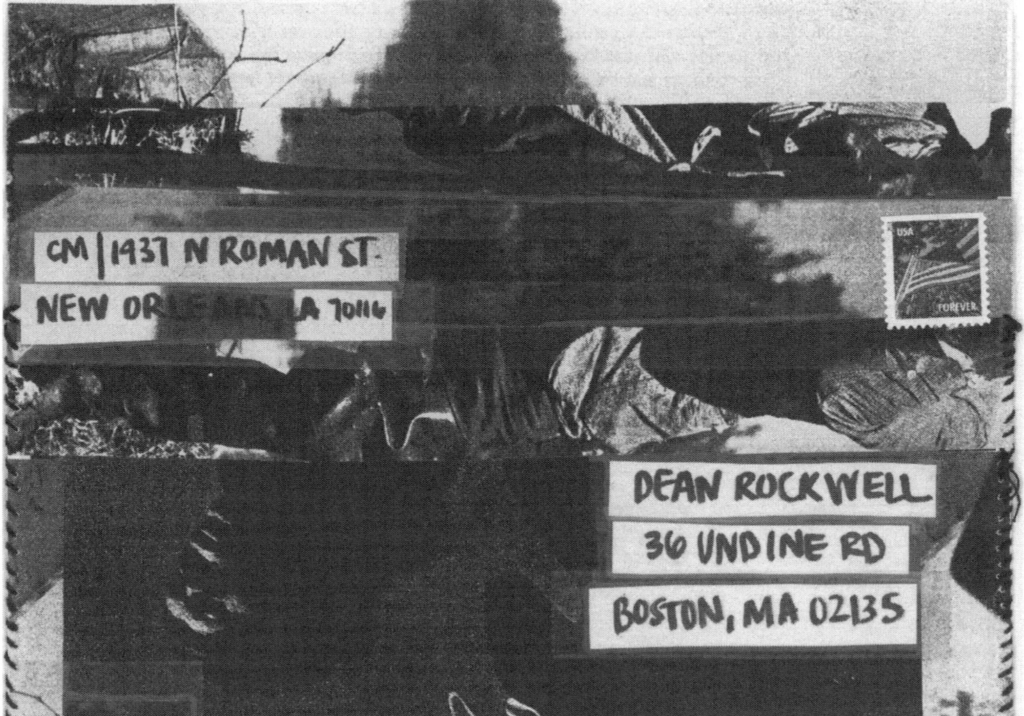

Figures 12.9–12.10: *A Much Mended Thing*, 2014. Courtesy of Cristina Molina and Dean Rockwell.

Dear Rocky,

I think a successful rebuild would be an urban plan that makes its residents to feel safe, included, and supported. Right now interstate 10 runs through the middle of New Orleans, over lower income neighbourhoods so that anyone from the wealthier uptown area can glide over Treme, Mid City and the Seventh ward without having to observe any poverty. All they see is LED billboards and an aerial view of the Mercedes Benz Superdome. The highway was built during the 1970s Brutalist period when successful urban planning meant high speed, efficiency and speedy movement of commercial goods through a space. What urban planners failed to mention is that some people were too scared to drive through these neighbourhoods and that this superhighway provided a solution for avoiding any contact.

When it comes to thinking about implementing structural change, I can't help but to have a Modernist mind and a Romantic heart. Structurally and visually, I want things to be organized, efficient, thoughtfully considered and functional. Socially, I want to nurture the people who live in these places by offering beauty, good standards of living and even pleasure and recreation beyond the rigid constraints of the efficient modernist model. That's why I think the work I do collectively with other artists is important; we emphasize a life beyond 'survival' and highlight the importance of creating a cultural capital.

Dear Cristina,

This idea comes through in one of your more recent letters. You describe urban development in New Orleans. The marker from the back side obscures the text because it bleeds through the paper, frustratingly undermining the prescriptive solutions you provide for rebuilding your city. You talk about 'divides' in the community and how the I-10 highway acts as a barrier. These structures, divisions and demarcations attempt to formally define the space in your city.

But what about the ever-present natural world? The menacing, salty ocean that made its way into the city in the first place?

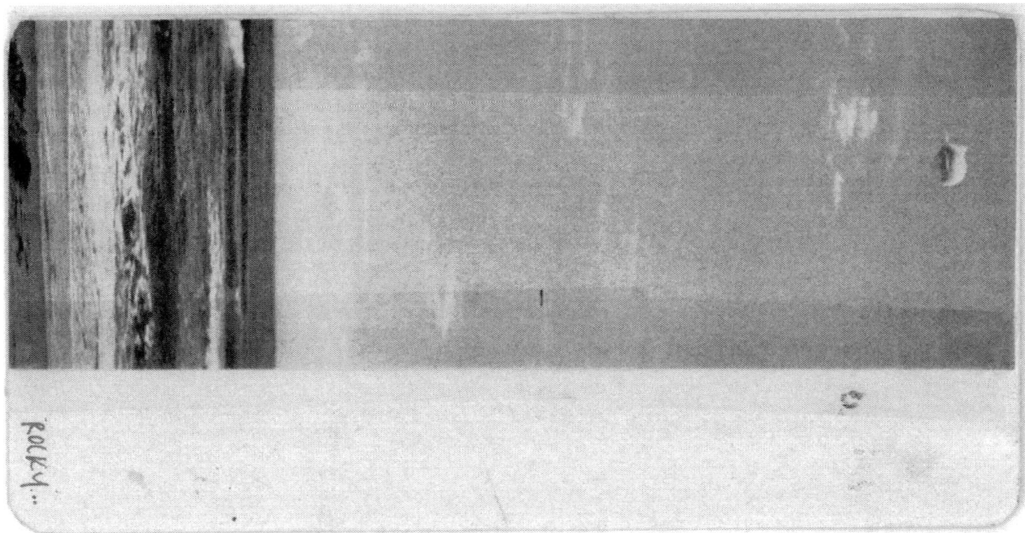

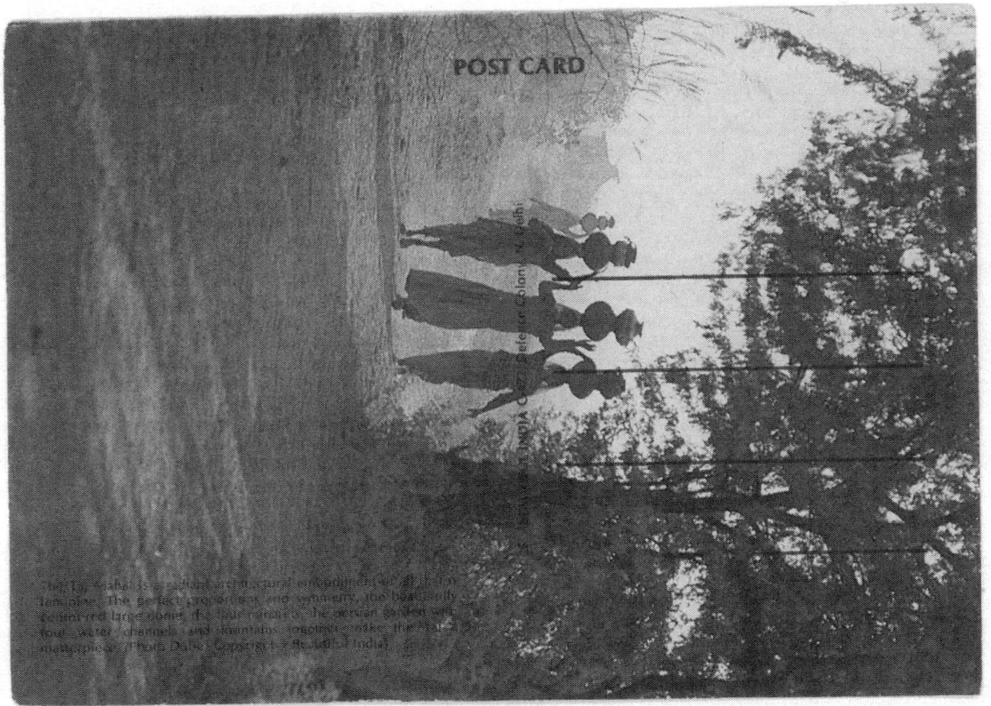

Figures 12.11–12.12: *A Much Mended Thing,* 2014. Courtesy of Cristina Molina and Dean Rockwell.

Dear Dean,

It's late for me, and the city is startlingly quiet tonight. There are stacks of clothing lying on the couch in my bedroom mixed in with books and receipts. Little piles of things have gathered around the house the past few weeks – they are waiting to be sorted and stowed away – tomorrow perhaps – but for now since I am on the subject of piles, I will tell you that you can't dig anywhere in New Orleans without finding a claw full of oyster shells. Within the soupy, spongy Orleanian earth are bits of these once pearlescent and muscular creatures. My grandmother told me that when she was pregnant with my mother, she had an intense urgency to eat several dozen oysters. Her desire was so feverish that she bought two buckets of them and sat down on a stoop, shucked and sucked them down, and flung the empty shells back into the aluminium can. As she ate them, she said a lunar eclipse was happening and she could not feel more alive. My mother was born the next day, and even still when my mom gets angry or a little flustered, you can see the birth mark (or 'lunar' as they call it in Spanish) spread over her forehead like some strange continent.

I am also quite fond of oysters and so wrongly thought that they were nothing more than the mucous membranes of the sea. Since I am mostly vegetarian, I thought at long last I can eat these slimy, ocean mushrooms, guilt-free. After a bit of research though, I found out that they are very much alive, even up until the moment you separate them from their shell and gulp them down. Needless to say, I was not very pleased by this news. However, some good has come from the consumption and disposal of fish carcasses safely deposited into the city soil. Mel Chin (celebrity artist and activist) worked with a team of scientists to develop a project in New Orleans called 'operation pay-dirt.' Together they found that if the contaminated, lead infested soil is mixed with the phosphate found in fish particles and shells, the soil then becomes neutralized and safe for kids to play in.

Dear Cristina,

It is interesting that you describe the benefits of the shells for the soil. You mentioned that artist Mel Chin worked with scientists to show how fish carcasses actually neutralized the soil and made it safe for kids to play in. This mending effect of nature enables children to experiment and explore. It seems that we need both physical structures and the natural world in this mending process.

Dear Dean,

It's true that the natural world is needed in the mending process, but we know that nature is not always benign; in the case of disaster it can create a threatening catalyst of events. Yesterday, I drove with a friend down I-10 headed East, and pulled over at the side of the road to a pile of rubble that obscured several hundred feet of road behind it. A yellow-spray-painted plume blocked our path, and we quickly hopped over it to explore.

One of my fellow artists has been fascinated by a series of abandoned exit ramps that at one point would have led commuters to their suburban homes in New Orleans East.

Once projected to be a middle-class utopia, a population of white flighters rushed the area anxious to start their cosy life style. Because the area did not develop at the pace they were expecting, many of them left, as a community of middle-class African Americans planted roots there.

After Katrina, a huge debate ensued, should the city's officials just let the swamp take over this now blighted land, should it return to its natural order? Although not so direct, or politically correct, the answer was clearly: yes. Now these exit ramps are over run with cat's claw, decomposing snakes are being devoured by fire ants, swamp insects dart straight into one's eyes as one traverses the once perfectly paved road – perhaps as a warning or a projection that says, 'I don't want you here, you don't belong.'

Reference

Clampitt, A. 1999. *The Collected Poems of Amy Clampitt*, New York: Knopf.

Notes on contributors

Valeria Biffi is a Lecturer in Visual Anthropology at the Pontifical Catholic University of Peru. She holds an MSc in Culture and Society from the London School of Economics and Political Sciences, UK. She researches indigenous representation, the uses of photography for social research and political ecology.

Vanessa Brulon is a Lecturer in Organizational Theory at Rio de Janeiro Federal University (UFRJ), Brazil and a psychologist. She is at the final stages of her PhD studies at Getulio Vargas Foundation, Rio de Janeiro, Brazil, examining spatial power in favelas in Rio de Janeiro. Her publications include 'Política das UPPs e espaços organizacionais Precários: Uma análise de discurso,' *RAE* (2013), and 'Organizações públicas e espaços às margens do estado: Contribuições para investigações de poder e território em favelas,' *RAP* (2013).

Diana Brydon, PhD (FRSC), is a Canadian Research Chair in Globalization and Cultural Studies and a Distinguished Professor in the Department of English, Film and Theatre at the University of Manitoba, Canada. She currently investigates transnational literacies, new postcolonialisms and global higher education. She has published on postcolonial cultural and literary studies and on ways communities adjust to globalizing processes. In addition to books on the authors Timothy Findley and Christina Stead, she has published the co-authored *Decolonising Fictions* (1993) and edited *Postcolonialism: Critical Concepts in Literary and Cultural Studies* (2000). Co-edited books include: *Shakespeare in Canada: A World Elsewhere?* (2002), *Renegotiating Community: Interdisciplinary Perspectives, Global Contexts* (2008) and *Crosstalk: Canadian and Global Imaginaries in Dialogue* (2012). Current projects include the Brazil/Canada Knowledge Exchange, a partnership development project funded by SSHRC, a co-edited book: *Concurrences: Archive, Voice, and Place*, and a research project: 'Redefining canada for a globalizing world: An "ecology of knowledges approach".'

Cristina Amélia Pereira de Carvalho, PhD, is a Professor in Organization Studies, Universidade Federal do Rio Grande do Sul, Brazil. She is currently researching cultural practices of resistance among groups, organizations and civil society movements. She obtained her PhD in Economics and Management at the University of Cordoba, Spain in

1997. Her publications include: *Cultura e transformação: políticas e experiências Culturais/ Culture and Transformation: Political and Cultural Experiences* (Eds) (Porto Alegre: Dacasa Editora, 2013), and *Organizações, cultura e desenvolvimento local: a agenda de pesquisa do Observatório da Realidade Organizacional/Organizations, Culture and Local Development: The Research Agenda of the Centre for Organizational Reality* (co-edited with Marcello Vieira) (Recife: EDUFEPE, 2003).

Lilian Fessler Vaz, PhD, is an architect, urban planner and a Professor in Urban Studies at the Federal University of Rio de Janeiro (PROURB/FAU-UFRJ), Brazil, where she coordinates the research group 'Culture, History and Urban Studies', in collaboration with the National Council of Technological and Scientific Development (CNPq). She obtained a PhD in 1995 in Architecture and Urban Studies from the University of São Paulo, Brazil. In 2003, she completed her postdoctoral research at the Maison des Sciences de l'Homme, Paris, France. Her publications include: *Modernity and Housing: Collective Housing in Rio de Janeiro, XIX-XX* (2002), *Der öffentliche Raum in der Planungspolitik. Studien aus Berlin und Rio de Janeiro* (Eds) (2006), *Public Spaces in Urban Policies: Studies of Rio de Janeiro and Berlin* (Eds) (2008) and *Other Spaces: Celebrating the Creativity of the Rio de Janeiro Periphery* (Eds) (2015).

Fábio Freitas Schilling Marquesan, PhD, is an Associate Professor at the University of Fortaleza, Brazil and an agronomist engineer. He holds a Doctorate in Organization Studies from the Universidade Federal do Rio Grande do Sul, Brazil with his thesis 'Terra e artesanato Mbyá-Guarani: polos da contraditória política indigenista no Rio Grande do Sul'/'Incentive policies for Mbyá-Guarani handicrafts in the state of Rio Grande do Sul, Brazil' (2013).

Miguel Imas, PhD (Editor), is a Senior Lecturer in Organizational and Social Psychology, the Kingston University, UK. He holds a PhD in Social Psychology from the London School of Economics, UK. In past years, he has been a Visiting Professor at the Getulio Vargas Foundation, Rio de Janeiro, Brazil and the University of Chile. He has undertaken ethnographic research in the Latin American context, where he has engaged with indigenous communities and local organizations. His work has been published in international journals on postcolonialism, art-resistance and 'barefoot entrepreneurs.'

Katarzyna Kosmala, PhD (Editor), is Professor of Culture, Media and Visual Arts at the University of the West of Scotland, UK and Visiting Research Fellow at the European Institute of Gender Studies, GEXcel, at Linköping University and Örebro University, Sweden. She is also an art-writer and curator. From 2010 and 2011, she was a Visiting Professor at Getulio Vargas Foundation, Rio de Janeiro, Brazil. Her research interests include gender and visual art, discourses of creative labour, alternative forms of organizing, arts-facilitated initiatives in peripheral locations and emerging economies. Her recent publications include *Sexing the Border: Gender, Art and New Media in Central and Eastern*

Europe (Ed.) (CSP, 2014); *Art Inquiry on Crossing Borders: Imaging Europe, Representing Periphery* (Eds) (ŁTN, 2013); *Imagining Masculinities: Spatial and Temporal Representation and Visual Culture* (Routledge, 2013). She writes regularly about video and new media art in international journals and catalogues. She is currently involved in the project Curating Europes' Futures (www.curatingeuropesfutures.net). She lives and works in Edinburgh, Scotland.

Daniel S. Lacerda is a Teaching Fellow and a PhD Candidate at Lancaster University, UK. He has been engaged with civil society organizations for more than fifteen years, managing free prep school educational provision and counselling at cultural organizations across favelas. His research interests focus on space production, critical discourse analysis and civil society organizations. His publications include 'Rio de Janeiro and the divided state: Analysing the political discourse on favelas,' *Discourse & Society* (2015), and 'Market rationality inside voluntary sector: An analysis of five organizations in Rio de Janeiro, Brazil,' *Voluntas* (2011). He also contributes to the LSE@Favelas blog.

Jacob Carlos Lima, PhD, is a Professor at the Department of Sociology, Universidade Federal de São Carlos, Brazil, a Vice President of the Brazilian Sociological Society and a Fellow Researcher at the National Council of Technological and Scientific Development (CNPq). He is also the leader of the research group 'Work and Social Mobility'. Between 2011 and 2014, he worked for the Coordination Centre for the Improvement of Higher Education (CAPES), at the Ministry of Education, Brazil. Currently involved in the project: 'Contradictions of Work in Contemporary Brazil: Formalization, Precarity, Outsourcing and Regulation' (2013–2017).

Cristina Molina is an artist and Assistant Professor of New Media and Animation at the Southeastern Louisiana University, US. Her work has been exhibited across the United States and internationally including El Palacio de Bellas Artes, the Dominican Republic; the Gallery at the Universita Degli Studi di Genova, Genoa, Italy; the Dialogue Space at Proyecto Ace, Buenos Aires Argentina; Makii Masaru Fine Art and Ginza Art Lab, Tokyo; ArteAmericas, North Miami MOCA; Frost Museum of Art, Miami; Harn Museum of art, Gainesville; Girls Club Collection, Ft. Lauderdale; the Ogden Museum of Southern Art, New Orleans. Currently lives in New Orleans, US.

Gonzalo Olmos is a photographer and a Research Associate at London Multimedia Lab for Audiovisual Composition and Communication, at the Institute of Social Psychology, London School of Economics and Political Sciences, UK. He obtained an MA in Photography and Urban Cultures at Goldsmiths College, University of London and an MSc in Organizational and Social Psychology at the London School of Economics and Political Science, UK. He was a curator of the Museum of Photography Lima (FOLi). He has exhibited at Canning House and the Hispanic Luso Brasilian Council, London; The Old Police Station,

Amersham Vale, London; Espacio Exhibe Gallery, Barranco, Lima; The Tavistock and Portman Foundation Trust Art Collection, London; and Sala Luis Miró Quesada Garland in Miraflores, Lima. His photographic work is in private and institutional collections of Lima, Athens and London.

Benjamin Parry, PhD, is an artist and curator based in London. He co-directs the arts organization Jump Ship Rat and has initiated numerous projects and interventions in the public realm internationally. He was recently awarded a practice-led PhD at the School of Media, Culture and Society, University of West Scotland, UK. His work explores tactical and informal urbanism; appropriations and interim uses of the unclaimed and the overlooked. He published *Cultural Hijack: Rethinking Intervention* (Ed.) (Liverpool University Press, 2011) and curated *Cultural Hijack* at the Architectural Association School of Architecture, London, which included an exhibition, conference and a program of live-interventions and happenings.

Alketa Peci, PhD, is a Professor of Public Administration and Organizations at Getulio Vargas Foundation (EBAPE/FGV), Rio de Janeiro, Brazil and a Researcher at National Council of Technological and Scientific Development (CNPq). Her research focuses on power and discourse analysis, particularly in the areas of (re)forming public administration and regulation of public utilities. Her current research projects focus on the limits and potentials of public-non-profit relationships in civil society contexts, characterized by scarce social capital bonds. She has been working closely with the President Office, the Federal Auditing Court, the Ministry of Defence and the Ministry of Planning, among others. She was also a Visiting Researcher at George Washington University, US.

Fernando Ramalho Martins, PhD, is a Lecturer at the Department of Public Administration, the Universidade Estadual Paulista (UNESP), Brazil and a Teaching Fellow at the Universidad Federal da Grande Dourados, Brazil. In 2010, he obtained his PhD in Sociology from Universidade Federal de São Carlos, Brazil. In 2009, he was a Visiting Research Fellow at the Social Science Department, Cardiff University, UK. He researches work organizations, control and resistance.

Maria Ceci Misoczky, PhD, is a Professor and Researcher in Organization Studies at the Federal University of Rio Grande do Sul, Porto Alegre, Brazil. She is also a Visiting Professor at the National University of the South, Bahia Blanca, Argentina and EAFIT, Medellin, Colombia. She coordinates two research groups: 'Organization and Liberating Praxis' and 'Health Management'. Her research interests include organizational practices of social movements and popular struggle, focusing on socio-environmental conflicts and anti-capitalist initiatives in Latin America. She also engages with a critique of the political economy of organization, social production and public policies as well as Latin American and Brazilian social thought.

Dean (Rocky) Rockwell is a PhD candidate in the Management and Organization Department at Boston College, US. He received his BA in Latin American Studies from the University of Richmond, US and his MA from the University of Florida, US in International Business. His research focuses on sustainability, non-profit organizations and social movements.

Claudia Seldin, PhD, is an architect, urban planner and a Research Fellow in Urban Studies, the Federal University of Rio de Janeiro (PROURB/FAU-UFRJ), Brazil. Her research fields include urban history, urban sociology, cultural studies, creative cities and public policy. She recently co-edited *Other Spaces: Celebrating the Creativity of the Rio de Janeiro Periphery* (2015). She obtained a PhD from FAU-UFRJ in partnership with the Institut für Europäische Urbanistik (IfEU) of the Bauhaus-Universität Weimar, Germany.

Aline Suelen Pires, PhD, is a Visiting Researcher at the Department of Sociology of Universidade Federal de São Carlos, Brazil where she also obtained a PhD in 2014. Currently involved in the project: 'The Y Generation and Information Technology Work: The Generational Flexibility Discourse on Flexible Work'. She is also a Researcher in the 'Contradictions of Work Today' research group at the Universidade de Campinas and 'Labour, Health and Social Vulnerability' research group at the Universidade Federal de São Paulo, Brazil. She researches cooperativism and cultures of work.

Leonardo V. C. Darbilly, PhD, is a Lecturer at Federal Rural University of Rio de Janeiro (UFRRJ), Brazil. He obtained his Doctorate in Brazilian School for Public and Business Administration, Getulio Vargas Foundation (EBAPE/FGV), Rio de Janeiro, Brazil. His research interests include arts and cultural management, power relations and conflict in organizations, and new technologies.

Alia Weston, PhD, is an Assistant Professor at OCAD University, Toronto, Canada. Her research is focused on creative engagements in social and organizational realms and within resource-constrained environments. In conjunction with her research, she runs practical workshops, in which participants engage with issues related to creative and sustainable work practices.